Schooling for All

SCHOOLING

FOR ALL

———

Class, Race, and the Decline
of the Democratic Ideal

———

IRA KATZNELSON

MARGARET WEIR

University of California Press

Berkeley   Los Angeles   London

A portion of chapter 7 also appears, in modified form, in *The Politics of School Reform 1870–1940*, by Paul E. Peterson, published by The University of Chicago Press.

University of California Press
Berkeley and Los Angeles

University of California Press, Ltd.
London, England

Library of Congress Cataloging-in-Publication Data

Katznelson, Ira.
  Schooling for all.

  Reprint. Originally published: New York : Basic
Books, © 1985. With new introd.
  Bibliography: p.
  Includes index.
  1. Public schools—United States—History.
2. Social classes—United States.   3. Politics and
education—United States.   4. Educational
equalization—United States.   I. Weir, Margaret,
1952–   II. Title.
LA212.K28 1988   371'.01'0973   88–4761
ISBN 0–520–06252–3 (pbk. : alk. paper)

Contents

Acknowledgments

THIS BOOK is rooted in a collaborative project undertaken by the National Opinion Research Center at the University of Chicago and funded by the National Institute of Education (Grant G–78–0100). We owe substantial thanks to Paul Peterson, who was the director of the project. Other staff members of the project who contributed to our work include James Christiansen, Carol Forster, Carol Peterson, David Plank, Sandra Prolman, Marcia Turner-Jones, and Kenneth Wong. Above all, we owe a special debt to John Bowman, John Echeverri-Gent, and Kathleen Gille for their exceptional research assistance. Kathleen Gille, in fact, should be considered coauthor of chapter 3 and a full collaborator in thinking through what our research was all about and what this volume might become.

These colleagues know of our appreciation and thanks firsthand. But we wish here to warmly acknowledge the role of Julia Wrigley—whom we have not met—in shaping our work. Her doctoral dissertation (revised and published as *Class Politics and Public Schools, Chicago, 1900–1950*) showed us how to avoid the usual pitfalls of treating workers simply as part of an undifferentiated citizenry enthusiastic about public education, as in the progressive view, or as a manipulated group coerced into schooling, as in much revisionist scholarship.

At important junctures in our work we received very helpful and supportive critical comments and advice from William Bullough, Elisabeth Hansot, David Hogan, William Issel, Jerome

Karabel, Michael Katz, Gail McColl, Gary Orfield, Kenneth Prewitt, David Tyack, Jules Tygiel, Wayne Urban, members of the Department of Education Seminar at the University of Chicago, the University Seminar on the Metropolis at Columbia University, and two anonymous reviewers for the *American Journal of Education.*

Like most scholars, we have depended a great deal on the thoughtful and generous assistance of librarians, who, in the nature of things, tend to remain anonymous. If we cannot name these individuals who facilitated our research, we can identify the libraries where they work: the Archives of the Archdiocese of San Francisco, the Atlanta Historical Society, the Bancroft Library, the Chicago Historical Society, the library of the University of California at Berkeley, the library at Emory University, the San Francisco History Room at the San Francisco Public Library, the library at Stanford University, the Teachers Library at the Board of Education of the San Francisco Unified School District, the library at the University of San Francisco, the Walter Reuther Library at Wayne State University, and, above all, Regenstein Library at the University of Chicago.

The caliber of Regenstein's holdings is characteristic of the extraordinary university where the great bulk of research and writing for this book was carried out. The University of Chicago's Department of Political Science and the Center for the Study of Industrial Societies make up a community of scholarship and critical thinking that challenged and sustained us as we worked.

Finally, we are deeply indebted to Steven Fraser, Senior Editor at Basic Books. His sympathetic readings, penetrating criticisms, and gentle proddings have made this book more clear, more coherent, perhaps even more lively than it would have been.

All this assistance—as well as the forbearance of the Katznelson household—we gratefully acknowledge, even as we take full responsibility for the arguments and evidence in this book.

Introduction to the
Paperback Edition

Schooling for All begins with a plea that education not be severed from considerations of social democratic policy initiatives in the United States. This entreaty is an analytical lament for the unthinking excision of education from most studies of social policy and the welfare state. But it is also a political claim that central characteristics of the tradition of schooling for all—universalism and a focus on the prerogatives of democratic citizenship—provide an important contrast to the categorical and efficiency-based features of most domestic public policies in the United States.

Underpinning *Schooling for All* is a set of assumptions and values that concern distributive justice. Although we did not aim to elaborate a political theory of education, an explicit theoretical discussion can illuminate our historical reinterpretation. In particular, concerns arising from democratic theory can help us discern how the historical heritage and the institutional realities of American public education both facilitate and constrain our ability to reverse its profound degradation.

Attempts to supply the missing ties between systematic democratic theory, history, and policy analysis must today begin with Amy Gutmann's *Democratic Education* (Princeton, N.J.: Princeton University Press, 1987), the only recent study of U.S. education written from within the analytical framework of democratic theory. Given our own focus on elementary education, it is Gutmann's chapter on the distribution of primary schooling that is most germane for *Schooling for All*. In this chapter, as in her book as a whole, Gutmann seeks to discover a democratic distributive standard.

In this quest, she takes up—and sets aside—three common standards in the literature and in debates on educational policy: (1) the maximization of life chances, a perspective insisting that we spend what is needed on education regardless of competing needs or resource constraints; (2) the equalization of life chances, a perspective seeking to bring all children up to the level of those with the best educational opportunities; and (3) a meritocratic standard that distributes education according to the abilities of children and their manifest willingness to learn.

Gutmann rejects each as inadequate, arguing the impracticality of the first, the imprecision of the second, the mean-spiritedness of the third. Instead, she proposes a standard for the distribution of schooling that is rooted in democratic theory. At its core is the appealing principle that "a democratic state . . . must take steps to avoid those inequalities that deprive children of educational attainment adequate to participate in the democratic process" (p. 134).

In elaborated form, this democratic grounding of the distribution of schooling has two parts: first, what Gutmann calls the democratic authorization principle, which stipulates that the democratic process should determine the relative priority of education compared to other social goods; and, second, what she labels the democratic threshold principle, which finds that inequalities in the distribution of educational goods can be justified only if they do not deprive children of the ability to participate effectively in the democratic process. These principles provide a nondiscretionary and democratic framework within which decisions about schooling and its distribution are made by imposing "a moral requirement that democratic institutions allocate sufficient resources to education to provide all children with an ability adequate to participate in the democratic process" (p. 136).

These deductive, universalistic principles are appealing in part because of their elective affinity both with actual nineteenth-century educational policies and with the most common justifications of these policies. Decisions to found egalitarian, free, common public schools and to organize school systems were made locally by city councils elected by a white male electorate composed of both propertyholders and nonpropertyholders. The leaders of the schools so created almost always justified their activities in language that resonates with Gutmann's principle of the democratic threshold (but in language that also reflects the dominant classes' worries that a mass franchise democracy of untutored voters might prove disastrous). Thus, for example, the inaugural report of Chicago's first superintendent of schools, J. C. Dores, argued in 1854 that

> Republican institutions are founded upon the virtue and intelligence of the people where they exist—they can be founded upon nothing else. . . . It is in the province of the Public Schools to educate each rising generation that it may be able to transmit our institutions, unimpaired, to each successive generation in turn. Tear down our School Houses and turn our children into the streets, and our political institutions would be involved in ruin.

A decade later, San Francisco's leading educator asserted "the duty of a republican or representative government, as an act of self-preservation, to provide for the education of every child." The schools, John Swett claimed, have a particular responsibility to be "the educators of the working men and women of the nation" because "the schools mold the character of the men whose will expressed through the ballot-box makes and unmakes constitutions and breathes life into all laws."

Rooted in democratic decision making and in republican values, schooling was the most robust "social policy" of the early Republic and the only one in the American experience, apart from social insurance, to be developed as a mass policy based on universalistic rights criteria. Within this frame, schooling expanded well beyond the economic requirements of early industrial capitalism.

The two main explanations for the expansion of primary education in the United States—what the literature has labeled the "progressive" and the "revisionist" positions—miss key aspects of this history. The former has well understood the elective affinity between democracy and schooling but has made the relationship too automatic. In fact, different social classes

and groups in the United States subscribed to Gutmann's democratic standard, but for quite different reasons. Working people
supported mass state schooling because it was an expression of
citizenship already achieved through the franchise. (By contrast, most European working classes resisted the imposition of
state education by governments that excluded them from the
franchise.) At the same time, the dominant classes supported
education for working people's children because they were concerned about the effects that uneducated voting citizens might
have on a democracy. The "revisionist" position, in turn, has
understood the class basis of support for schooling, but in its
zeal to show the capitalist biases of education it has frequently
missed the point that education expanded far beyond basic labor market requirements. Indeed, it was this expansion beyond
an economic minimum that characterized the single great "social democratic" achievement of the American regime before
the New Deal.

   If the expansion of nineteeth-century schooling for *all* (white)
children as a universal right was rooted in a democratic-repub-
lican ideology, it was also underpinned by a felicitous conjunction of this ideology with a variety of social and economic factors in antebellum America. These included the specific bases
of support for schooling by the various social classes already
alluded to (citizenship proved a bridge across class lines), as
well as a pattern of urban social geography that permitted
a cross-class educational experience for children of different
backgrounds.

   Within this distinctive, and partly fortuitous, context schooling for all as a normative goal and as an institutional reality came to have three interlocked meanings by the mid-
nineteenth century: equal access to primary schools; the same
curriculum for children of all social backgrounds; and, where
possible, the sharing of the same classroom by children with
different demographic characteristics.

   These universalistic principles and practices began to erode
almost as soon as they were instantiated, as early debates about
high schools and language issues reveal. Much of our book is
concerned with the complicated story of the decomposition of
the formula of schooling for all, and the ways this story was

shaped by the dynamics of class formation and race relations in the American regime. But what of today? Can political assertiveness on behalf of schooling for all help revive the best egalitarian and democratic features of American public life? Can education, once again, complement its economic role with a profound commitment to the values of citizenship?

The period since World War II yields a contradictory report. On the one hand, black Americans have been included within the framework of democratic access and to some extent have been integrated into schooling experiences with whites (more so in the South, as things have turned out, than in the North). On the other hand, there have been even more powerful countertrends toward more segmented curricula and toward education that is sharply segregated by the class position of parents, a trend that in many places has deepened the pattern of segregation based on racial divisions.

The decay of schooling for all in the postwar years has been caused in large measure by basic shifts in precisely those characteristics of American society that once underpinned universalistic distributive guideposts. Much of *Schooling for All* is concerned with this theme: how the coalition in support of egalitarian public education has been seriously compromised both by the narrowing of concern and the declining influence of American labor and by the contraction of community-based working-class ethnicity into the defensive category of "whites." Perhaps most important in shaping the meaning and possibilities of the social bases of politics has been a series of changes in the distribution of people and jobs in metropolitan areas. With the explosion of suburban development, more and more Americans have come to live in political units that have very homogeneous populations (in Weberian class terms), where local politics is concerned mainly with exclusion (based on zoning and the operation of real estate markets), and where schooling is ancillary to property values.

Accompanying this changed social geography has been a whole new set of demands on the schools, which are called on to cushion the effects of economic and social transformation. As in the first two decades of this century, the schools' responsibilities and capabilities in preparing students for the marketplace have become worrisome and contentious. Further, as in the earlier period, the business community has taken the lead in pressing for reform. Faced with mounting economic competition, business leaders have become concerned with the efficiency and quality of their work force and have looked at the public schools with renewed interest. Some corporate leaders have expressed their dissatisfaction in harsh terms, calling the public schools a "failed monopoly" that turns out products with a "50 percent defect rate" (*New York Times*, 27 October 1987, p. A30). From such discontent, business leaders have begun to articulate an agenda of educational reform.

Teenage sexuality and the growing number of unmarried mothers (seen both as cause and as measure of shifting family and social mores), as well as the emergence of a definable underclass, likewise have focused new attention on the role of public schooling. Traditional concerns about sex education have been supplanted by calls for the schools to go beyond informing students to more direct forms of intervention, such as dispensing contraceptives. Less controversial, but perhaps more challenging in terms of the allocation of resources, is the problem of "latch-key" children. What can and should the schools do to cope with the increased numbers of two-wage-earner and single-parent families?

Narrowed and increasingly segmented participation in school politics leaves us in doubt as to whether the egalitarian impulses that characterized American schools at their founding can guide current educational innovation and responses to these new agenda items. Yet without such guiding principles, the prospects for reinvigorating public education remain bleak. Untempered by wider debate, business concerns that schooling more closely serve the needs of the marketplace could lead to more formal segmentation of public education—the kind of segmentation providing different benefits for different social classes that was resisted by a coalition of educators and labor at the turn of the century. But if the schools fail to address the mounting criticism of their performance, the current degradation of public education will continue unabated. The universalistic character imprinted on public schools in the early years of the Republic will have been lost, perhaps irretrievably.

The very real dangers of political failure and irrelevance confronting public schooling in the United States underscore the importance of renewing the democratic debate that Gutmann so persuasively convenes. And yet the complexity and fragmentation of contemporary school politics raise a number of basic questions for the principles of schooling as outlined by Gutmann: What political limits on the traditional egalitarian standards of schooling have been established by current institutions, strategies, and local political cultures? Given Gutmann's insistence that democratic processes determine levels of schooling and that a minimum of schooling appropriate to democratic citizenship be provided for all, is the appropriate locus of democratic decision making the traditional notion of the locality, or is it larger, more heterogeneous units? Should the level of schooling and its content be determined by local decision makers, or should we insist on national minimum standards? In short, if we accept Gutmann's democratic authorization principle, who should do the authorizing? And if we are prepared to accept her democratic threshold principle, is its actualization impeded or assisted by a tradition in which schooling decisions are made by the most local units of the federal system?

This condensed discussion of a democratic basis for questions of distributive justice in education has implications for the questions that guide educational research. Progressivism versus revisionism and standards versus equity have provided the principal axes of debate. The first of these antinomies has proved incapable of defining some of the most interesting questions about the American tradition of education; if *Schooling for All* is about nothing else, it is concerned with demonstrating this claim. The second antinomy makes sense only within a restricted framework that accepts without comment current political boundaries and the discourse they engender. Educational research conducted within the parameters of this debate produces a truncated and skewed vision of the possibilities for pursuing equality and high educational standards simultaneously.

The traditional fault lines of scholarly and practical debates about schooling, in short, are insufficient and misleading. We propose instead that the story of American education be located within the interplay, first, of capitalism and democracy; second, of class formation and local school politics; and, third, of the social structure and social geography of American cities.

We reconstruct the various dimensions of the history of American schooling in these terms in the pages below. Here, we would like to suggest that such a history, in tandem with the kinds of democratic concerns articulated by Gutmann, can help refocus and reinvigorate discussions about public policy as they concern both education as such and the larger possibilities of a more equitable regime. We need a standard against which to measure reality and with which to strive, as well as a keenly honed sense of the conditions that inhibit or facilitate its realization. Only by such a joining can we avoid the usual pitfalls of policy debates: unexamined premises about efficiency drawn from the kitbag of microeconomists and utopian aspirations far beyond our reach.

Schooling for All

1

Urban Education and
the Working Class

SCHOOLING is today a fashionable political and academic subject. Scarcely a day passes without another book, journal article, newspaper story, or task force report on the state of American education. "The Schools Flunk Out," one reviewer of such evaluations trumpeted in a recent headline. A fine study of public schools in the Great Depression ends with a comparison to current "hard times," while another treatment labels the period 1945–80 the time of "the troubled crusade." Considerations of secondary education have searched for examples of "the good high school," on the assumption that such schools are rare, and they have compared private and public schooling only to find the latter deficient. On what now seems like a routine basis, governmental and foundation commissions discover that our schools are at once mediocre, in a state of crisis, and ill-equipped to serve the national economic or military interest.[1]

Not long ago, educational disputes were concerned with equality and race. Today, in a manner that reflects a more broad ideological shift to the right, school conflicts are mainly about educational standards. One not-so-hidden assumption is that the quest for equality—one that has enmeshed the federal government to an unprecedented degree—has produced a threatening erosion of standards. The reader of these complaints might assume that public education is much like New York City's subway system: in neglected surroundings it provides an unsafe passage presided over by bored and low-productivity employees.

The recent critiques of mass schooling are actually versions of an old, conservative lament about the idea and practice of schooling for all. In this view, public education with few or no barriers to access will, by necessity, dilute intellectual rigor, make victims of gifted children, and reduce incentives to academic achievement. This familiar line of argument has found unwitting colleagueship in the attack on the idea of the common school in both the deschooling tradition of Ivan Illich, which sees organized schools as innately oppressive, and some Marxist critiques of the public school as an agent of capital.

Indeed, much of the debate about schools in recent years has been dominated by those who think common schools in capitalist democracies are a bad idea (albeit for very different reasons). The defenders of common, mass public education, on the other hand, almost to a person, have stood within the "progressive" camp, which in a much too simple way has viewed the "past as a morality tale linking the evolution of American democracy to the triumph of public education."[2]

While newspapers and journals are chock full of stories about educational standards and the fit between schools, work, and society, this conversation has been an impoverished one. Cast in a language of crisis suffused by nostalgic sadness and loss, it reflects a very limited reading of American educational history and is almost entirely lacking in a vision of schooling committed to equality and democratic citizenship.

"Schooling—like education in general—never liberates without at the same time limiting," Lawrence Cremin reminds us. "It never empowers without at the same time constraining. It never frees without at the same time socializing. The question," he concludes, "is not whether one or the other is occurring in isolation but what the balance is, and to what end, and in light of what alternatives."[3] This contradictory and dialectical view by a liberal student of American education provides a helpful orientation to how to think about schooling. Often, schooling is excised from treatments of the welfare state and, more generally, from social democratic attempts by governments to protect ordinary people from the ravages of unfettered markets. The public provision of goods such as social security pensions, as well as the regulation of working conditions, planning to minimize unemployment, and other public policies, though contradictory in their effects on the market system, are nevertheless thought to fall clearly within the social democratic ambit. Moreover, as programs they tend to be associated with working-class movements, organizations, parties, and demands.

Not so with conventional treatments of education. At the very beginning of his book *The Welfare State and Equality,* for example, Harold Wilensky announces that "education is special." Schooling, he claims, promotes meritocracy rather than equality. Education underpins the social structure; it sorts people into the empty places of the occupational order; and it reinforces differences between social groups rather than eliminating or reducing them.[4]

We are not without sympathy to this line of argument, as will be amply demonstrated later. But we reject the excision of schooling from the social democratic package of policies. We do so because we think Wilensky has portrayed tendencies, not certainties. The issues he raises are historically conditioned and variable ones. Schooling may promote equality; it can reshape social structures; and it has narrowed differences between social groups. Just as the expansion of public education in the western countries has usually been promoted by dominant social groups, so, too, has it been resisted by ruling classes. And just as working people have often tried to keep state-imposed schooling at bay, so, too, have educational access and expansion been at the core of working-class politics.

The relationship between schooling and the various national working classes, in short, has been historically contingent. To gain perspective on this historicity it is useful to attend to the lectures R. H. Tawney presented at Williams College in the summer of 1924. Tawney came to America as a well-known socialist, historian, and intellectual leader of the British labor movement.

He came just after the Labour party had returned about one-third of the members of Parliament and had been asked to lead a coalition government. In his lectures he sought to explain to Americans the party's policies and aspirations.

Public education was central to this vision. Tawney's lectures discussed the party's constitution, its stance toward the nationalization of the coal industry, its internationalist orientations, and its commitment to democratic socialism. He spent only a few minutes on social legislation but devoted an entire lecture, the second longest of the six he presented, to "The Labor Movement and Education."

In this account of "the main educational ends at which the Party now in power in England aims," Tawney identifies schooling with egalitarian ends and with ordinary people's aspirations. Labour was at war, he reported, with "a system which graded the quality of education and the opportunities for obtaining it not according to the capacities of children but according to the vulgar irrelevancies of their parents' income." He stressed, by contrast, the Labour movement's belief that "social inequality is at best bad manners and at worst involves a grave waste of character and intelligence."[5]

Schooling was important not only to Tawney's socialist aspirations but to his democratic ones. For without the cultivation of a high standard of the universal provision of education, working people could not be effective actors within their own communities and as citizens. Schooling is necessary to rational, non-manipulated opinion; that is, to the constitution of a public capable of democratic participation.[6]

This association of schooling and citizenship would have been familiar to an American in the 1830s or 1840s. Indeed, Tawney recognizes not only these parallels but the differences between the history of schooling in the two societies. "The fundamental characteristic which distinguishes English education from that of America, and which sets the English reformer his first problem, is that in the former, unlike the latter, public education developed late in the history of an old and stratified society, was for the first two generations subdued to the medium in which it worked, and only after prolonged effort succeeded in asserting its own standards and canons against the pressure of a tough and unyielding environment of social tradition."[7] This one statement of explicit comparison in the lecture challenges us to treat the obverse case, where schooling came early to a relatively permeable social structure and where school officials were able to create links between schooling and citizenship that the various social classes found congenial.

Tawney's lectures are also useful for their speculations about the role that mass pressures in general and working-class activity in particular might have in shaping the expansion of public education. He notes that in the nineteenth century "the impetus to educational reforms in England came from above, from the churches, from the universities, and from the State; and its results were accepted with acquiescence rather than enthusiasm by those for whom they were designed." Only in the twentieth century did this situation alter. "The new thing in the last decade is the emergence of a demand for the extension and improvement of educational facilities among the rank and file of the population. . . . The statement common twenty years ago that public opinion was indifferent to education is today less commonly met than the criticism that it exaggerates its importance."[8]

Although Tawney does not explicitly make the connection, there is an implied relationship between this development and the full expansion of the franchise in 1918 to adult males and to women over thirty, as well as to the supplanting of the Liberal party by Labour as the main alternative to the Tories. From the vantage point of American politics, these correlations provoke questions about the active role of the working class in the United States, where workers could vote and where, early on, they achieved the kind of access to schooling that organized English workers had to fight for in the twentieth century.

Finally, Tawney provides us with a good starting point for his enumeration of those factors and social forces that he considers most important in the history of nineteenth- and early-twentieth-century English education: "religion, class organization, economic interests, and the thought of educationalists and teachers."[9] In our treatment of schooling in the United States we return again and again to a parallel list (even as we find race supplanting religion as a dominant force in shaping conflicts about schooling for all).

Tawney's themes and suggestive, if tantalizingly brief, conceptualization of how to think about schooling resonate throughout this volume. We hope the readers of *Schooling for All* will find in the book a historical elaboration for the United States of Tawney's normative and analytical commitments.

I

THIS BOOK is a memorial to public education as the guardian and cultivator of a democratic and egalitarian political culture in the United States. It is also a call to political assertion, because social resentments and racial divisions in our present commercialized society—one divided by suburban-based social geography into homogeneous polities lacking even a common political forum—mock the idea of schooling for all.

We examine the history of class and education in the United States. If our reading of this history is accurate, however, its telling is of current significance, for the changing relationship between public schooling and the American working class is at the root of our current educational and civic afflictions.

American public schools are in trouble. Characterized by racial and class segregation, grossly unequal teaching, learning, and facilities, mammoth bureaucracies, lost confidence, and a plethora of contradictory policies and goals, the school systems of the United States seem far removed from the powerful early-nineteenth-century vision of the common school for all.

The American working class is also in trouble. Social scientists debate the size of this group, but the number of employees (and their families) who work for a wage, who do not own productive property, and who do not supervise the work of others constitutes the great bulk of the population. Yet as a self-conscious, political group, the working class is a diminishing force. Much of American politics is defined by other factors; even the proportion of workers organized by the trade union movement has declined to only one in five.

The troubles of the schools and the troubles of the working class are connected, just as in the past the achievements of the American working class and the contours of public education were closely bound, if often in surprising ways. The main purpose of this book is to explore these relationships, not only for the present, but in the sweep of the last century-and-a-half of American educational history. *Schooling for All* thus asks two reciprocal questions: how has the American working class shaped the development of public education? And, how have schools shaped the development of the working class?

Mass common schooling under public auspices was created in part because of the support of working people in the decades before the Civil War. They joined in a coalition favoring such schools while at the same time many of their counterparts in Europe were resisting state schooling because, unlike European workers, white male working-class Americans were voting citizens.

The resolution early in American history of the issue of access to public primary education had a paradoxical effect on the working class. The concerns that were most likely to shape a class-based politics—rights to the franchise and public education—were off the public agenda. As a result, school disputes focused less on access to education and more on other issues, some of which were concerned with very specific links between the workplace and the school, such as vocational education, and some of which were concerned with the links between ethnic working-class neighborhoods and the schools, such as language instruction. Over time, this pattern of school politics reinforced divisions between working-class culture at work and at home. As school politics accommodated to these divisions, class as a basis of political action became limited and domesticated—so much so that when the traditional commitment to the common school came under stress both after World War II (when blacks demanded access to it) and in recent years, the working class had virtually disappeared as a force able or willing to fight for schooling for all.

A second aim of this book is to ask what has been special about the American experiences of class and schooling. For if, as David Tyack rightly says, "analysis of urban schools can offer a way to ask questions about the whole society while retaining a particular institutional focus,"[10] then a focus on schooling and class can help us understand distinctive features of culture, social organization, and public policy in the American past and present.

One way the United States distinguished itself from other industrializing capitalist societies of the early nineteenth century was by an early commitment to a civic culture of democratic participation (albeit one restricted by race and sex) irrespective of property and class relations. Yet the United States, like other capitalist societies, did not—indeed, could not—abolish distinctions based on class.

The inescapable tensions between the public and private realms, and battles at this boundary about the extensiveness of equal citizenship and popular sovereignty, took place in and were moderated in part by the system of schooling for all. The commitment to educate all children in primary schools paid for by the government was the most distinctive American public policy of the early nineteenth century. By charting the intertwined story of class, democracy, and schooling we can thus examine the fate of basic features of the American regime.

II

BOSTON established free elementary schools in 1818; New York in 1832. By the end of the Civil War, virtually all large American cities in the North and West had significant educational institutions providing free public primary schools for all potential voting citizens (and for many girls). Their leading characteristics, from the perspective of the other western industrializing countries, was their availability and their interclass basis.

By the middle of the nineteenth century an American working class, as distinct from the working classes of other societies in western Europe and North America, had also been created. What made this working class special was the unusual and stark division between the ways it thought about, talked about, and behaved toward the occupational order, the workplace, and labor struggles, on the one hand, and the residential community, the ethnic group, and political conflicts, on the other hand. Class-based political conflict did not materialize as sharply as the main fault line of politics as it did in other industrializing capitalist countries. The very openness of the American political process to worker participation had an important role in muting holistic class-based responses to industrialization. Therefore, political agitation was not generally organized around workplace relationships (rather, a more narrow but also fierce set of labor issues developed at the site of capitalist firms). Instead, ordinary electoral politics came to be organized around the communities where workers lived and the governmental institutions (police, welfare, and education) that delivered services in these residential spaces. The community, increasingly separate from the workplace, became the basis for ward-based political parties and for ascriptively defined social groups.

The central questions addressed in this book concern the relationships between this special pattern of educational provision and this manifestly unusual working class. Because of the twin developments of early mass-based public schools and a distinctive early pattern of working-class formation, schools became important locations in the shaping of American political culture. In the crucible of education many political and economic leaders sought insurance against social upheaval, and many working families looked to education to alter both individual and group possibilities. School politics, for some, meant the preservation of order; for others it has meant an avenue of opportunity and a lever for altering the social structure.

In *Schooling for All* we explore the connections over time between the exceptional social class and educational features of the American experience. Each has conditioned the other in ways that have changed over time, and that we seek to specify. In making these connections we have focused mainly on Chicago and San Francisco from the period when common schools were founded to the recent era of profound challenge to the ideas and practices of common schooling.

A recurring theme in the chapters that follow is the oscillation between class and ethnic definitions of schooling and the politics of education in the United States. Unlike some European societies, as in Belgium or Holland, schooling has not been understood primarily in ascriptive or religious terms. Nor has education been comprehended mainly in class terms, as in other European societies like England and the Scandinavian countries. In the United States the dynamic relation between the two kinds of definitions, organized by different working-class institutions, has shifted from time to time and from issue to issue. Even where class definitions have predominated, as in Chicago in the late nineteenth and early twentieth centuries, these understandings of class have been restricted to the realm of work and labor.

Since their founding, public schools in large U.S. cities have been neighborhood and community institutions. The units of city politics more generally—ethnic groups from particular residence communities organized on a ward basis—have also been the units of the school population and, at times, of school governance. Thus, from their founding, urban schools were potential objects of ethnic and territorial conflict.

But no school system can entirely escape the potential for— indeed, the strong likelihood of—being understood in terms of class. Although the relationship between capitalist industrialization and the expansion of public school systems has been uneven from one American city to another, and even more so from one European and North American country to another, the existence of this relationship is not in doubt. There simply are no data to contradict Jean Floud and A. H. Halsey's assertion that in capitalist industrial societies "it is inevitable that the educational system should come into very close relationship with the economy."[11] Further, since schooling manifestly prepares children for the labor market (though how well and how precisely it does so is of course a matter of much heated debate),[12] school politics elicit work-related concerns. It was hardly an innovation of Samuel Bowles and Herbert Gintis (the contemporary authors most identified with the analysis of the intertwining of schools and the class structure)[13] to note that "the center of interest in the field of education today is undoubtedly the subject of the relation between education and industry," or that "the rapid growth of modern industry, and the growing importance of industrial and commercial occupations, have exercised an increasing pressure upon the public educational system and have compelled extensions of certain types of educational services and changes in the emphasis upon others." In fact, these citations are drawn not from Bowles and Gintis but from publications written in the 1920s.[14]

In pursuing the connections between schools, workplaces, residence communities, and politics we have been aware that education is multidimensional in two respects: in the *types* of conflict (such as ethnic or class-based ways of organizing struggles about schools) and in the discrete *issues* around which conflicts focus (such as compulsory education, language instruction, and vocational education). Key issues may change even as the definition of what school politics is essentially about may stay the same; and such issues as those of attendance and curriculum may be understood primarily as being concerned with ethnicity and territoriality at one moment and about the workplace and labor relations at another moment.

These questions are explored in the chapters that follow. Taken collectively they represent a particular cut into the vast and complex story of American public education. We think this dissection forces a basic reconsideration of American educational history. Our aim is to change the conventional debates about schooling —confessedly an immodest goal for two political scientists who are not specialists in the domain of education.

In the chapters to come we examine the creation of mass schooling before the Civil War and the development of complex, differentiated school systems later in the century. We discuss the reforms of the Progressive Era and contests over the organization of schooling between 1930 and 1950. And we explore the special features of vocational education and the significance of race. Finally, we speculate about the future of public education.

Each of these themes is familiar, but none has been adequately explored from a perspective focusing on the relationship of class, democracy, and schooling, which we think essential. Since so much hinges on our basic premises and questions, we begin here by clearing through the thicket of approaches to public education in order to find an appropriate place for the analysis of the working class.

It is by no means self-evident, however, that working-class organizations, concerns, and struggles belong at the center of considerations of schooling in America. Indeed, with few exceptions, they have not been at the center. Much traditional scholarship has focused exclusively on the significance of democracy, with a complete lack of concern for social class as an important feature of society. Much of the critical radical and Marxist work of the past two decades has emphasized the functions of schools as agents of social control and as key mechanisms for sustaining inequality in capitalist societies. A reader in search of the working class as an intentional actor would more easily find such an analysis in the pages of an early-twentieth-century progressive economist like Frank Tracy Carlton or a current defender of the liberal vision of schooling like Diane Ravitch than in the work of such critical contemporary analysts as Joel Spring, Clarence Karier, Samuel Bowles, and Herbert Gintis.[15] We take issue neither with the focus on democracy nor with the focus on capitalism but with the disappearance of the working class from educational analyses and the glib dismissals of education from the agendas of social democratic and egalitarian movements and aspirations.

For far too long now, discussions about education, social structure, and politics have been dominated by a discourse, once suggestive but now stale, between traditional progressive historians, on the one hand, who have identified schools as democratizing institutions that, in relatively unproblematical fashion, opened up opportunities to all social classes, and revisionist critics, on the other hand, who have stressed elite domination of schools and the capacity of education to domesticate a potentially insurgent working class. In the former vision, schools transcend class; in the latter they manipulate and reproduce the social structure.[16]

In neither perspective are working people and their children taken seriously, even though they have been the objects of school policies and are actors in their own right. Even such leaders as party politicians, union organizers, and the heads of ethnic and nationality associations are usually treated with only passing references. Without serious considerations of working-class people, organizations, and leaders the debates between progressives and revisionists remain very partial indeed.[17]

When, in the early twentieth century, for example, school reformers advocated administrative centralization, were they principally concerned with educational quality for all children, as the progressive tradition claims, or, as the revisionists argue, with social control? Many speeches by reformers suggest that the latter was more important, for reformers claimed that schooling would increase productivity and dampen political protest. But the meaning of such advocacy changes with its context. If addressed to conservative businessmen to encourage expansion of a proeducation coalition, such speeches may have been tactical assertions designed to gain political support for other unstated ends. But if reformers persisted with such arguments in the face of strong working-class opposition to their plans, the revisionist interpretation of reform as an elite alliance in the interest of social control becomes all the more persuasive. It is impossible to provide this kind of context if the working class is absent and if only the reformers' motives, objectives, ideologies, and successes are discussed in detail. It is precisely this kind of context that is missing from both the progressive and the revisionist accounts.

Consider briefly the work of Lawrence Cremin, a leading exemplar of the progressive tradition. His magisterial series *American Education* represents a landmark contribution to our understanding of educational history. Written without the polemical and tendentious tone typical of the literature on schooling, it acknowledges the importance of some of the themes we stress, including the significance of the separation of work and home and the ways in which schools may prepare students for productive work outside the household. The themes it stresses above all, however, concern the ways in which the schools have formed an integral part of the development of the democratic idea, buttressed by the institutions of family, church, printing press, and library, in addition to that of public education. Schools, in Cremin's view, have been successful in shaping a democratic citizenry:

> Contrary to the drift of a good deal of scholarly opinion during the
> past ten years, I happen to believe that on balance the American

education system has contributed significantly to the advancement of
liberty, equality, and fraternity, in that complementarity and tension
that mark the relations among them in a free society.[18]

The logic of schooling, from this perspective, is the logic of democracy.

The progressive portrait is one of the extension of mass schooling to all children through the secondary level as a happy accom-
paniment of democracy. A society without class-based barriers to
voting produced schools without class-based barriers to access.
The fit between school and society was relatively frictionless and
functional. Schooling, democracy, and the cultivation of individual talent went hand in hand.

While there is much to be said even for this summary version
of the progressive account, its most striking weaknesses are clear.
Its logic of democracy is timeless. Its content might vary over
time, but not its essence. That which is contingent is asserted as
a given. Further, progressive history is history devoid of class
content and contests. Even after the achievement of mass access
to public schools, working people had distinctive interests concerning curricula, ethnic and religious identities, governance, and
the links between schooling and work. About these issues the
progressive version of educational history is silent.

By contrast we have the revisionist camp, whose best work
remains Samuel Bowles and Herbert Gintis's *Schooling in Capitalist
America.* "There is, we believe, a logic to the educational system,"
they write, but on examination it is less a logic of education than
of capitalism. "The mixed record of schooling in capitalist America is a capsule history of the successes, failures, and contradictions of capitalism itself."[19]

If it is clear that our treatment of the relationship between
educational development and working-class history is reserved
about the progressive tradition's tendency to avoid grappling
with social class, it is less obvious that we would have major
differences with the emphasis by Bowles and Gintis. Since theirs
is the most coherent revisionist account, we spend some time
explaining what we think are its shortcomings. But even before
turning to this task, it is worth stressing that Cremin's view of

the schools as an aspect of democracy and Bowles and Gintis's appreciation of education as an aspect of capitalism are not mutually exclusive, even if the advocates of each position think they are.

III

THE WORK of Bowles and Gintis has been exceptionally important and influential for many critical scholars. Its great merit is to locate schools as a key part of capitalism. Their work treats the genesis, expansion, curricula, and organization of schooling and the making of educational policy as the structured, dependent outcomes of the logic of capitalist accumulation. By attending to their arguments we should like to specify why, in contradistinction to them, we think an appropriate starting point for an account of "schooling in capitalist America" is the mutual relationship of working-class formation and public education.

We take issue with neither their attempt to link schooling and capitalist development nor their claims that public schools have had functional consequences for capitalism as a system and for business people as a class. Rather, we differ with how these connections are made and how their account of the functions of schooling is carried out. How Bowles and Gintis conduct their analysis and why the working class disappears from view in their book have important implications for our own analysis, largely because they so directly challenge our premises.

The provocative association in time between capitalist industrial development and the expansion of American public schooling, and the symmetry between what happens in schools with changes in the organization of work, provide Bowles and Gintis with the main evidence for their claim that the logic of public education above all is the logic of capitalism.[20] The core of their argument begins with the assertion that "there can be little doubt that educational reform and expansion was *associated with* the growing ascendency of the capitalist mode of production."[21] Second, they claim that "the educational system helps integrate youth into the economic system . . . through a *structural correspondence* between its social relations and those of production."[22] This "association" and this "correspondence" are more than descriptive claims, they are attempts to explain *why* these relationships hold. "For the past century at least, schooling has contributed to the reproduction of the social relations of production largely through the correspondence between school and class structure."[23] To claim an association and a correspondence in this sense is to claim that mass public schooling was generated and continues to exist *because* it provides for the development of capitalist social relations. In this view the logic of capitalism and the logic of schooling are inextricably bound:

> We have been able to show more than a correspondence between the social relations of production and the social relations of education at a particular moment. We have shown that changes in the structure of education are associated historically with changes in the social organization of production. The fact that changes in the structure have preceded parallel changes in schooling establishes a strong prima facie case for the causal importance of economic structure as a major determinant of educational structure.[24]

These claims are at least as plausible as the progressive argument that democracy creates schools that, in turn, help sustain democratic life. It is in the development of their claims, however, that Bowles and Gintis fall short. They never quite decide whether there are actual far-seeing capitalists who understand the importance of schooling for the market system and who act to promote public education. Their ambivalence on this point can be seen in the passive voice they sometimes adopt, as when they write:

> Since its inception in the United States, the public school system *has been seen* as a method of disciplining children *in the interest* of producing a properly subordinate adult population.[25]

and,

> More fundamentally, the contradictory nature of liberal educational reform objectives may be directly traced to the dual role *imposed* on education in the interests of profitability and stability.[26]

More frequently, a collective subject is provided. Following the last citation Bowles and Gintis write of "these overriding objectives of the capitalist class." Later, they talk of the "two main objectives of dominant classes in educational policy." They also wrote that in periods of crisis

> . . . the capitalist class—through its use of the police power of the state in suppressing anticapitalist alternatives, through more general power attending its control over production and investment, and through extensive control over the financial resources for educational research, innovation, and training—has been able to loosely define a feasible model of educational change, one which has appeared reasonable and necessary in light of the "economic realities" of the day.[27]

With the exception of their short treatment of vocational education and of the high school at the turn of the century, Bowles and Gintis provide virtually no evidence for these claims (though, to be sure, other revisionist historians have provided some of the evidence that *Schooling in Capitalist America* lacks, and the paucity of evidence does not mean that their claims are wrong). More important from our point of view, however, is that the working class never appears in their account as an actor of importance. It is thus impossible to assess whether the connection between capitalism and the schools was ever contested by members of the working class. Nor is it possible to assess the scope for contest, or the content of contest, within the framework of the relationship of the schools and the capitalist system. In the absence of such treatments the working class appears automatically as merely the object of history and public policy, an epiphenomenon of capitalist desires and activities.

By contrast, we think it is impossible to develop accounts of the relationship of schooling and capitalism (and, for that matter, of schooling and democracy) without treating schools and school systems as institutions actually or potentially contested by members of the working class. If we are serious about inquiring after the role of business in shaping public education we must look empirically at moments of indeterminacy, conflict, and change in the character of the public schools. Such examinations demand that we look not only at capitalists but at workers as well.

Bowles and Gintis, by contrast, do not avoid a focus on the working class as much as they explicitly reject it. They treat workers as political actors only when they consider, and put aside, what they call the "popular demand" explanation for the rise of mass education, which argues that the emerging working class before the Civil War provided the support needed to place common schools on a tax-supported basis.

In revised form this view, first proposed by Frank Tracy Carlton,[28] plays an important role in our analysis in chapter 2 of the origins of public education. Bowles and Gintis raise two main objections to it. First, they say that workers' organizations made many demands, education being only one of them; yet only this demand was readily achieved: "What explains their ability to achieve a larger school system when their other demands were not met with such conspicuous success? The answer, we believe, is that the expansion of public education was supported by employers and other powerful people as well as by organized labor."[29] Second, they claim that the evidence presented on behalf of the "popular demand" interpretation is based on the views of skilled and articulate workers, not the majority, who may well not have sought the expansion of schooling.

These objections are very weak. It is far too simple to say that workers counted only when they were part of a larger coalition. On Carlton's evidence this assertion is not correct, or at least is not always correct. But even when it is true the question of what might have happened had the workers staunchly opposed the expansion of public schooling still requires an answer. In America, where workers could vote, would schooling have developed as it did against their opposition?

The claim that evidence of working-class support for schooling in the antebellum period is based on the statements and actions of skilled workers is simultaneously correct and misleading. The workers who articulated and fought for a vision of democratic, common education were not skilled workers in the modern sense but artisans whose very existence as a class was threatened by industrialization. The common school in the East was forged during a period when this class attempted unsuccessfully to organize to secure its future and when the new wage-labor working class was still too weak, too unorganized, and too small to have a coherent political voice. The artisans who supported the common school were attracted by its *common* features, which, through democratic control and supported by mass taxation, the lack of tuition payments, and a shared curriculum across class lines, could cushion their children against social change.[30] Bowles and Gintis are correct to say that this working class had influence only as part of a broad coalition, but they are surely wrong to generalize from the experience of early-nineteenth-century artisans to later eras of working-class history.

More important is their conflation of capitalism and the American experience. While they treat capitalism and schooling in just one society, they present an analysis that hinges almost entirely on what all capitalist societies have in common in spite of their differences (economic accumulation, hierarchical workplaces, differentiated systems of schooling). Since patterns of working-class formation and the particularities of the creation, organization, and content of public school systems differ from society to society, the story of the connections between the working class and the schools in any single society must in part be the tale of comparative differences, not just the similarities Bowles and Gintis emphasize.

IV

"SCHOOLS produce workers,"[31] but how? Bowles and Gintis tell us that schools have been created to see that people are suited for the hierarchical organization of modern firms, but they have nothing to say about whether or how schools reinforce class organizations, languages, and aspirations in different societies. To take up these issues requires a basic understanding of what was special about the working class in the United States in the early to middle nineteenth century at the moment when mass common schooling was brought into being.

We come back to this issue time and again in the chapters that follow. For the moment we should like to illustrate the kind of analysis we shall pursue. One of the key features of early capitalist industrialization in the United States, as in the countries of western Europe, was the growing separation in the large cities between work and residence. The process of separation entailed three main elements. First, the household ceased to be a locus of production. Work moved outside the home. Second, whole districts came to be defined either as places of residence or as places of work. Third, the new residential neighborhoods became increasingly homogeneous in class terms.

The ways workers interpreted and acted on this new social geography varied from society to society. In the United States, working people might have interpreted the new order in holistic terms that would have comprehended society as divided along a single class cleavage at work, in politics, and in community life. Or they might have understood this separation, and the complicated process of negotiating between the new divided spheres of life, in wholly ethnic, communal, and territorial terms. But the pattern that prevailed was different. By the Civil War most American workers in the big cities of the Northeast had developed a separate consciousness of work and home. In this sense American workers were formed as a class only by labor. Outside of work, they developed a multiplicity of affiliations based mainly on ethnicity and territory.[32]

Early school politics contributed to the making and the remaking of this segmented pattern of class and group life. If most urban Americans supported the common school in the antebellum years, not all agreed about its content. American workers, who were divided between older artisans and the emerging wage-earning modern working class and at the same time, in overlapping ways, between Protestants and Catholics and between the native-born and immigrant Irish and Germans, defined school issues in this period primarily in ethnic terms. The ward organizations of big-city school systems, as well as the withdrawal of some Catholics from public education, provided mechanisms for the resolution of these ethnic conflicts in much the same way as emerging local party organizations managed political life on the basis of ethnicity and territoriality.

School issues before the Civil War, in short, helped create a distinctively American working class by providing a sphere of conflict for nonclass definitions of politics outside of work. Workers' parties and unions articulated what they saw as the interest of labor, while the mainstream political parties for which most workers voted, as well as working-class local institutions like gangs, secret societies, and churches, treated schooling in cultural and ethnic terms.

The analysis of school politics and the analysis of class formation, as this brief initial example suggests, may be appropriately joined. Especially in the United States, where the history of the working class has been so caught up with the separation of work and community, a focus on schooling can help reveal both the limits imposed by the American system of class relations and the movement within these limits.

V

THE OBJECTIONS to a focus on working-class attitudes and behavior that Bowles and Gintis discuss are not limited to the early period of mass schooling. "We find little support," they conclude, "for the view that our educational system took its shape from the demands of common people."[33] When we began this study we were certain that this conclusion was facile and based on very little research on the connections between schools and the working class. Although our hunch was that Bowles and Gintis's conclusion was wrong, or at least vastly overstated, we began with an agnostic position. We decided to look and see.

Our answers, which are often speculative, follow in detail. Here a preview is in order. Chapter 2, "Creating Public Education," provides an analytical account of the creation of primary school systems in Chicago and San Francisco. It explains the paradox of the early and vigorous development of public schooling in a country with a relatively weak and inactive state. By examining the assumptions and processes that produced mass state education even in these cities created de novo in the decades just before the Civil War, we show that by mid-century a remarkable consensus about the minimum provisions, levels, and content of public schooling spanning class lines had developed.

Whereas the United States was late and unenthusiastic, in comparative terms, about the creation of modern welfare state policies, it was early and enthusiastic about the creation of modern public schools. Most of the voluminous literature on the founding of public education stresses either industrialization or democracy as the fundamental cause. We reinterpret these suggestions in a framework that does not choose one or the other but argues that early capitalist industrialization created a potential for disorder that was managed by the creation of public schools as one way to protect the political regime and the economic order. The participatory federalism of the American political system helped spur the creation of public education by local elites in coalition with working-class voters. Citizenship, schooling, republicanism, and civic virtue went hand in hand.

The same causal factors that explain the early, vigorous expansion of public education in the United States also help account for the creation of a working class distinguished by the degree to which it developed a split consciousness dividing the work and off-work dimensions of social life. The relationship between the development of these patterns of schooling and of class formation, moreover, for the reasons we have already noted, was mutually confirming.

In the period 1870–1900, discussed in chapter 3, the polarized pattern of working-class formation crystallized, and school systems became more organizationally complex than the common primary schools of the antebellum years. The working class did not provide the central impetus to the expansion of the public schools in this era. Nor did workers engage in school politics as a class with a self-consciousness opposed collectively to other classes or to the state. Rather, workers fought school battles in more narrow terms. Sometimes they assumed an identity as labor. At these moments they were concerned mainly with the links between schools and the workplace. At other times, their ethnic identities came to the fore. Then, members of the working class focused on the cultural, territorial, and political interests they shared with other people spanning class lines. This dichotomous pattern was the result of the open quality of education for white working-class children and of a split consciousness that workers had inherited from the pre-Civil War years.

In chapter 4, which discusses the progressive era of school reform, from 1900 to 1930, we argue not that workers have been overlooked as the central agents of reform, but that they played a distinct role that must be understood both to make sense of the positions and choices of other actors and to understand key sources of variation in the reform experiences of different cities. Without a careful consideration of the relationship between education and the working class in this era it is impossible, for instance, to discover variations between cities in their histories of school reform or to discover why teachers in some places chose to identify with organized labor and in others opted to remain aloof from the working class in the interest of developing an autonomous professional persona. In Chicago, for example, where workers in this period tended to engage in school politics as labor, they managed to extract many concessions from the business and professional advocates of reform. But in San Francisco, where workers utilized their community-based ethnic identities in battles over school reform, they were unable to win concessions from the reform coalition.

Students of school politics usually leap from the era of reform to the 1960s, when educational conflicts are understood to have been the product of the consolidation and growth of the reform impulse. The disappearance of the years 1930 to 1950, dealt with in chapter 5, from the literature on schooling has had the unfortunate consequence of significantly understating the contested character of school organization and policy and of the role of working people in these school conflicts during these decades. Many issues concerning the governance and centralization of the schools, including questions of popular and neighborhood control of education, were repoliticized. The role that workers played in these disputes, however, was more domesticated and even more narrowly instrumental than in earlier periods.

"Training for the Workplace," chapter 6, argues that workers,

acting strictly as labor, were central to the development and expansion of vocational education. Rather than being the hapless
victims of a system imposed from above, workers favored such
training and, through their unions, actively participated in shaping the new programs and in fighting to control them. By desig-
nating vocational education as an appropriate arena of narrow
labor concerns, the outcome of these school disputes re-created
the segmented pattern of working-class participation in school
politics.

In chapter 7 we also break with the periodization of the earlier
chapters to take up the theme of the relationship of blacks to
public education from Reconstruction to the early 1970s. We
show how, for blacks, school issues were concerned precisely
with those questions that had been settled early for whites: access
to schools and citizenship. As a consequence, black school aspirations and struggles resembled those of white European workers
more than those of other Americans. These characteristics became manifest in the 1950s and 1960s, when race became increasingly important as the defining element of urban school politics.
By contrast, class—in either its labor or its ethnic incarnation—
ceased to provide a main fault line of school disputes. Indeed, the
absence of class was as striking as the presence of race at the
center of the urban school movements of the 1960s. In "The
Significance of Race" we show how this shift in the social basis
of the politics of education was the result not only of the special
place of education in black demands for full citizenship but also
of the domestication of class that had taken place over the course
of a century-long engagement of the working class with the
schools.

Finally, in chapter 8, our speculative conclusion proposes that
the long histories of class and race in American public education
have interacted with more recent trends to reopen many fundamental questions about the public schools that had long seemed
resolved. The narrowing of class to instrumental concerns of
labor, together with the breakup of traditional white ethnic city
communities, their dispersion to privatized households in the
rims of the cities and the suburbs, and the increasingly pronounced correlation between places of residence, income, and

styles of life, have transformed the historical notions of *common* schooling subject to *public* political discourse and decision. More and more Americans, including members of the working class, have been able to purchase particular kinds of public schools by purchasing specific kinds of residence areas protected by defensive zoning to ensure their homogeneity. Housing and schooling markets have displaced educational politics as key forums of decision making. As a result, public education, which had been the repository of egalitarian aspirations and opportunities, has become more and more a force for social division and inequality. Education and the market have become increasingly entwined.

If these trends are to be reversed, popular movements and democratic decision making will have to assert themselves on behalf of schooling for all. The future of public education and the character of the American working class are both at stake. Whether and how class and public schooling will exist in the United States thus remain questions that are inescapably connected.

2

Creating
Public Schools

THE HISTORY of public education before the Civil War is
replete with puzzles. In the United States the commitment to
state schooling and to high primary school enrollments came
much earlier than in other major Western societies. Most of the
major industrialized countries achieved almost universal school
attendance by World War I, and all others achieved it just after
World War II. This goal had been achieved, at least for white
American children, in large measure by mid-century and in full
by the end of the nineteenth century.[1]

A second puzzle concerns the auspices of the new public
schools. Most public schools outside the United States have been
founded by central governments. This sponsorship is not surprising because the development of state education in the West has
been an aspect of a larger process by which nation-states became
differentiated and autonomous from other organizations and in
which the state eliminated competitors in a number of spheres
(most crucially, control over the means of legitimate coercion and
taxation). This process of state formation, one of the chief hallmarks of modernity in the West, has been one of the erection of

increasingly sharp boundaries between the state and civil society and of the heightened capacity of government in the areas over which it claims jurisdiction.

From this point of view, the early enthusiasm for state schooling in the United States presents the paradox of the early and vigorous development of public schooling in a country with a relatively underdeveloped state apparatus. The Constitution of the United States is silent about education. Schooling is a power reserved to the states and, in turn, delegated to localities. The founding of public school systems, accordingly, has been undertaken at the local level within the framework of state laws. In other Western societies it took the forceful intervention of the kind of strong nation-state that did not exist in America, often against the wishes of the parents of school-age children, to achieve comparable results. No equivalent of Britain's Education Act of 1870 ushered in a national system of public education in the United States. Instead, the expansion of public education was a repetitive process, with each instance of state schooling disconnected from every other instance.

A third puzzle concerns the bases of support for the new common, or public, schools. The very principle of free, mass public schooling that proved so contentious for ruling groups in other countries and was so often resisted by working classes as an unwelcome state intrusion was accepted as a given by virtually all of the social classes and groups in the United States. This broad consensus can be seen on both the "supply" and the "demand" sides of schooling. With the singular exception of the animosity of Catholic clergy to the early primary schools it is simply impossible to find opposition to state schooling at the primary level by political and social elites or by working-class organizations. The supply of schooling was a given that was beyond public political speech. So, too, was the demand for schooling. Throughout the founding period the demand outstripped the rapidly growing supply.

Schooling for all as a policy for white children has been much examined and debated by educational historians, but these three features of the genesis of public education have remained puzzling. We argue in this chapter that the combination of federalism and voting rights for white male citizens created special structural conditions that facilitated the early and enthusiastic support of public education at a time when early industrial capitalism was reshaping the class structure. Key connections between state-building, economic needs, political culture, and education were provided in the years before the Civil War by using primary schools to cultivate civic responsibility among the working class in the name of republican virtues. The newly emerging working class of this period, in turn, found such appeals alluring because, unlike most of their counterparts in Britain and on the Continent, they were voting citizens.

With access to schooling and to the franchise, America's working class became enmeshed in a politics of education that had less to do with social class and the state than with questions of neighborhood, ethnic diversity, and cultural assimilation. In this way, the federal political system of voting citizens that was so basic to the creation of a distinctive kind of public education also contributed to the development of a special kind of working class, distinguished by the degree to which it developed a split consciousness dividing the work and off-work dimensions of social life. Especially in the large American cities, workplace militancy, which often cut across ethnic lines, was divided from the solidarities of the residential community.

Most considerations of early American primary schooling understandably focus on the Northeast. We have chosen to look mainly at Chicago and San Francisco precisely because they were *not* among the first American cities to create public school systems. By examining the assumptions and processes that produced mass state education even in these cities, which were created de novo in the decades just before the Civil War, it is possible to identify the basic elements of an American consensus regarding minimum expectations for the provision and content of public schooling. To the extent that Chicago and San Francisco confirm each other's development and in this way also confirm the main features of schooling in the East, it is possible to infer a widely shared American pattern of state-sponsored schooling. And it is this distinctively American pattern that commands our attention.[2]

I

THE preeminent historian of American education, Lawrence Cremin, has stressed that education refers to a process more encompassing than formal schooling. He defines education as "the deliberate, systematic, and sustained effort to transmit, evoke or acquire knowledge, values, attitudes, skills, or sensibilities."[3] It is by no means obvious that *state* schooling is required to achieve these purposes. The development of *public* schools must be regarded, therefore, not only as a special kind of educational vehicle but as an aspect of the formation of modern states.

From this perspective, the development of government-controlled schooling is part of the larger organizational history of the state's displacing family, church, and voluntary association controls over various spheres of life. Such was the case as much in the United States as in France and England, where church-state conflicts and issues of secularization provided central axes of debate about the formation of state schools. That the United States (or England or France) would opt for an organized state solution as the principal way to deal with education was not a preordained outcome.

Public schooling as an aspect of state-building demanded, above all, that government assert its legitimate and authoritative claims to make educational policy and control institutions that were independent of the church. It had long been accepted in the Catholic and Protestant countries of western Europe that schooling was the principal responsibility of the clergy, in tandem with the family. Thus, in France, education was not a public function under the ancien régime. Leaders of the French Revolution wrote and spoke often about compulsory and universal education sponsored by the state, but it was not until the Third Republic that free state education dislodged the monopoly of the church in primary schooling. Elementary schooling in England was also mainly the preserve of the Anglican church and the nonconformist churches until 1870. The secularization of the schools in Prussia was achieved in the early nineteenth century, nearly a century after Frederick William I declared himself in favor of universal state schooling and a half century after Frederick the Great created a state secondary and university system (he was compelled to leave elementary schooling in the hands of the clergy).

The family and the church were the preeminent instruments of education in colonial America. The patriarchal household provided for schooling in values and for apprenticeship. Piety and civility were transmitted in part by example and in part by the ability to read and ponder the Bible. Access to trades was also the responsibility of the household, especially since extrafamilial institutions for training, such as guilds of artisans and merchants, were weaker in America than in England or on the Continent. The various American religions—from Anglican and Puritan, to Quaker and Dutch Reformed, to Catholic, and, in small numbers, Jewish—taught their congregants in both informal and formal settings. Like other institutions in the New World, the churches tended to be intensely local bodies that expressed and shaped the culture of the residents of the geographical communities in which they were located.

In these communities schools came and went under a variety of sponsorships, usually religious. Most striking about these schools was their lack of differentiation from other organizations that were part of civil society. As Cremin writes, there was a

> . . . blurring of lines between institutions, which makes it exceedingly difficult to assess the number and concentration of formally established schools. What the sources clearly indicate is that schooling went on anywhere and everywhere, not only in schoolrooms, but in kitchens, manses, churches, meetinghouses, sheds erected in fields, and shops erected in towns; that pupils were taught by anyone and everyone, not only by schoolmasters, but by parents, tutors, clergymen, lay readers, precentors, physicians, lawyers, artisans, and shopkeepers.[4]

Schooling was a patchwork in the larger port cities of Boston, New York, Philadelphia, and Baltimore, one that cut across divisions between the private and the public, the religious and the secular, the workplace and the residence.

This diverse pattern was complemented by a growing interest

in education by the governments of many towns and cities in the prerevolutionary era. As historian Geraldine Murphy has shown, various localities in seventeenth-century Massachusetts began to concern themselves with the provision of some free schooling.[5] Outside of New England such efforts were more sporadic but were never wholly absent. A much more common form of schooling, however, was provided by schoolmaster-entrepreneurs of the kind who later founded the first primary schools of Chicago and San Francisco. Of the schoolmasters Cremin has identified in New York City and Philadelphia between 1689 and 1783, the parochial and town-sponsored schoolmasters numbered 103, but the entrepreneurial teachers numbered 413.[6]

Schooling was rather more available in the New World on the eve of the American Revolution than in the countries from which most Americans came, but it was still relatively scarce. In the three decades before the revolution there was an average of 175 children per teacher in Philadelphia and 254 children per teacher in New York City. Mass public schooling did not constitute a fact of public life. Although the Founders had a good deal to say about the importance of schooling for a republican nation of citizens, their ideals took a very long time—some seven decades —to begin to be translated into action.[7]

During that period, spanning the postrevolutionary and the antebellum years, a radical transformation occurred in the expectations and practices of Americans. The school systems of Chicago and San Francisco are indicators of just how extensive this change was. What had been problematical in 1780 had become conventional by 1850. "For the nation as a whole," Cremin observes, "schooling was established in those areas where it had been nonexistent, regularized in those areas where it had been intermittent, and systematized and extended in those areas where it already had been prevalent."[8] These new schools, which were parts of school systems, provided the rudimentary infrastructure for the dramatic increases in enrollment, expenditure, physical plant, standardization of curricula, and the grading and classification of students that were the hallmarks of mid- and late-nineteenth-century educational development.

By 1850 public primary schools had become commonplace.

The creation of government-sponsored school systems in Chicago and San Francisco summarized and telescoped a long history of educational development, one in which the state of Massachusetts, under the leadership of Horace Mann, had been the most visible pioneer. Scholars have debated whether the process of founding Massachusetts' schools was a conflictual one, a subject to which we return later, but it is clear that by mid-century in new cities like Chicago and San Francisco the great majority of people of all social classes agreed that mass primary education was desirable and that the Massachusetts model was indeed appealing. The schools of Massachusetts and more generally those of New England and New York defined for Chicago and San Francisco residents the kind of public schooling they wanted.[9] In fact, Chicago's success in instituting such Eastern methods as the grade classification system and an age-specific curriculum allowed San Francisco to look to Chicago as a model as well as to New England and New York.[10]

II

LIKE the other states carved out of the Northwest Territory, Illinois was enjoined by the Ordinance of 1787 to establish a constitution with a commitment to schooling. The state's first constitution set aside land in each township for public schools. Shortly after Chicago was incorporated in 1833, local citizens petitioned under state law for the sale of school lands to create a school land fund. The interest earned from this fund was apportioned among schools on the basis of number of pupils.[11]

The first schools to receive such funds were public only insofar as they had a governmental source of income and, in exchange, were compelled to permit a measure of public oversight. They were not public in the modern sense of being demarcated clearly from the private sphere. The boundary between public and private was hazy. The first schools to receive a governmental subsidy (there were three in 1834) had been founded as private schools by teacher-entrepreneurs and used their government moneys to offer free education to white children whose parents could not afford to pay their fees.[12]

The boundary between public and private, between state and civil society, became less permeable in 1835 when a special act of the Illinois State legislature created a structure of governance and finance that permitted the development of a publicly initiated school *system.* The act provided for the organization of school districts in Chicago and for the election of trustees for the "common schools" to oversee school property and the processes of levying taxes and hiring teachers and to "see that the district schools are free, and that all white children in the district have an opportunity of attending them, under such regulation as the inspectors shall make."[13]

Chicago was granted its first charter as a city in 1837. With the charter, control over public schools was transferred to officials of the city government, with ultimate authority vested in the Common Council. A coherent system of school government and finance was created.[14] Although relatively primitive by later standards, these new arrangements clearly were public, not private; secular, not sectarian; and common to all white children, not segregated by class.

Some two thousand miles to the west, San Francisco replicated key features of the Chicago situation. There, too, the creation of the city and the establishment of public schooling went hand in hand, and there, too, the first attempts at a public role in education both predated the formal establishment of the city in 1851 and depended on an inchoate and permeable boundary between private and public.[15]

The first public school in San Francisco was an ad hoc affair. In 1849 a local teacher established a private school and petitioned the San Francisco Common Council for an appropriation. Financial support was awarded to the school a year later; the teacher became a public employee and the council regulated the duration of the school day. The council created a school system the next year by taking advantage of provisions of a new state law that distributed funds from the sale of public lands to counties on the basis of a census of children between the ages of six and eighteen. In September 1851, the San Francisco Common Council voted to establish a network of free common schools, dividing the city into five districts with the capacity to levy new real estate taxes to supplement state aid.

In the two decades that followed their founding, the school systems of Chicago and San Francisco grew rapidly and developed from primitive organizations into increasingly complex decentralized structures of governance and administration.

Chicago had only 21 teachers on the public payroll, an enrollment of 1,919 pupils, and a school budget of $6,038 in 1850. Just two decades later, the system employed 537 teachers, schooled 38,939 pupils, and spent $527,741. San Francisco's enrollment likewise increased more than thirtyfold between 1851 and 1870 from its initial 1,000 pupils; the number of teachers in these years grew from 15 to 371 and the budget rose from $23,125 to $526,626.

The schools not only grew but became organizationally differentiated, coherent public bureaucracies. Chicago's first school superintendent was appointed in 1854, and a board of education was created in 1857. These two developments separated schooling from other functions of the city government and made possible the coordination of curriculum and grading levels across district and ward lines. "It was nothing less than a revolution," Hannah Clark wrote in her historical survey in the late 1890s, "when the superintendent began to examine classes, organize departments, and insist on the use of uniform text-books."[16] In San Francisco, separate ungraded schools were superseded, as in Chicago, by a system governed by a superintendent and a board of education that presided over numerous graded primary schools. The earliest San Francisco schools, like those in Chicago, had not provided printed courses of study for teachers to follow but had given teachers the authority to devise curricula. These schools were also ungraded. Not until 1859, after the institutionalization of the superintendency, was a printed course of study drawn up, and not until 1861 was the division of students into separate grades introduced into all the primary schools.

III

IF it is clear that the development of public schooling is an aspect of state formation, it is equally clear that the elements of state-building vary enormously in timing and content from country to country. An identification of the founding and expansion of American public education with the state's assertion of a distinction between the private and the public provides a useful starting point, but it cannot distinguish between the various kinds of states and civil societies that affected the process of founding public schools. Consider, for example, the key relationship between church and state.

In the context of state formation it should come as no surprise that conflicts about religion dominated other forms of conflict in the early history of public schooling in the United States. "The gravest obstacle to the development of an effective common school system throughout the United States," educational historian Rush Welter observed, "was neither urban taxpayers' parsimony nor rural complacency but religious intransigence." During the 1830s and 1840s prominent spokespersons for most of the Protestant sects and for the Catholic church insisted that sectarian religious training was "indispensable to the maintenance of public morality."[17] More particularly, the nativist zeal of the antebellum decades produced both an assertive Protestantism and a defensive reaction among fearful Catholics.

The centrality of religious conflict to the formation of American public education is not, as much educational scholarship interprets it, a reflection of exceptional religious pluralism or of the importance of ethnicity in American life. On the contrary, religious conflicts in the United States highlighted the same issues that defined the formation of states and the creation of public schooling throughout the West.

But if the issues were the same, the outcome was different. Public education became nondenominational earlier, and the public realm imposed itself against opposition in the educational sphere more emphatically and completely in the United States. Religious challenges to public schools did appear, but, in comparative terms, these conflicts were at the fringes of a broad consensus on public schooling. Their comparatively mild character was the result of the country's constitutionally limited role for religion in public life, the diverse and divided character of religious organizations and affiliations, the relative newness of Catholicism in large cities, and the less entrenched character of church-run schooling. Religious bodies, in short, were weaker, had less to defend, and had fewer incentives to resist the encroachment of the state into the area of education than their European counterparts. Nonetheless, religious conflicts about education are worth attending to because they provide significant confirmation of the key features of the American educational experience we have identified.

The history of Chicago schools was unlike the typical Old World pattern in that Catholic schools did not predate public schools. In fact, they arose later. Although there was considerable diversity and decentralization in the schools established by the church—most Catholic schools were attached to a particular parish and supervised by a parish priest, and many were considered the province of a particular ethnic group—together they constituted a coherent system in competition with the public schools. When the first two Catholic schools were opened in 1846, public schools were already well established in each of Chicago's four school districts. By the early 1850s, eight Catholic primary schools, in addition to a Catholic academy and a university, were in existence.

At this time there were six Irish Catholic schools with 600 students among them and two German Catholic schools with an additional 300 students. The total number of students in Catholic schools rose to 10,612 in 1870 (one-fourth of the public school count) when fifteen of the twenty-one parishes in Chicago had schools attached to them. The largest proportion of students at this time were enrolled in the city's eight predominantly Irish, English-speaking schools. The next largest group went to the five German schools, and the remainder were divided between the city's one Bohemian and one Polish school.[18]

Throughout this period a strict separation between Chicago's public and church schools was maintained. Early school legislation made no provision for state funding of parochial schools, and the 1870 Illinois constitution expressly forbade it. This separation between public and church schools was reinforced by the strong anti-Catholic sentiments prevalent in Chicago and by the Catholic hierarchy's strongly expressed animosity toward the public school system. The *Western Tablet,* a short-lived Catholic newspaper, characterized the public schools in the early 1850s as places where

> . . . either no religious instruction is imparted, or if any connected with what is called religion be inculcated, they [Catholic children] are taught to feel ashamed of the creed of their forefathers, which is often assailed, travestied and ridiculed by anti-Catholic and prejudiced teachers.[19]

To counter these influences Catholics requested, unsuccessfully, that priests be permitted to instruct children in the public schools about their religious obligations.[20]

In the early 1850s, Catholic objections to the public schools went so far as to challenge their right to exist. The *Western Tablet* argued:

> The system of public schools supported by taxation as established in many States of the Union and chiefly in this city, is entirely at variance with the notions which the members of the Catholic Church entertain of a *good education*. . . . Religion is, by the Catholic Church, considered an essential branch of education, and without religion she conceives no *real education* possible. . . . We Catholics look upon the system now pursued in our public schools not only as unfit for the education of our children, but we regard it as unjust, as unconstitutional, and as either Godless or sectarian. . . . We are forced by compulsive taxation to pay for the schooling of the children of others, and have to impose a voluntary tax upon ourselves to educate our own.[21]

The Catholic hierarchy and press frequently warned parents that they were violating their duty to the church if they allowed their children to attend public schools. Throughout the century the Catholic establishment aspired to obtain public funding for parochial schools, eliminate the taxing of Catholics for public education, and have Catholic teachings incorporated into the public schools, but they lacked the power to make such demands a serious political issue.

Unable to secure broad public support (even among the Catholic laity) for the type of schooling they preferred, Catholic leaders retreated to much weaker claims that implicitly recognized the legitimacy of the public schools. Instead of contesting the public schools' right to exist, they sought to remove what they saw as anti-Catholic religious influences from the schools. Their campaign to proscribe the teaching of the Protestant Bible in the public schools became a subject of keen debate in the late 1860s and achieved success in 1874.[22]

In San Francisco the local government and the church had a less acrimonious relationship and reached a more formal rapprochement, but the substantive outcome was the same in the sense that religious conflict was marginalized.

The ordinance establishing the public schools of San Francisco provided that schools "formed by the enterprise of a religious society in which all the educational branches of the district schools shall be taught" should be eligible to receive city funds. In 1852 the California legislature ruled that this provision was illegal. But the following year the state's Superintendent of Public Instruction recommended to the legislature that the school law be amended to allocate some public funds to denominational schools, which were helping to ease the burden of overcrowded public schools. The result was the passage of the Ward School Act of 1853, which, once again, made the Catholic schools eligible to receive public funds.

The practice proved short-lived. Three Catholic "ward" schools, providing for 1,421 students, received just under $40,000 between 1853 and 1855. In 1855 the legislature ended the practice of funding these schools by requiring that parochial schoolteachers pass an examination and obtain a public school certificate in order for their schools to receive public funding.[23]

While the Catholic hierarchy continued to voice its preference for a school system that would allocate public funds to denominational schools, unlike its Chicago counterparts it did not oppose the principle of free public schools. It did, however, continue to seek public funds by pointing to the savings to the public purse provided by church schools. But with the exception of a grant of $15,000 to the schools run by the Presentation Sisters in 1870, the ward school experiment was never revived.[24]

Catholic opposition to the public schools of San Francisco was tempered by the public schools' hiring of Catholic teachers after the ward schools were abolished in 1855. Historian R. A. Burchell argues that "although the city went along with the state prohibition against passing local tax money to the Church schools, the San Francisco political situation was too delicately balanced after 1855 to permit a Protestant crusade against Catholic teachers in the public schools." Because the public schools were not "aggressively Protestant," clerical zealots had trouble convincing Catholics that their " 'immortal souls' were in 'fearful danger' . . . in the present common school system when the system seemed altogether indifferent to religion."[25] Thus, while the relationship of religion and the schools was by no means resolved by 1870, the fundamental principle of providing tax-supported nonsectarian public schools was not challenged even by those who advocated that the state should also support denominational schools.

IV

RECENT scholarship on the origins and expansion of state schooling in western Europe can help sharpen the questions we ask about the development of American public education. As in the United States, modern school systems were created in nineteenth-century France, Germany, and England. By the end of the century each of these countries was committed to universal primary schooling, to the proposition that basic schooling should be the province of state, and to the idea that schooling was the path for children to learn civic responsibility and acquire occupational training.[26]

There are many broad similarities, as well as some subtle differences, between the formation of public schooling in colonial America and in eighteenth-century western Europe. Throughout

Europe the various state-established churches had the most formal responsibility for schooling; in practice, their supervision was intermittent, and local parishes and communities were very much left on their own to fashion the schools as they saw fit. Schoolteachers were supported by various methods—by local taxes from the tithe, by subscription of the local population, or through endowments. Overall, there was an extremely uneven distribution of schooling. In southern France, for example, most villages had schools, but there were virtually none in Brittany. Eighteenth-century surveys show that between one-third and two-thirds of parishes in England had schools of some sort. In all of these settings, as in the United States, the schools varied enormously in their permanence, formality, security of finance, and size.

By the early nineteenth century the European and American patterns of schooling had begun to diverge. There was, of course, a great diversity of school reform patterns in nineteenth-century Europe, but a number of important differences between Europe and America stand out. By contrast to the massive popular demand for schooling in the United States, European school reforms were not based on popular support. After an exhaustive survey, educational historian M. J. Maynes concluded:

> What is surprising and telling about the history of school reform in the late eighteenth and early nineteenth centuries . . . is that the impetus for school reform did *not* come from parents. On the contrary, even if many parents throughout Western Europe silently acquiesced to the reform of the school, the records of popular response to educational innovation suggest that these reforms often met with a great deal of active or passive resistance.[27]

Not only did popular movements opt "for outright rejection of the offer, held out by reformers, of schooling for the people," but they created alternative, often utopian visions of what schooling might be.[28]

To the extent to which it is possible to generalize about the diverse European experience, the principal impulse to create mass, state-sponsored schooling originated in ruling groups and classes. In elite discussions the view that elementary education should be accessible to all was at first very much a minority view. Over time, the opinion that mass schooling was dangerous was overtaken by the position that the best way to maintain the social order was not through ignorance but by carefully modulated and limited access to state-controlled schooling.

This view was in some measure motivated by the view that the new capitalist order might benefit from a better-educated labor force. But far more prevalent were state-building motives. From the middle of the eighteenth century bureaucrats in the German states, and especially in Prussia, began to pressure the church-administered schools to contribute to the economic prosperity underpinning the regime's fiscal health, to mold a more patriotic citizenry, to consolidate military organization, and, in these ways, to secure the state apparatus. With the goal of assuring the implementation of these aims, the central state asserted in the Prussian state law code of 1894 its responsibility for developing schooling with relatively uniform characteristics across the various localities through such mechanisms as teacher training and inspections.[29]

Although French and English school reforms proceeded at a slower pace, they were animated by very similar central-state-building impulses. Popular education in France, though discussed in the ancient régime, was very much the product of the French Revolution and the Napoleonic reforms that followed. These were national and centralizing reforms, thought to be essential to the political success of the regime. In England, resistance by the dominant classes to mass public education lasted longer, in part because they feared Europe's first industrial working class, but by the middle of the nineteenth century state subsidies and state inspections had created a de facto, if uneven, national system of schooling.

Popular resistance and central state leadership, in tandem with initiatives by industrialists and landowners, were the key features of European school reform. In the interests of state building, "enlightened" elites managed by the end of the nineteenth century to create school systems that imposed obligatory schooling on the majority of school-age children and state controls over teaching and curricula. The pace of reform hinged largely on the rate at which various elites came to see the schools as a tool for the assertion of state authority in opposition to the traditional view that the ignorance of the bulk of the population is a sure guarantor of social control.[30]

In all of these respects the expansion of state schooling in the Old World differed radically from the American pattern. To be sure, on both sides of the Atlantic schooling had become more regular, more formal, and more encompassing by the end of the nineteenth century. But in the United States patterns of popular resistance were largely absent (indeed, as this chapter will show in some detail, public education was a central concern of working-class organizations in the antebellum years); school expansion was mainly a local affair; and the political coalitions supporting the schools transcended class divisions.

The explanations most commonly offered to account for the variation in the pace of school expansion in Europe appear to have only limited applicability to the United States. Sociologist Marzio Barbagli, for example, attributes the Italian elite preference for keeping the masses ignorant to the traditional character of the society—its low social mobility, its rigid stratification, the importance of the church, and the low degree of differentiation between the family and the units of the economy. But if the implicit counterfactual is that the most modern of the industrial societies would opt for rapid expansion of schooling—a position consistent with the American experience—then why was the most industrial and the least agrarian of the European countries, England, among the last to institute mass, free, state-sponsored primary schooling? Indeed, much comparative work has established that while there is a broad correlation between capitalist and educational development over the long haul, throughout the nineteenth century the pace of school reform, the enthusiasm with which it was greeted, and the actors who pushed for it neither were dependent on a proximate relationship with capitalist development nor were a direct consequence of the rate of capitalist development.[31]

More specifically, the differences between the American and English cases cannot be accounted for by reference to the factors Barbagli cites for Italy. With regard to this comparison, Maynes suggests that English elites feared a self-conscious, organized working class. But in the United States fear of a well-organized working class did not prove to be a barrier to elite support for public schooling. In yet another comparison, between the rates of school expansion in Germany and in France, Maynes proposes that French liberalism retarded the development of public schools because it permitted local resistance to central-government school reform plans. This relationship between liberalism and slow school expansion is implausible for the United States, where liberalism and schooling went hand in hand. But it does indicate that in regimes that allow for local options the attitudes of local governments and local populations are critical factors.

V

IF the explanations most frequently offered to explain the variations in educational development in Europe have only limited applicability to the United States, how shall we explain the American pattern? With so little class conflict or resistance, why did schooling come so early?

Among the key factors, we will argue, was democracy in a federal state where a language of republicanism was shared by the citizenry at a distinctive moment of capitalist development. By shattering preindustrial patterns of social control that centered on the household as a unit of production, capitalist industrialization created massive new problems of order that were expressed, in part, as problems of citizenship in a republic. The dominant classes feared disorder, articulated their concerns in terms of civic virtue, and pursued educational reform as an instrument of order. The working classes, like working classes elsewhere, strongly desired schooling for their children. But, unlike some other working classes, they were prepared to join in political coalitions favoring public schooling because they had already been mobilized by political parties into the state as voting citizens.

This interpretation, which will be developed later in this chapter, differs substantially from both the "progressive" and the "revisionist" views. Unlike the revisionists, we think it mistaken to singularly stress class conflict and the economic functions of schooling, at least in this period. Unlike the progressives, however, we think that not just democracy but capitalism mattered. Let us see how.

In "The Origins of Mass Public Education," based on evidence from Massachusetts, Samuel Bowles and Herbert Gintis argue that the founding of public schools was characterized by class struggle—"a jarring and conflict-ridden course of struggle and accommodation." The shift to state-run schools, in their characterization, is to be explained mainly by changes in the organization of production and by the desires of "an ascendant and self-conscious capitalist class . . . [whose] needs were to profoundly shape the evolution of the educational system." In this view, the shifts in the labor force and its skill levels "required a system of labor training which would allow the costs of training to be borne by the public" and brought about a school system that could dampen opposition by workers to the new capitalist order.[32]

In short, their view—which is elaborated in a sketch of Lowell, Massachusetts, where industrialization and the creation of common schools coincided—is that capitalist development was the most important cause of American educational expansion. They recognize that in an equally capitalist England state schooling lagged by a half-century, but this gap they explain by the resistance to state schooling by landowners and the Church of England against the wishes of both workers and businesspeople. In the United States, where such resistance was weaker, professionals and capitalists led the way to schooling for all, often against the opposition of perplexed working people, whose resistance in Lowell took the form of boycotts and even an attempt to burn down a school in an Irish neighborhood.[33]

As we shall soon demonstrate, we agree with Bowles and Gintis's very broad assertion that "educational reform and expansion in the nineteenth century was associated with the growing ascendency of the capitalist mode of production."[34] When put this way, it is difficult to disagree. But we think Bowles and Gintis are far afield in the manner in which they tackle this relationship, as well as in their interpretation of the details of working-class attitudes to schooling.

The central problem with placing capitalism at the center of explanations of schooling for all in the United States is not that other capitalist societies seemed to require less public education; it is, as educational sociologist Robert Dreeben has put it, that "American schooling has expanded in excess of occupational demands."[35] The problem to be explained is why the "minimum" level of schooling in mid-century America represented a "surplus" beyond what capitalism appeared to require, either in Dreeben's analytical terms or by comparison with other capitalist societies.

Further, more exhaustive studies of Massachusetts confirm our findings for Chicago and San Francisco that the introduction of common schooling by local governments was a process that took place with very little conflict. Economic historian Alexander Field, for example, has found that instances of intense political conflict about public education were very rare and more often than not focused on issues of immigration and nativism rather than on schooling as such. Most commonly, school professionals were able "to implement their policy solutions largely without opposition." Kaestle and Vinovskis likewise found that in mid-nineteenth-century Lynn, Massachusetts,

> . . . the public in general consistently supported the growth of the system and expected it to train up literate and virtuous citizens who would be integrated into the work and social life of the city and nation. From all that we could learn, both the most complacent and the most disenchanted elements of the adult population agreed about the ends and means of the schools. We have found no evidence to indicate that any group, at any time during the century, actively resisted either the aims or the organizational arrangements of the public school system except some Roman Catholics, who objected on religious grounds.[36]

If Bowles and Gintis press for too direct a relationship between capitalism and schooling, our own approach, focusing on state-building, citizenship, and federalism, is nevertheless nestled within a broad understanding of the school-capitalism connection. But our understanding of this relationship is more indeterminate.

The brilliant, if unfocused, reconstruction of Massachusetts educational development by Kaestle and Vinovskis demonstrates that the shift from private to public schooling was less a shift in the number of children in school than a shift in locus of enrollments. But once the state took over the bulk of schooling, it could authoritatively intensify the educational experience by lengthening the time children spent in school in a given school year. This new capacity, they show, broadly coincided with, or even anticipated, surges in economic growth.[37]

This link, however, was *not* narrowly and instrumentally *economic* in character:

> Because the major trend was toward expanded common school enrollments, not more intensive secondary education, and because the different levels of education were not well coordinated or regulated, little meritocratic selection and training of talent was going on, quite apart from discriminatory attitudes that have always compromised the "sorting" process. Besides, early industrial development did not require upgraded skills; on the contrary, skill requirements were reduced by factory production.[38]

How, then, did capitalism figure in the early development of American public education?

Field's careful empirical work helps define the relationship. In his comparative study of Massachusetts townships he finds that the *length* of school sessions varied in a remarkably consistent way with the percentage of Irish in the population, the number of families per dwelling, and the share of male merchants over the age of fifteen in the labor force—all measures of industrialization. He concludes: "It was a particular type of social environment associated with a particular type of manufacturing that along with commercial development tended to induce long school sessions."[39]

Note that in this analysis the tie between capitalism and schooling does not hinge on a human-capital argument, nor does it depend on the schools' adopting a curriculum to train children to be productive workers. Instead, Field stresses that local political actors, faced with the dislocations and problems of social order created by industrial change, tried to create schools as a way to protect the social structure and the economic order.[40] This suggestive formulation provides a starting point for an argument that connects economic developments to state-building, participatory federalism, the political coalitions that supported public education, and American patterns of class formation.

It is important to remember that the dislocations of capitalist industrialization were not just changes in the nature of work; they were cultural and spatial in character. Under the impact of industrialization the family workshop, the locus of most late-eighteenth- and early-nineteenth-century production, broke up and was succeeded by new divisions in city space that sundered old patterns of social control. In industrializing cities and towns, the place of work and the place of residence increasingly separated; and the various social classes more and more came to live apart.

Everywhere in the West, working people experienced and resisted the massive transformations of economic and social life where they worked and where they lived. In addition, as Katznelson has written,

> The state responded in pursuit of order in unprecedented ways. These responses were hardly identical from place to place, but they did always have three constituent elements: the attempt to regulate, and often to proscribe, combinations of workers at the point of production; the use of the franchise to incorporate workers and their leaders into the polity in ways that least threatened social cohesion; and the development of a new nexus of political relationships linking residence communities to government. Collectively, these responses by the state replaced traditional "private" forms of social control with public authoritative activity. One consequence was the displacement of conflict between capital and labor into relations between the state and citizen.[41]

In the United States these general trends were reinforced from the perspective of local elites by the fact that workers were *citizens,* whose voting patterns and bases of solidarity at best were unpredictable. Further, in a federal system with a central government concerned mainly with securing its own existence at home and in the international arena, and with the issues of tariffs and internal improvements, local governments had to find their own solutions to the problems of order.

Within this economic and political crucible public education was forged. At the level of local government, schooling was one of the available mechanisms to incorporate citizens into the regime and, in this way, to secure authority and property. In the United States, where the state was diffuse and decentralized (so much so that educational historian David Tyack argues against state-centered explanations like ours on the grounds that in the nineteenth century "it was by no means clear what the 'state' really was")[42] and where white males were voting citizens, the political functions of schooling were expressed by politicians and school reformers in a rhetoric of republicanism that emphasized the socialization of citizens for civic responsibility.[43]

Connections among education, republican virtues, and stability were commonplace in the discourse of school officials and political leaders. The first superintendent of Chicago's schools observed in his inaugural report that:

> Republican institutions are founded upon the virtue and intelligence of the people where they exist—they can be founded upon nothing else. . . . It is in the province of the Public Schools to educate each rising generation that it may be able to transmit our institutions, unimpaired, to each successive generation in turn. Tear down our School Houses and turn our children into the streets, and our political institutions would be involved in the ruin. . . . Education is necessary not only for the public safety but for the happiness of the individual.[44]

The defense of the common school system in San Francisco rested on similar grounds. The city's most important educator, John Swett, often asserted that "it is the duty of a republican or representative government, as an act of self-preservation, to provide for the education of every child" and that the schools have a particular responsibility to be "the educators of the working men and women of the nation" because "the schools mold the character of the men whose will expressed through the ballot-box makes and unmakes constitutions and breathes life into all laws."[45]

This kind of language provided a discourse about education capable of spanning class lines. It appealed to political and economic elites as a formula for order, and it appealed to working people as a formula for citizenship.[46]

Working-class trade unions and organizations without doubt were strong supporters of schooling for all in the years just before and after the Civil War. Based on his reading of this evidence and on the support that working-class voters gave to tax referenda to support the public schools, Frank Tracy Carlton concludes that the working class was "chiefly instrumental in placing our schools on a tax supported basis."[47] This view is the mirror image of the position advocated by Bowles and Gintis and other revisionist scholars, who see the founding of state education as a process of imposition. Both positions treat the establishment of public education in terms of class struggle.

Carlton's view is significantly more compelling than those provided by the revisionists. He points to the votes of the working-class electorate, to the importance that urban Workingmen's parties assigned to mass schooling, and to craft union support for the schools in the 1830s and 1850s in the port cities of the Northeast. For these groups, as for other Jacksonians, schools were a means to break monopolies of the dominant classes.[48]

If there is no question that working-class organizations and citizens in the main supported public education, it does not follow that they were its key advocates or that they had to struggle mightily against others to realize their goals.

Surely this was not the case in Chicago or San Francisco; nor, as historian Philip Curoe showed six decades ago, was this the case more generally. Curoe's findings, in fact, have held up remarkably well. Workers were part of the political coalition supporting the schools: "They worked with other groups toward stirring up an interest in educational reform among the complacent members of legislatures and among the general public. They helped to 'sell' the idea that a voting citizen cannot discharge his obligations without a modicum of education and some leisure for self-improvement." In short, they appealed for schooling assuming their identity as citizens, not their identity as workers. More-over, their attention to this issue was sporadic and episodic. "Here and there a labor group touched upon a vital educational problem, but there was no sustained 'drive.' "[49]

This pattern is not surprising in a country where workers were voting citizens and where workers were not excluded from access to schooling on the basis of class. On the Continent and in Britain demands for the vote and for common schools under popular control were demands made on a class basis *against* the state. In the United States, working-class men quickly entered the world of citizens, and their children entered the public schools. As Katznelson has written elsewhere, "Workers as citizens did not feel they had to battle the state, for they were included in its embrace."[50]

Neither the franchise nor the schools were objects of class struggle. The parallels between the extension of voting rights and that of access to common schools are striking. In both instances issues of citizenship were debated on the ground of common liberal assumptions about representation and sovereignty that left little legitimate room for opposition. And in both instances the elusive, diffuse, decentralized character of the American fed-eral state facilitated an inclusive polity. With respect to the vote there was no unitary state for ruling classes to defend or for working classes to transform. Likewise, with respect to public education the multiple levels of the political system created thou-sands of different arenas where political coalitions for schooling could come together, arenas that became elements of a continent-wide pattern of policy diffusion.

It is worth noting that access to citizenship in the American federal regime—recorded primarily in the early franchise but also in early access to public schooling and in the relatively tolerant legal climate for the formation of urban craft unions—was also the central factor in shaping the formation of the American work-ing class in the antebellum period. During that time the experi-ence of industrialization was understood and acted on by workers in a way that distinguished between the work and off-work parts of working-class life. At work, the working class was formed as labor, represented by trade unions. Off work it was mobilized into politics by a decentralized party system, stressing territorial and ethnic rather than class identities and the delivery of services, including education, to citizens in their residential communities. The federal state was permeable to working people when they thought, talked, and acted in nonclass ways. The result was a cultural and political dissociation of work and home.[51]

This new spatial separation between where people labored and where they lived made possible the development of an urban politics in which the various social classes could join in cross-class institutions. Its most important feature was machine-style politics. Urban political parties were decentralized, ward-based institutions. As a result, working people could think of the party machine as belonging to "us" because of where they lived, even though it did not belong to them in other meaningful ways.

The same held true for public education. The schools, organized on a neighborhood basis, were relatively homogeneous in class and ethnic backgrounds. For working people schools were genuinely local institutions, even if, at the city level, they were controlled by and served the purposes of the dominant classes.

The participatory localism of American public schooling thus contrasted powerfully with the situation on the other side of the Atlantic. There (if we may be permitted the profound simplification of talking about a European pattern), workers confronted unitary, centralized states from which they were excluded. In that context schooling *was* an imposition. Struggles for schooling were subordinated to struggles for citizenship rights, for only with the granting of the latter could state schooling become an arena belonging to "us" rather than to "them." In this context the dominant classes had ample reasons to identify demands for popularly controlled mass schooling with disorder. The working-class yearning for education was expressed not by support of state ventures but by sending children in very large numbers to schools controlled by working-class churches and self-help neighborhood institutions—what historian Thomas Laquer, writing about England, calls "the ramshackle, improvised network of schools patronized by the working classes." These schools, he notes, "were an important part of the community and one of the most important reflections of its educational aspirations."[52]

VI

STRUGGLES about schooling in western Europe were conflicts about citizenship and access. As a result, they were based on class distinctions; they resonated with mutual distrust between the classes; and they were marked by working-class assumptions that the state belonged to "them," not "us."

Educational conflicts for white Americans presumed citizenship and access. While the support given to public education by the different social classes was distinct, and while the dominant and working classes sought to secure different goals through their backing of common schools, schooling per se and the role of the state in providing it were not at issue. As a result, the educational issues most hotly debated in the United States were very much like the issues that dominated machine politics more generally: issues of ethnicity and space. Only in the few instances where school professionals, politicians, or businesspeople sought to impose class boundaries within the educational establishment, as in the attempt to create high schools, did the American working class act more like its European counterparts. Then they resisted.

Germans migrated to Chicago in large numbers after 1848 and soon became one of the largest ethnic groups in the city. In 1865 German organizations pressed for the inclusion of German language classes in the public schools. This proposal was opposed by other ethnic associations, especially the Irish, who argued that such instruction conferred preferential treatment and that, moreover, the function of the public schools was to eliminate rather than promote ethnic diversity. The school board's response was to introduce German language instruction as an experiment in a predominantly German elementary school. The next year the board, under pressure from German parents, decided that German instruction could be introduced in each area of the city. Soon after, German was taught in at least one elementary school in each district. By 1870 about one in fifteen pupils received German instruction on a voluntary basis, and the issue, though it was later revived, seemed dormant.[53]

In San Francisco, language debates likewise were fierce for a brief period. There such teaching was offered in the city's brief-lived cosmopolitan schools. The first was established in 1865, initiated as a result of pressure from the German Turnverein and an outspoken school reformer, John Pelton, who argued that immigrant children be allowed to learn in their parents' native tongue. Pelton's view that the "city is of a mixed character: schools must adapt to the city" drew on a popular current for support, but it was challenged by other school leaders who thought the schools should homogenize diverse cultures into an American hybrid. After an initial period of intense conflict when genuine bilingualism was attempted, the program of study was altered so that most of the students' time was spent in English studies with only a short period allotted to foreign-language instruction. Over time, as German political capacity decreased, so did the time spent on German instruction. By 1874 the cosmopolitan schools were eliminated.[54]

The differences between the Chicago and San Francisco outcomes can be explained by differences in numbers and in organized ethnic group capacities, but these divergences are much less interesting than the terms of conflict. Rather than quarreling about whether to have primary schooling for all, the participants defined the substantive issue as one of ethnic diversity versus assimilation. Likewise, disputes about secondary education hinged on common understandings about primary schooling; they also showed that the cross-class consensus on elementary education did not by any means eliminate divisions about schooling across class lines. Issues of access and citizenship continued to have the capacity they displayed abroad to mobilize workers on explicit class bases.

The early high schools of Chicago and San Francisco were initiated by school professionals who explicitly aimed to serve the well-to-do. Two years after the first high school opened in San Francisco in 1856 (the same year the doors of Chicago's first high school also opened), the school superintendent remarked, "The high school elevates and gives character to the city, making it attractive to a better class of citizens who may be seeking a home." Six years later, his successor observed, "With such a school in midst, there no longer exists a necessity that parents should at pecuniary loss, send their children out of State to be prepared for credible matriculations at Harvard or Yale."[55] In this way the schools' professional leadership sought to build the clientele for the new state schools in the upper classes, who, in turn, became vocal supporters of them. These citizens benefited tangibly from the school system's divergence from the principles of universal and common education. With the opening of the public secondary schools a demarcation in the length of study became institutionalized in the system because many children could neither afford the time nor meet the examination requirements to attend. Further, diversification of the curriculum into Classical, English, and Normal departments in both cities divided pupils according to their courses of study, thus heralding future departures from the principle of equal schooling for all.

That such departures proved controversial is confirmed by the attempts school superintendents in this period made to defend the high schools by claiming that services were provided to all social classes, at least indirectly. Chicago and San Francisco superintendents, while noting that the high schools were often "a subject of warm discussion," argued that secondary schools were a natural extension of free and common primary schooling ("It is necessary to complete a system of free schools that provision should be made for a thorough course of instruction in the higher as well as the lower branches of study and discipline, and such an education Chicago now freely offers to the humblest of her children"). They also adduced other arguments in favor of the high school: the curriculum would provide home-grown teachers for the primary schools; high schools created access to universities for all social classes; it was wrong to think that the "high schools serve the rich alone," and in fact graduates were "found to be from families in very moderate circumstance, some supporting themselves while at school by labor"; high schools provided skilled employees for local business; and high schools benefited the entire school system by encouraging students to strive for higher levels of achievement.[56] The sheer variety of these claims and their strained character attest to the controversial character of an aspect of the school system that so manifestly departed from the egalitarian traditions of the common school. As late as

1870 only about 3 percent of the children in school were enrolled in institutions for secondary education.

Language conflicts and disputes over the high schools pointedly contrast with the broad consensus about primary education and the comparatively limited terrain of disputes about public education in mid-nineteenth-century America. The cultural silences about schooling—those points that were taken for granted —in retrospect are far more impressive than the political noise that seemed deafening to the participants at the time.

The existence of primary schooling for all paradoxically had the effect of highlighting such conflicts as there were, but these disputes were circumscribed. By 1870 the most fundamental questions about access to schooling for white Americans had been resolved. And by 1870 a distinctively American working class had been formed. The relationship between these schools and this working class in the last three decades of the century is the question to which we now turn.

3

Schooling for All

IN the last three decades of the nineteenth century the idea of schooling for all at the primary level was realized, at least for white children. Equal access to public elementary education became a matter of right and practice. With the passage of compulsory school attendance laws it also became mandatory.

In this era of explosive capitalist growth, massive immigration, and urban development the public schools expanded and became organizationally complex. As Chicago grew into a booming industrial metropolis and as its population expanded from 300,000 in 1870 to nearly six times that size by 1895, its school population and budget increased spectacularly. The average daily attendance jumped from 25,000 in 1870 to 166,000 a quarter-century later. In the same period, the budget rose from half a million dollars to six million. San Francisco emerged at this time as the commercial hub of the West. Its growth, though more measured than Chicago's, was substantial. The city's population and public school attendance more than doubled, and its school expenditures nearly tripled (see table 3.1).

From one standpoint, capitalist development, on the one side, and schooling for all, on the other, went hand in hand. The impulse of common public education, however, had not been just quantitative. As conflicts over high schools had revealed, for members of the working class schooling was linked inextricably

TABLE 3.1

Expansion of the Chicago and San Francisco Public Schools, 1870–1900

	Chicago				San Francisco			
	1870	1880	1890	1900	1870	1880	1890	1900
Average Daily Attendance[a]	25,300	42,400	89,600	231,400	15,394	28,150	31,352	36,940
Total Current Expenditures ($)	527,742[b]	691,536	4,706,299	7,462,899[c]	388,736	755,654	954,203	1,202,936

SOURCES: Chicago Board of Education, *Annual Report*, 1870, 1880, 1889, 1891, 1901; San Francisco Superintendent of Public Instruction, *Annual Report*, 1870, 1880, 1890, 1900.

[a] Average daily attendance (ADA) was the figure most commonly used in the nineteenth century to measure school enrollment. It is the average count of the number of pupils attending school each day. ADA figures for Chicago are rounded to the nearest 100. The data given for 1890 are interpolated from the data for the years 1889 and 1891, because the 1890 attendance data were unavailable.

[b] Total amount paid for support of the schools.

[c] Expenditure data for Chicago in 1900 are taken from a 1901 school report; 1900 data were unavailable.

to egalitarian republican and democratic interpretations of civic culture.

This linkage came under very great pressure in the late nineteenth century. Capitalism and schooling for all proved contradictory. As modern class divisions became more extreme and as living space in the city was divided more and more along class lines, school populations in different neighborhoods became homogeneous. The vision of common, interclass schooling was defeated by the new political economy and its geographic expression.

The tensions between democratic schooling and the new capitalism were of two types. The first concerned links between schools and the increasingly differentiated residence communities. These communities were divided from each other not only by class but by nationality and ethnicity. With the rapid growth in scale of the city, the introduction of new kinds of mass transit, the shifts in the nature of work, and the further segregation of workplaces from residential communities, members of ethnic groups sharing income levels could choose to live close to one another. More and more the large American cities took on the aspect of an urban mosaic. With a face to this differentiated world, schools grappled with such new issues as language instruction and even bilingualism.

The second kind of tension concerned work. By the end of this era the great majority of employed people in the cities were proletarians who did not own the means of production, who did not control the labor power of others, and who worked for a wage. The economy of the period was further characterized by an increase in large factories, more integrated labor markets, and shifts in occupational structures which, by the turn of the century, favored the growth of a new group of "semiskilled" workers. It was in this period that schools ventured into new territory by adding courses in manual training, pointing toward the later establishment of vocational education.[1]

These educational and societal developments, in short, created a new situation. The vision of schooling for all split in two, distinguishing between equal access and common cross-class education. School issues also bifurcated, into those of work and those of community.

At this point, the working class did not provide the central agency for the expansion of the school systems created before the Civil War. Nor did capital. Rather, educators finding their professional voice took the lead in extending the domain of the public schools. At times they were joined by allies from business or labor when school expansion coincided with these groups' more narrow organizational interests, but in most cases educators played the central role. Their activities can be understood best in organizational and state-building terms.

Not surprisingly, however, the depreciation of common schooling and the major changes in the ties among school systems, work, and community engaged the attention of working people and their organizations. At times they struggled for the larger vision of schooling for all. Although the working class did not generally push for expanded schools, it did resist attempts to pare down the curriculum of primary schools for working-class children and actively defended a varied curriculum for them. Nevertheless, the working class did not engage in school politics *as a class,* that is, with a self-consciousness of itself as a class in action against other classes or the state. There is a painful irony here, for just at the moment when the reorganization of schooling and society challenged working-class interests in common education, the heritage of an earlier period—the narrowing of school questions once issues of access had been resolved and the split pattern of class formation dividing between the rhetoric and politics of work and residence—militated against such a collective assertion.

Rather, working-class Americans engaged school issues and conflicts in more limited ways. When they fought school battles they did so in more narrowly defined terms, either as labor, concerned with the links between schools and the workplace, or as ethnic groups, attentive to the cultural, territorial, and political interests they shared with other group members of all classes. This pattern of selective attention and of selective influence may be accounted for, first, by the fact that white workers had not had to struggle against significant opposition to secure entry to free common public schools; second, by the features of class formation that post–Civil War Americans inherited from the antebellum period; and, third, by the elective affinity between the di-

vided consciousness of the working class and the divided nature
of school issues.

I

IT IS important to think of the formation of a class as a conditional process. Whether people who share objective traits in the
material organization of society will form a class in action cannot
be predicted from profiles of the social structure, nor can the
rhetorical and practical bases of their action be deduced from
such profiles.

Consider a central feature of the industrialization process, the
growing separation of work and home. This trend actually entails
three kinds of separation: work leaves the home; neighborhoods
may become differentiated on the basis of production or residence functions; and the social classes may come more and more
to live apart from each other in increasingly homogeneous communities. As a result of the early and very much incomplete
separation of work and community in antebellum America,
workers had to interpret the new industrial and urban realities.
They might have interpreted the new order in holistic class terms
that would have comprehended society as divided along a single
class cleavage at work, in politics, and in community life. Or they
might have understood both realms in ethnic terms. But the
pattern that prevailed was different. By the Civil War most
American workers in the larger cities had developed a split consciousness that separated the politics of work from that of home.
American workers were formed as a class only as labor. Outside
of work they developed a multiplicity of affiliations based mainly
on ethnicity and territory.[2]

Workers brought this inheritance with them into the late nineteenth century, when the differentiation of urban space became
better defined. As transportation lines opened up, workers migrated to previously remote sections of the cities, establishing
residential neighborhoods and leaving behind areas now primar-

ily devoted to industrial or commercial activities. In San Francisco major changes in residence patterns occurred between 1880 and 1900. Workers who had previously clustered in the crowded quarters in the "South of Market" area moved to the more spacious western and southern regions of the city. Accompanying this exodus was an increase in commercial construction in the South of Market, which became a zone of industry and warehouses. Likewise, the downtown area north of Market Street lost population as commercial and industrial activities supplanted residential dwellings. The Chinese, restricted to a single cramped district, were the only large group to remain in this growing commercial and industrial area. Each newly established residential area had distinctive characteristics. Market Street still separated classes, as artisans and laborers settled below and middle classes above the divide. Laborers were more likely to remain behind in the central city while artisans flocked to the better working-class districts in the newly opened sections and, to a lesser extent, to some middle-class districts.[3]

The great Chicago fire of 1871 hastened that city's spatial transformation. Vast areas were devastated, and some required complete rebuilding. Reconstruction proceeded with greater regard for functional specificity than would have been possible had change been gradual. This was particularly true of the downtown section, which merchants rebuilt as a huge commercial center. A second effect of the fire was to accelerate the growing spatial separation of the rich from the poor. A new city ordinance required that all new buildings within a specified range around the city's core be constructed with noncombustible materials. The expense of such buildings combined with soaring land costs served to exclude workers and many middle-income residents from the central locations. Those who could afford to commute settled in the newer residential districts on the outskirts of the city, but the vast majority of workers crowded into an intermediate zone that grew increasingly cramped as immigrants flooded the city.[4]

As working people tried to interpret and manage this patterning of urban life they grappled with the basic issues of class formation. The institutional separation of workers' activities at the workplace from those in political and communal life was reproduced in this period. The failure to bridge this gap was not a matter of default. Several groups attempted to alter the pattern; some political parties sought to mobilize workers in class terms, and, more often, organizations formed at the workplace tried to enter the electoral arena with labor parties. Yet no explicitly worker-based political organization endured into the twentieth century in either San Francisco or Chicago.[5] The political arena continued to be monopolized by mixed-class parties that based much of their political appeal on ethnic concerns. Some unions sought to forge ties with local politicians in the quest for jobs, contracts, and other perquisites dispensed by municipal government or continued to press for favorable treatment on legislation or policies of particular concern to organized labor. But early visions of a movement representing a broad social and political agenda of working-class concern did not materialize.

The disjunction between economic and political organization was well established among San Francisco working-class organizations before the 1870s. In this era of economic prosperity, virtually all the trades were organized. But activism at the workplace was not matched by an equal interest in labor-based politics. Electoral endeavors were controversial among trade unionists, and more than one organization split over the issue of independent political action. The Democratic party attracted the largest share of the working-class vote, recruiting members on the basis of their ethnic affiliations. The Irish in particular provided the backbone of the local Democratic organization.

The depression and labor surplus of the 1870s undermined the position established by San Francisco's trade unions. Under these circumstances, the presence of large numbers of Chinese immigrants became the major focus of working-class discontent. The Workingmen's party of California (WPC) capitalized not only on the anti-Chinese agitation but on the resentment toward the railroads and land monopoly that had been brewing in the state for nearly a decade. Rising to power on the demagogic oratory of Denis Kearney, its Irish leader, the party briefly eclipsed the Democrats at both the local and the state level. Its name notwithstanding, the Workingmen's party did not have a strong base among trade unionists; its primary constituency was among the unemployed. Unlike the traditional political parties, however, it stressed working-class concerns.

The party had a short, if incandescent, life. It elected a mayor, won three seats on the school board, and captured several other offices in 1879. Without a coherent program and a secure social base, however, it found itself burnt out just two years later. The party's impact on working-class activism thus was short-lived, limited mainly to influencing the Democratic and Republican parties, which were alarmed by the demonstrated potential of working-class disruption, to be more solicitous of working-class support.

The electoral successes of the Workingmen's party had also broken the power of many ward politicians, a situation that Christopher Buckley, an Irish immigrant who had arrived in San Francisco in 1862, exploited in his successful attempt to build a centralized Democratic party machine along ethnic lines. Throughout most of the 1880s, "Blind Boss" Buckley was the city's pre eminent politician. The Democratic party under his rule was deeply embedded in working-class communities, and ward clubs were not just political organizations but centers of social life and employment. Although various labor organizations sought to challenge his control over the working-class vote, Buckley remained a dominant power until he was defeated by reformers and publicly discredited by an indictment for bribery.

Though diverse, San Francisco's labor organizations retained their predominant emphasis on the workplace. The short-lived Trades Assembly, led by socialist Frank Roney, was forbidden by its constitution from embarking on partisan political campaigns. Roney circumvented this prohibition by forming the Mechanics League to act as a political arm, but the group's endorsed candidates fared poorly. Two organizations, the Knights of Labor and the International Workingmen's Association (IWA), absorbed many of the activists from the Trades Assembly in the mid-1880s. The Knights of Labor, though not strictly a trade union, maintained a workplace orientation, emphasizing commonalities among all producer groups. The IWA (led by Burnette Haskell, editor of the paper *Truth,* who alternately espoused socialist, communist, and anarchist ideals) made little effort to transcend the gap between working-class political and economic activity, expending most of its energy organizing trade unions.

By the late 1880s these organizations had been overshadowed by the Federated Trades Council, presided over by Frank Roney. Its leadership had an avid interest in politics, and in 1886 the FTC joined with the Knights of Labor to form a Labor party to enter the municipal elections. In spite of the role of unionists in its formation, few labor organizations endorsed the party. Its defeat by the Democrats caused a crisis within the labor movement centering on the issue of political action. Those who believed in a nonpartisan economistic trade union movement assumed positions of leadership, and politically active labor leaders were purged.

Over the following decade the San Francisco labor movement remained divided about the extent to which labor should engage in political action. The San Francisco Labor Council, formed in 1892, shunned political involvement, as did many of its affiliated locals. In contrast, the Building Trades Council, which reunited several years later, strongly advocated participation in electoral politics as a central means of consolidating its strength. At the end of the nineteenth century, politically conscious trade unionists had not managed to fashion organizations that crossed the barriers between labor organizations at work and the political parties that dominated off-work concerns.[6]

In Chicago as in San Francisco, workers in many trades organized shortly after the Civil War. And, as in San Francisco, there was a vigorous challenge to the split political culture of the working class during the depression of the 1870s. Founded in 1873, the Workingmen's party, transformed later into the Socialist Labor party, had striking electoral successes late in the decade. But, as in San Francisco, its success proved short-lived and provoked renewed debate within the labor movement about the appropriate limits of union political activity.

The socialists were overcome, too, by more traditional ethnically and territorially based political party organizations. These tended to be highly decentralized, organized by independent entrepreneurs who owed their influence to personal political acumen rather than to their position in a formal party organization.

Not until the 1880s, when five-time mayor Carter Henry Harrison dominated the Democratic party, was a centralized political machine constructed. Harrison won support from capitalists and workers alike and, though ambivalent to union labor, convinced workers by his rhetoric and tact that he was their friend. Above all he appealed to working people's ethnic consciousness. An opponent described his masterful knack for ethnic politics this way: "On St. George's Day, Harrison blooms out like an English rose. On St. Andrew's Day, he is stuck full of thistles. On St. Patrick's Day, he looks like a clover field."[7]

As Carter Harrison consolidated the Democratic party on ethnic terms, Chicago's labor movement prospered. Union membership soared. Various groups—socialists, anarchists, the Knights of Labor, and the Trade and Labor Assembly—competed to articulate working-class demands. In the tumultuous 1880s working-class activism was not limited to the workplace. The repression that followed the Haymarket bombing precipitated the formation of a trade union–based labor party, the United Labor Party (ULP), which ran successful candidates in 1886 and 1887.

This heyday of labor influence dissipated quickly, however. The regular political parties allied against the ULP and promoted a general fear of radicalism that quashed prospects for labor's independent political action. Nonetheless, the increase in trade union strength and the threat of political action caused the dominant parties, especially the Democrats, to be more attentive to the interests of labor. In 1888 gubernatorial candidate John Palmer denounced the Pinkertons. Four years later, John Peter Altgeld won the state's highest office by supporting the eight-hour day and workers' compensation.

This support for labor's workplace goals, together with the ethnic basis of ward organization, reinforced the dominant split pattern of working-class politics and helped undermine the Knights of Labor and the more political elements of the labor movement. In spite of sporadic efforts in the 1890s to revive independent political activity (such as the People's Party of 1894, an alliance of populists and local labor), the triumph of pure and simple unionism and machine politics was clear-cut.[8]

II

IT WAS this particular working class, whose political and work-place concerns were institutionally separated, that engaged in the educational struggles of the late nineteenth century. What was its relationship to public education in this period of school expression and differentiation? What were the terms of working-class participation in school struggles? How important was this class in the resolution of these battles?

To restate: We shall claim that state-building educators were more significant in pressing for school expansion than were workers or businesspeople. Workers did not act in the school arena as a class. Instead, they selectively attended to educational issues, sometimes as labor, at other moments as ethnic groups. This pattern of participation reflects not only the peculiarities of American class formation but also the early entry of workers into the public schools. We make these claims on the basis of our research into the issues of compulsory education, language instruction, and manual training, the dominant school issues of late-nineteenth-century Chicago and San Francisco.

Because the question of access to the public schools had been settled early, American workers did not identify educational issues as a central target of struggle. The lack of a major working-class education movement, however, does not indicate that workers were indifferent to schooling. Indeed, their rhetoric routinely affirmed wholehearted support for the public schools. Under particular circumstances and on particular issues, moreover, workers actively pushed to extend public schooling beyond the common school minimum. One such issue, central in the late nineteenth century, was compulsory education. Legislative efforts to enforce school attendance highlight the circumstances under which unions actively participated in school politics and illuminate the conditions that mobilized workers on the basis of ethnic affiliations.

Active though unions were in supporting compulsory education, educators, not workers, formed the backbone of the movement in San Francisco and Chicago. The earliest and most persistent advocates of compulsory schooling were public school officials, particularly superintendents, seeking to secure the future of public schools as a central municipal institution. Yet educators alone did not carry sufficient weight to entice legislators to consider the issue seriously. They actively solicited support among other groups to strengthen their position. They found allies among reformers and middle-class women's organizations, who responded to the promise that education would remedy crime, vice, and social disorder. Labor was drawn in on quite a different basis. Unions acted to support compulsory education only when such laws seemed necessary to secure or enforce child labor legislation. Because of this need to build coalitions, legislation proposing compulsory education occasionally included provisions that had little to do with school attendance but were needed to secure adequate support. Such provisions often aroused substantial opposition, and labor supporters dropped into the background as ethnic groups and political parties entered the fray, transforming the issue into a contentious partisan affair.

The earliest efforts to enact compulsory education in Chicago and San Francisco reveal both the inability of educators alone to pass the issue and the potential for controversy when the educators' allies tacked on additional provisions that differentially affected ethnic groups. In Chicago, professional educators began to call for compulsory education in the late 1860s. At numerous educational conventions, teachers and school administrators praised education in terms calculated to appeal to propertied members of society. Thus, a speaker at the Illinois State Teacher's Association convention in 1868 defended the state's right to compel school attendance by claiming that it would help to secure both the property which constituted the state's legitimate tax base and the "social and political institutions which law represents."[9] A later statement by a member of the Chicago Board of Education typifies this argument:

> We should rightfully have the power to arrest all these little beggars, loafers, and vagabonds that infest our city, take them from the streets and place them in schools where they are compelled to receive education and learn moral principles. . . . We certainly should not

permit a reckless and indifferent part of our population to rear their children in ignorance to become a criminal and lawless class within our community.[10]

The effort by educators failed to attract sufficient support. Legislation proposing compulsory education was defeated five times between 1871 and 1881. Not until 1883 was a law passed requiring children aged eight to fourteen to attend twelve weeks of school annually or be subject to a fine levied by the board of education.

In contrast, California passed a similar compulsory education statute in 1874. There educators met with early success by linking mandatory school attendance with a measure to prohibit the dispersal of public moneys to religious schools, thus appealing to anti-Catholic prejudices.[11] Proponents of mandatory schooling also made explicit appeals to German voters by claiming that the measure had been inspired by the Prussian example. Defined in such terms, the issue was at once ethnic and partisan. Republicans strongly supported the measure; Democrats, with their base of Irish Catholic support, denounced it.

So strongly was the issue defined by partisan and ethnic loyalties that even educators split over the matter. The most vocal supporter was German-born Henry Bolander, Republican state superintendent of schools from 1871 to 1875. Bolander praised education as "the only force sufficient to diminish and remove the causes of crime" and as "the first condition necessary to the prosperity of a nation."[12] His predecessor, Democrat O. P. Fitzgerald, did not deny the virtues of education but argued against compulsory attendance. He attributed the popularity of the issue to the recent military success of Prussia but maintained that Americans had proven compulsory attendance unnecessary by fighting battles successfully with *volunteer* soldiers, the graduates of *free* schools."[13]

The most vocal opponent was the Catholic church, which stood to lose the most. A provision denying Catholic school funding would have shut off any hope for a return to the public aid to Catholic schools that had existed in the 1850s. It also raised fears that compulsory education would be but a first step in a process that could regulate the curriculum and lead to the destruction of the parochial schools.[14]

Labor was divided on this proposal for compulsory education. The leading spokesman of the nativist National Labor Union strongly supported the campaign and denounced the use of public funds for religious schools. The Mechanics State Council, however, the first statewide labor group, debated the issue, but its members came to no agreement. Support for the measure was not included in the council's platform.[15]

In neither San Francisco nor Chicago did the passage of the first compulsory education laws satisfy educators. They pressed for stronger enforcement mechanisms and sought to attract allies to their cause. As in the first stage, the experience of the two cities varied. In San Francisco the issue lay dormant for nearly a quarter-century, but in Chicago it became a focus of controversy involving reformers, labor organizations, and ethnic associations. The distinct way in which compulsory education meshed with the priorities of potential allies accounts for the difference between the cities.

In Chicago, educators and reformers again emphasized education's potential as an antidote to the social disorganization and disruption that engulfed the city. Their arguments were now more compelling as class violence threatened to rip Chicago apart. In December 1888, a month after the Board of Education argued that the 1883 law was "insufficient and incapable of enforcement," the *Tribune* campaigned for the board to take more decisive action.[16] Meanwhile, the Chicago Woman's Club sent the board the following resolution:

> WHEREAS, the appalling increase of crime among youth, the large number of vagrant children, and the employment of child labor in the city of Chicago is fraught with danger to the commonwealth, therefore, we, the Chicago Woman's Club, respectfully ask your honorable body immediately to take the necessary measures to secure the inforcement of the Illinois Statute of 1883, providing for compulsory education.[17]

Animated by quite a different set of concerns, Chicago's labor unions were also taking an interest in compulsory schooling.

Labor's entry into the discussion cast the issue in a new light by explicitly tying it to child labor legislation. Though declining in this period, child labor was prevalent enough for union leaders to identify its restriction as a central legislative objective.

The Board of Education took advantage of this broader and more intensive support for compulsory education by convening public meetings in 1889 to draft new compulsory attendance, child labor, and truancy legislation. The board showed its political shrewdness by rolling the provisions into one package, appealing for support of compulsory education to both middle-class reformers and labor unions. This combined support secured the passage of a new compulsory attendance law. Besides providing that every child aged seven to fourteen must attend school for sixteen weeks, the 1889 "Edwards Law" also stipulated that. instruction be in English. This provision threatened the state's large German population, many of whose children attended private and parochial schools where English was not the sole medium of instruction. Lutherans and Catholics, many of them German, also feared that local authorities would begin to exercise control over parochial schools.

The earliest organized opposition to the law focused on the defense of parochial schools, but the language issue soon overtook it in importance. Chicago's two German-language dailies launched a concerted opposition to the Edwards Law, expressing their preference for legislation that would require *some* instruction in English. Compulsory attendance per se no longer was the issue.

Seeking to attract the German vote, Democrats attacked the Republicans for sponsoring the Edwards Law and vowed to repeal any provisions that restricted the right of parents to control the education of their children. German votes helped elect Democrats to major state offices for the first time in twenty years. Two years later Democrats made compulsory attendance their main issue. This time the Republicans, fully warned of the unpopularity of the Edwards measure, pledged to replace it. The opportunism of this switch was transparent, however, and the Democrats triumphed once again. The Edwards Law was repealed in 1893, leaving Illinois with no compulsory attendance law.[18]

Labor maintained a low profile throughout the controversy, eager to preserve harmony within the labor movement. Class-based concerns thus gave way to ethnic and partisan loyalties. After the law's repeal, however, labor participated once again. Unions played a significant role in drafting new legislation. In January 1893, at a meeting attended by numerous prominent reformers, a committee consisting solely of trade unionists was selected to sponsor a compulsory education bill in Springfield. Once again labor's efforts on behalf of compulsory education went in tandem with support for child labor legislation. The 1893 compulsory education law required children between seven and fourteen to attend school for sixteen weeks annually with enforcement by truant officers appointed by the board of education. Subsequently, a series of revised laws were passed, culminating in 1909 with an extension of the age limit to sixteen and a requirement of attendance for "the entire session, not less than 6 months of actual teaching."[19]

Educators were notably less successful in arousing a broad interest in tougher compulsory education legislation in San Francisco. With a much smaller influx of immigration and less industrial development than in Chicago, San Francisco had fewer episodes of severe disruption and no comparable coterie of reformers, which in Chicago had formed the core of support for educators seeking to enforce compulsory education. In San Francisco's single major outburst, the anti-Chinese riots of 1877–78, school officials pulled out the familiar arguments supporting compulsory education as a remedy. It would be cheaper, argued Superintendent A. L. Mann, "to educate people at the public expense than to pay the cost of their arrest, conviction, and imprisonment for crime."[20] But the plea received little attention and was largely forgotten as agitation died down.

On labor's part as well, there was less incentive to press for compulsory education or even for child labor laws. Most labor platforms included demands for compulsory education and child labor legislation, but these were never actively pursued as important organizational goals. San Francisco's unique economic development was responsible for this lack of urgency. San Francisco had a very low percentage of unskilled occupations, which were filled disproportionately by Chinese. Thus, child labor in San Francisco was not enough of a problem to generate a strong and early movement to restrict its use and to enforce compulsory schooling. Instead, labor's efforts were directed at excluding the Chinese.[21]

By the turn of the century, however, educators were able to attract more support for their cause. Although no group of reformers comparable to Chicago's developed, a variety of upper- and middle-class women's organizations expressed an interest in compulsory schooling. In this period problems of truancy were on the rise as a major wave of immigrants flooded the city for the first time in over twenty years. It was among these newcomers, primarily Italians, that nonattendance was most common.

The passage of a strengthened compulsory education law in 1903 owed much more to the pressure of women's clubs and to a generalized fear of newcomers than to the activities of organized labor. Unions did support this legislation but paid it less attention than they did to the last vestiges of child labor. The Labor Council and the Seamen's Union, for whom child labor was a problem, successfully lobbied for the child labor law passed in 1905. The two issues, therefore, were not coupled as they were in Chicago, because reformers were able to achieve compulsory schooling and child labor legislation quite independently. As a result, union interest in compulsory schooling was perfunctory.[22]

In San Francisco, then, as in Chicago, educators led the movement for compulsory education. Attempting to attract support, they argued in terms designed to attract allies, in some cases explicitly linking compulsory education with other issues. Provisions tacked onto compulsory education legislation to appease political allies, however, often served to arouse the hostility of ethnic groups, transforming the terms of discussion and changing the main actors.

III

IN the early nineteenth century, when Americans spoke of a "common" school system they meant not only schools that were open to all (or at least to all whites) but also schools whose curricula offered all children education with similar content.

Training for citizenship in a democracy provided a rationale for the early assumption of state responsibility for education, and considerations of equality dictated that the curriculum be narrowly directed to this end. Access to a common school system, defined in this way, became part of what Americans expected as a minimum right of citizenship.

After the Civil War, public schools diversified, embracing a variety of subjects never envisioned by the architects of American common schooling. This expansion resulted both from new group demands and from a process of state-building. An array of social groups sought to reshape the public school system to their cultural and economic needs, needs no longer limited to the tasks of citizenship. At the same time, school officials used curricular innovations to extend the reach of state policy to new groups and to prevent competing institutions from capturing their clientele. Although the diversification of the curriculum incorporated new groups into the public school system, it also generated opposition, first, from those who objected to particular changes and, second, from those who opposed the general growth of public school expenditures. Especially during periods of financial crisis, critics coalesced to attack what they saw as the extravagance of schooling beyond the primary grades and basic subjects.

In the two most important cases of curricular expansion during this period, the introduction of foreign-language instruction and the establishment of manual training, groups with strong roots in the working class demonstrated interest in changing the content of public education. However, the fragmented character of America's working-class experience meant that neither issue was fought effectively in class terms; instead, ethnicity and labor provided distinct bases of group mobilization. In the late nineteenth century, ethnicity proved to be a relatively effective base of action, because urban politics was typically sensitive to demands phrased in ethnic terms. Labor, however, played a much more peripheral role in curricular issues, partly because most of these did not directly affect the workplace but also because labor organizations were not well integrated into the local political structure. This pattern was temporarily challenged in Chicago in the 1890s, when business groups tried to reduce the number of special subjects and restrict the curriculum to a basic, practical core. In response, a coalition of ethnic and labor groups united to defend the diversified curriculum and articulate an alternative view of the role of the working-class education. Yet school officials avoided an overarching class confrontation on educational issues by making concessions to the ethnic groups involved, thus restoring the fragmentary, issue-specific character of working-class interest in school politics.

The large number of Germans in the population created a potential for significant political leverage. By 1870 German-born residents constituted 9 percent of the population in San Francisco and 18 percent in Chicago. When several German organizations pressed for the inclusion of their language in the Chicago public schools in 1865, the school board approved German-language courses as an experiment in one school. Demand proved so high that within a year German was taught throughout Chicago. San Francisco's public schools initially went even further. So-called cosmopolitan schools, in which French and German were the languages of instruction, opened in 1865. By 1871 enrollment in these schools had grown to more than 5,000 pupils in eight schools; by 1873 foreign languages were taught in every school of the city.[23]

Ethnic groups won concessions on the language issue not only because of their political influence but because many school officials thought German instruction would cause German students to transfer from private to public schools. The chairman of Chicago's committee on German languages, for example, noted that

> . . . among the scholars of German birth or parentage, who took part in the study of German, your committee observed a considerable number who formerly attended sectarian or private schools and who left those institutions as soon as the public schools gave them the opportunity to study in their native language, the number of private schools now to be found in every nook and corner of the city, will decrease, and the children of all nationalities will be assembled in the public schools, and thereby be radically Americanized.[24]

Thus, many school officials sought to strengthen the public school system through curricular modifications that met the demands of important ethnic groups.

The teaching of foreign languages in public schools had its opponents from the outset. Some ethnic groups objected to preferential treatment for Germans. But, more important, the attack on language instruction in San Francisco in the late 1870s and early 1880s was part of a broader movement to control the costs of government in a period of fiscal crisis. In education, attempts to cut the school back to the basics included an attack on high schools and all special subjects that were not necessary "to perform the ordinary duties of citizenship."[25] Although Germans initially deflected assaults on language instruction, their position was weakened by the financial crisis of the 1880s and the mobilization of a large segment of the conservative press. German influence was also undermined by the rise of the Irish-dominated Buckley machine. The teaching of foreign languages was not eliminated, but it was curtailed.

The most forceful attack on language instruction came later in Chicago. In 1893 the *Chicago Tribune* launched a campaign against "fads," urging that teachers of special subjects such as "singing, drawing, mudpie-making and modern foreign languages should be cut to the lowest figure."[26] Several members of the Board of Education who were sensitive to the *Tribune*'s position (including the president, who was also the *Tribune*'s attorney) took up the crusade. Antagonisms surrounding the "fads" ran much deeper in Chicago than in San Francisco. The issue was immediately perceived as a question about the fundamental purposes of public education. The aggressiveness of the antilabor *Tribune* prompted responses from a wide array of groups including organized labor.

According to the *Tribune,* the expansion of the curriculum interfered with the primary purpose of the common school—to provide the "children of the masses" with an "education for breadwinners." This meant restriction of the curriculum to rudimentary subjects. Special subjects were "costly luxuries" that "fritter[ed] away" the time of the pupils.[27]

The labor movement took up this gauntlet, embracing these curricular reforms. In the view of Thomas Morgan, the most articulate educational spokesman of organized labor in the 1890s, democratic government required the "widest, deepest, and best

education of every member of the state and nation.[28] A similar
position was expressed by P. H. McLogan, a Chicago printer:

> We consider it as the duty of the appointed protectors at our school
> system to provide for the mass of the people, not a scant education,
> instruction in those branches which may be deemed necessary for the
> immediate bread-winning, but a liberal one. . . . We think that in-
> struction in our public schools should be so ample as to dispense
> absolutely with the necessity of private schools.[29]

While the opponents of special studies viewed them as more
appropriate for private schools or for more advanced students,
the labor movement defended their place in the primary grades.
Morgan was fond of pointing out that only 22 percent of workers'
children ever went beyond the fourth year of school, so that
unless the remaining 78 percent received drawing, singing, and
the other special studies in the primary grades, they would never
get them.[30] The attempt to limit special studies to the higher
grades was seen by workers as an expansion of the educational
opportunities open to wealthy families at the expense of the
"common schools."

In early February 1893 the *Tribune* renewed its assault, this time
singling out the German language as the chief culprit among the
"fads." The inclusion of German in the controversy was of crucial
importance in determining the development of the war against
German language instruction. Leaders of the German community
convened mass meetings and sent vocal representatives to school
board sessions. The labor movement joined them in support of
the "fads."[31] In response, the school board used evasive tactics to
stifle discussion of the "fads," especially the German-language
issue, until well after the upcoming mayoral election. Then it
proposed a compromise to allay the fears of the German community. Each "fad" would be dealt with separately, and German
instruction would be eliminated from the first four primary
grades. This resolution was acceptable to the German community. In exchange for their acquiescence, prominent Germans
were guaranteed a veto over future school board appointees by
Mayor Harrison and were thus given insurance against further
incursions into German-language instruction. In the meantime,

the Committee on School Management met and hammered out a solution to the teaching of the other special subjects. The committee's report, which was adopted by the board, noted that special studies had great educational value and stipulated that the time devoted to them should be reduced but not eliminated. For a moment a broad working-class mobilization about "fads" spanning labor and ethnic concerns appeared imminent. But it never occurred. The board effectively severed the German issue from the other curricular questions, and the compromises it proposed were sufficient to cool the dispute.[32]

The school curriculum issue that the labor movement cared most about was manual training. Labor was not alone in its concern for how public education might adapt to sweeping economic change. In this it was joined by business and some educators as well. Manual training was a diffuse concept. For labor, it meant a broad instruction in skills that could be useful for a variety of jobs. For business, it often meant training in more specific skills. Many educators dissented from such vocationally oriented interpretations and argued for the introduction of classes in drawing, woodworking, sewing, and other activities. They emphasized the pedagogical goal of integrating hand and mind or the social value of inculcating respect for manual labor.

Working-class organizations of the 1870s and 1880s were early supporters of manual training. In San Francisco, the Mechanics State Council favored the teaching of trades in the public schools. The Mechanics Deliberative Assembly recommended to the legislature a bill proposing that labor schools be attached to the public school system. Later, San Francisco's leading labor paper, *Truth,* expressed admiration for labor schools in vague terms, saying only that the school curriculum must emphasize "practical useful knowledge."[33]

Chicago working-class groups also rated manual training high on their agenda of educational issues. The *Knights of Labor,* the most important labor paper in Chicago in the mid-1880s, asserted that "much of the degradation of labor may be traced to ignorance, and this is caused to a great extent by sending young children out into the world to battle for bread before they have been taught anything that will put them on even ground with their fellows." The market for labor was undergoing rapid change during the period, and without some form of manual education, the labor paper contended, workers would be ill equipped to make the switch from one trade to another. What was needed was to teach "the principles of technical education which prepare a boy for no trade in particular and yet give him the rudiments of any and all trades."[34]

Protection against the vicissitudes of the labor market was not the only advantage attributed to manual training by the *Knights of Labor*. Universal industrial education would place workers on firmer ground within the workplace itself. The apprenticeship system of training and job security no longer existed, according to the labor paper, and no system of job training had arisen to replace it. The *Knights of Labor*'s solution was the establishment of free manual training and public technical schools.[35]

The labor movements of the time limited their efforts on behalf of manual training to rhetorical exhortations. Although various labor groups ran candidates for political office, they were not well integrated into the political structure of either Chicago or San Francisco. They also lacked the capacity to establish institutions that could compete with public schools in providing manual training. Finally, in a period when labor had to fight for survival, manual training was pushed to the periphery of their concerns.

Chicago's business community agitated for manual training earlier than San Francisco's. In 1881 the Citizen's Association of Chicago, whose members included some of the city's most important businesspeople, issued a report criticizing the public schools for failing to provide "practical training, that training of hand and eye which would enable those leaving our schools to be useful and productive members of society almost immediately after leaving school."[36] At the same time, the *Chicago Tribune* took up the cause. For over a year, weekly articles advocating "practical education," "manual training," and "industrial education" in the public schools appeared in the paper.

In 1882 several prominent businesspeople, including Marshall Field, Richard Crane, George Pullman, and John Crerar, began efforts to open a private manual training school. Over the next two years the plans were carried out by the Commercial Club, and in 1884 the Chicago Manual Training School was opened. Although the school's curriculum included some traditional academic subjects, its major focus was on the use of "shop work" to train both the hand and the mind.

By the early 1890s San Francisco's business community showed considerable interest in the problem of industrial training. Here, too, leading businesspeople concentrated on founding private industrial arts schools. The first of such schools was the Lick School, which opened in the early years of the decade and offered training in the machinery trades. At the same time, an endowment had been procured from a leading San Francisco merchant, J. Clute Wilmerding, who desired to found a school where "our boys shall be trained to earn a living with little study and plenty of work."[37] The major business organization in the city, the Merchants Association, mounted a drive to locate donors to supplement the endowment. When it opened at the turn of the century, the Wilmerding school offered a course of instruction geared primarily to the building trades. Both the Lick and Wilmerding schools were private institutions but did not charge tuition.

Most educators initially opposed manual training. Although most of the educational community accepted the notion that education should serve a utilitarian function, many school officials felt that this did not require specialized education for trades. Tradition-minded school officials recoiled at the suggestion that the curriculum should be so differentiated, seeing such attempts as a violation of the common school ideal.

Only when businesspeople founded their own schools of industrial education did public school officials make a thorough commitment to manual training. By the mid-1880s substantial segments of the educational community now argued that manual training could be justified in pedagogical terms. The value of training the hand as an important aspect of training the mind was invoked to rationalize the introduction of courses like drawing and woodworking; these courses ostensibly made education more practical without undermining the public school's primary role as an institution cultivating Western culture.

By 1895 manual training was offered in all Chicago's elementary and high schools, and a separate school of manual training had been established. Changes in San Francisco were not quite as extensive, but by 1894 most of the city's high schools and half of its grammar schools taught manual training, as did the Commercial High School. By the turn of the century, the Polytechnic High School, equipped with tools to train skilled workers, had opened. Thus, spurred by competition from private industrial schools, educators recognized that "if we are to carry more pupils beyond the grammar schools we will find the greater proportion of them attracted to the business and manual training courses rather than the classical."[38]

As manual training became identified with preparation for specific trades and as a business-backed policy, the attitude of organized labor changed. Craft unions, which by the mid-1890s had become the dominant mode of workplace organization, began to perceive threats to their control over the labor market. In San Francisco, the newspaper of the Building Trades Council remarked that "trade schools have been proposed and in a feeble way have been grafted upon our public school system . . . [but] nothing can take the place of practical experience . . . trade unions must for self-protection take action, else they will be overrun with incapables."[39] The San Francisco Labor Council also opposed manual training in the public schools. Although the more pedagogical forms of manual training were well established in San Francisco's public schools and (as evidenced by the approval of a series of bond issues for manual training) enjoyed wide popular support, more specialized forms of trade training were not instituted there until the 1930s. In Chicago, too, labor unions tempered their support for vocational training as business enthusiasm highlighted the dangers for unions. In the early years of the twentieth century, these differences would erupt into a major controversy as business pressed for a separate business-controlled system of vocational education.[40]

Organized labor showed an interest in manual training beginning in the 1870s because the issue was one of the few school agenda items that affected the workplace directly. Workers' mobilization as labor, however, was relatively modest in intensity and effect. With the labor movement in flux, indeed with its survival in question, school issues were of secondary importance. And even when labor was directly engaged in school struggles its isolation from regular party politics left unions without the organizational strength and political influence to make an independent mark. Despite the special concern unions had for modifying the curriculum to improve the fit between schools and work, manual training did not become part of the educational minimum until business and school officials took up the issue.

Ethnic mobilization, on the other hand, proved to be of more direct effect in securing language instruction and in defending it with partial success against powerful adversaries. The urban political system resonated to ethnic claims and was equipped to accommodate them. Overall, the pattern of the demands, identities, alliances, and effectiveness of the working class in school politics was determined most fundamentally by its divided political culture.

IV

IN the late Reconstruction period the American educational minimum consisted of common primary schooling. Its provision was sporadic, even primitive; and the legitimacy of the state, rather than the church or family, as the key purveyor of education was still shaky. By the turn of the century the state's role was much more secure. Students were compelled to attend primary schools, and the vast majority enrolled in public institutions. No longer rudimentary, urban school systems had become significantly more developed and differentiated as organizations. This process of school expansion expressed and managed the central contradictory aspect of state-building in a market society: that between democracy and capitalism. The schools served democratic imperatives by equalizing formal access to basic primary schooling. At the same time, the new curricula and levels of schooling adapted public education to the economic forces of the second industrial revolution.

In part, the higher level of minimum schooling at the turn of the century was the result of attempts to deal with problems generated by the post–Civil War minimum. Crowded classes, mentioned in virtually every superintendent's report; the gap between the ideal of common schooling and the realities of a school system that could not find places for all; and family strategies that kept some children out of school impelled officials, politicians, and citizens to press for more buildings, more teachers, and compulsory attendance.

Yet the policy changes in the last three decades of the century were not immanent ones, inherent in a "natural" trajectory. Various actors pressed their interests as they saw them. Educators pushed for an expansion in the scope of state activity. In so doing, they claimed a monopoly of skill and knowledge and acted to ensure the desirability of the service they offered. As state officials they fought to extend government's bounds, just as they presented public policy as classless and neutral. Capitalists expressed an interest in a harmonious relationship between schools and labor markets. They fought not to exclude working-class children from the public schools (unlike many of their European counterparts, who did try to maintain class barriers to schooling) but to teach children in ways that meshed with the class structure. Reformers sought to obtain social peace. Workers, as this chapter has shown, also engaged in school politics but with an orientation and a capacity limited by their heritage of class formation. Their interventions as workers or as ethnic group members were highly selective. Workers achieved their demands only insofar as they found allies among educators or businesspeople, who reached similar policy conclusions for different reasons. Accordingly, working-class influence on school expansion was not only selective but limited. Their fragmented orientation to schools and to politics more generally impeded the development of a *working class* capable of using the instruments of democratic politics to achieve collective goals.

These features of intervention in school politics do not mean that workers were wholly ineffectual or irrelevant to the shaping of American education. On the contrary, workers helped define the contours of cultural transmission and the fit between work and schooling *at those moments* when there was a distinct ethnic or labor interest that allowed them to mobilize resources and when their goals corresponded sufficiently with those of others to permit them to find allies. They also emerged as one of the staunchest and most effective defenders of the common school when it was under attack in this era.

If in these ways workers helped produce schools, the schools also helped produce workers. That is, the functioning of urban school systems in the cities where massive concentrations of workers lived re-created the split pattern of class formation in at least two ways. First, because workers were voting citizens and because they did not have to struggle against the state to achieve access to primary schooling, education did not help form the working class as a collectivity spanning work and community. Second, the issues that workers pressed in school politics found a resonant response in the society's party and industrial relations systems. Workers' concerns as ethnics for language instruction or as laborers for child labor legislation—which were the basis of their support for compulsory education—were confirmed by others as legitimate grounds for posing policy demands. Using these identities, workers could struggle to achieve their ends with reasonable chances of success. The boundaries of class formation and the boundaries of school politics thus were mutually confirming.

4

The Eclipse of
Democratic Schooling

ACOALITION of professional educators allied with businesspeople and politicians "reformed" American public education in the first three decades of this century. In all the major urban centers, including Chicago and San Francisco, organizationally primitive and politicized school systems were recast. The corporation replaced the political party as the desirable form of organization. Professionalism, merit, and efficiency became the guiding values as an effort was made to reshape the schools into economically functional institutions and to insulate them from democratic politics.

Citizenship is often thought of only in terms of voting, as a legal right, without inquiring about the purposes and programmatic possibilities of political mobilization. Because mass participation is fraught with uncertainty for economic and political elites, such elites often seek to develop mechanisms to soften or eliminate the uncertain results of democratization. One typical strategy is the insulation of key areas of decision making from popular pressures.

Early-twentieth-century educational reform may be understood, in this light, as one attempt to narrow the meaning of citizenship for working-class people. It succeeded not just because elites tend to get their way but also because the political culture of the American working class, even in its most effective labor aspects, was unable to put up an effective contest.

Thus it is not without irony that R. H. Tawney chose in his 1924 explication of Britain's labor movement to contrast American education favorably with his country's class-riddled and exclusionary educational system. Tawney was impressed most by the egalitarian features of New World schooling; he was blind to the dissipation of the most democratic impulses of schooling for all.

When Tawney visited Massachusetts, educational bureaucratization was marching alongside professionalization of the educational craft under the banner of reform. By 1930 the organization and rationales for autonomous school bureaucracies directed by self-regulating educational professionals were, if not wholly uncontested, established as features of municipal life. One result was the institutionalization of a set of interests and people committed to a "nonpolitical" characterization of the problems of the public schools. There were now full-time specialist advocates to defend the existing provision of schooling and to seek the expansion of the offerings by the schools. These professionals within urban school systems, together with those outside (mainly in major university schools of education) constructed a discourse and a practice of schooling that appeared classless. The schools stressed individual solutions to the problems of mobility. The school system appeared class-blind even as it reproduced the class structure; its ostensible purpose was to transmit knowledge without class implications.

These ideas of expertise, political neutrality, and classlessness were characteristic illusions of the era, which saw the progressive treatments of schooling as an aspect of democracy. The mystification of class exacted a stiff price for democracy itself, however. The schools became less hospitable to cultural difference, and the public realm was severely contracted.

The facts of reform are by now ably chronicled and very well known. In most major cities, battles over school governance constituted the central drama in urban education. The first major push for school reform in Chicago came in 1899 with the report of the Harper Commission, which was headed by University of Chicago president William Rainey Harper and included prominent members of the Chicago business community. Asserting that Chicago had long since outgrown the administrative structure of its schools, the commission recommended a smaller board appointed by the mayor. It proposed that daily administrative matters be split between a superintendent and a business manager. The superintendent would have charge of all educational affairs, including personnel, and was to be "employed as an expert, just as a physician is and in the range of work in which he is so employed he is independent of dictation."[1] The report maintained that the schools' efficiency could be greatly enhanced by giving the superintendent control over the hiring and firing of teachers and by linking promotions to merit rather than length of service. The business manager would enjoy a similar autonomy in running the business affairs of the schools.

These recommendations were presented to the state legislature, which rejected them. Unruffled by repeated failures, proponents of school reform persisted and presented similar bills in 1901, 1903, and 1905. Each bill was defeated. Reformers next attempted, again unsuccessfully, to win in a different arena by inserting their recommendations into the new city charter slated for ratification in 1907. Only in 1917 with the passage of the Otis bill did educational reform triumph in Chicago.

In the same year a survey of educational conditions in San Francisco provided the basis for school reforms passed three years later. Unlike that of Chicago, San Francisco's school governance had been substantially modified in the 1898 city charter. Rampant and blatant corruption throughout the 1890s had prompted the charter's drafters to include provisions for a small professional board of education appointed by the mayor. However, to placate Catholic resistance to reform, an elected superintendent was retained. As early as 1901, prominent educator Ellwood Cubberly urged further reform of the system, warning that this mix would produce an administrative nightmare.[2]

Reformers, however, preoccupied with the major scandals uncovered in the municipal administration of the Union Labor

Party, did not direct their energies toward schools until 1911. In that year the elite Commonwealth Club launched a discussion of the quality of education in San Francisco, initiating a process that culminated in a study of the city's schools. Conducted by a team of professional educators, this Claxton Survey's recommendations paralleled those of Chicago's Harper Commission: institute a professional superintendency named by a nonprofessional appointed board of education and clearly divide responsibilities between the two. In accord with "sound business practices" the board would act as "the board of directors of a business corporation," not taking an active hand in the daily affairs of the schools but allowing the superintendent to function as its "technical expert and executive."[3] The initial effort to enact the recommendations was rebuffed by voters in 1918. After an intensive campaign reform supporters managed to pass the measure, by a close margin, two years later.

The terms of debate about the character and meaning of this history of school reform are also well known. Our contribution is to enter the room of debate by the side door, as it were. We wish to demonstrate the variation in the process and outcomes of reform in each city, showing how the distinctive role of the working class contributed to these differences. We do not argue that workers have been the overlooked central agents of reform. Rather, we wish to properly insert their organizations and actions into the story for two reasons.

Reform was not interpreted and disputed on the same terms in every city. In some places, such as San Francisco, the controversy over school reform was engaged as an ethnic issue, while in other cities, most notably Chicago, reform became the focus of labor opposition. The introduction of working people into the analysis of school disputes is essential to understanding the different terms on which reform was fought for. One important determinant of such differences, which inclusion of the working class clarifies, is the positions and choices of other actors. This is especially true with regard to schoolteachers who, in this period, were struggling to find a distinctive identity and voice. The development and elaboration of urban school bureaucracies defined an organizationally specific, but substantively ambiguous, place for teachers

at the bottom of the new organizational hierarchy. Their relationship to the children they taught, and to parents, was inherently
unclear: were teachers to be outsiders in or members of the communities of their students? With the feminization of school teaching, teachers were recruited increasingly from the relatively cheap
labor pool of women in immigrant and working-class neighborhoods. Much like the children they taught, if a generation or two
removed, teachers had to define a relationship to the locality in
which they taught. As low-paid workers in a bureaucracy undergoing self-conscious professionalization, teachers had possible
identities as workers and as professionals. Obviously subordinate
in prestige, discretion, and pay to predominantly male administrators, teachers were torn between a close identification with their
hierarchical superiors, whose professionalism was attractive, and
the collective gains to be secured from a solidarity with organized
labor. It is impossible to make sense of the resolution of these
tensions or of the political role of teachers in the story of reform
without introducing the working class into the story. Even further: as we shall show, the behavior of workers on educational
issues is not explicable without a treatment of the strategic choices
teachers made for themselves.

Without an understanding of the distinctive roles played by
the working class it is impossible to make sense of the variation
in the outcomes of reform in each city. In San Francisco, where
workers took their ethnic identities into the battle over school
reform and allied with teachers and the powerful Catholic hierarchy, the advocates and opponents of reform did not seek to
compromise their differences, each group believing that it had
sufficient strength to win. The outcome was a "pure" version of
reform that left a substantial bloc of the population unreconciled
to the changes. In Chicago, where workers engaged in school
conflict as labor, joined by teachers and occasionally but not
consistently by various middle-class elites or ethnic groups, there
was considerably more pressure on both sides to compromise.
The reform that was ultimately adopted reflected concessions on
both sides and, by dissolving the united opposition to reform,
paved the way for a reorganization of alliances on educational
issues.

Insertion of the working class into this history thus offers a way of moving beyond the self-contained quality of the existing historiographical debate. Distinct positions are taken by those who argue that reform was the product of business elites seeking to control schools unfettered by democratic representation and those who see reform as a democratic process in which citizens became convinced that administrative change was necessary to provide the efficient high-quality education they wanted. This debate has reached an intellectual dead end as each side has proven to its own satisfaction the exclusive validity of its own position. A priori adoption of either position limits the questions one can ask about educational reform and, most importantly for us, restricts one's view of workers to either manipulated or passive actors on the one hand or undifferentiated "citizens" on the other. Our focus on workers will make use of each of the two dominant perspectives, deriving questions from each to illuminate the logic governing working-class participation in school reform. We will also consider a third, less prominent explanation for school reform that borrows from organization theory. This perspective views reform as a response to the growth and increasing complexity of school systems that make modification of existing administrative arrangements technically necessary. In this interpretation, change is introduced mainly by school administrators and is neutral in its implications for different classes.

Although we will draw on each of these perspectives to make sense of the role of the working class in educational reform, we will show that the ultimate impact of reform was to diminish the potential for a broad working-class influence over wide areas of school policy. By pointing to the particular ways in which workers participated in the reform struggles, however, we hope to give this assertion a more precise meaning that can encompass the substantial variation that occurred among cities.

Schools span the divide between work and home. School politics, therefore, is capable of invoking either of the main identities of American workers: as laborers and as ethnic group members. Conflicts about school reform in Chicago and San Francisco in very large measure are stories about why these different identities were mobilized and what the consequences were.

With regard to some issues, such as vocational education, the choice of identity is obvious. School reform, however, was multifaceted and thus was capable of invoking alternative identities. Some school reforms stimulated conflicts about teachers as members of the union movement; other reforms challenged traditional patterns of ethnic politics and patronage. Thus, *how* workers engaged in the politics of reform was conditional.

These alternatives had an important impact. Where workers mobilized as labor, our Chicago case suggests, they were able to impose compromises more effectively than when they based their actions mainly on ethnic and religious identities. In San Francisco, where confrontation was cast in these terms, reformers could impose their goals without being compelled to make concessions. Labor identities proved capable of forging the politically active working class into an effective political actor. Labor unions had the cohesion and resources needed to fight battles in multiple political arenas and to secure the allegiance of teachers. Ethnic politics, by contrast, proved more susceptible to divide-and-conquer strategies. Its intense localism, the absence of broad visionary appeals, and a tradition of patronage made effective collective action by working people on issues that transcended ethnicity very difficult.

Where workers engaged in educational politics as members of ethnic groups they could do so only with respect to highly particularistic claims about jobs, positions on the school board, or contracts for construction and maintenance. The representation of society in ethnic terms imposed limits on what could be said and fought about in political life. The schools, from an ethnic vantage point, could not even be discussed in terms of their relationships to American capitalism, labor markets, or social mobility.

If the ethnic perspective that dominated San Francisco school politics imposed these blinders, the Chicago experience shows how, even when the terms of school conflict were those of labor, these had become very narrow terms indeed by the 1920s. The role of labor had become limited and stylized: limited to substantive issues of teacher employment and vocational education, and stylized in terms of labor slots on boards of education and concerns about building-site work, plumbing, and maintenance.

In short, the nineteenth-century pattern of working-class formation operated in the first three decades of the twentieth century as a powerful constraint on the political capacities of the working class to effectively resist school reform. Quite simply, there was no working-class political movement or party system capable of successfully opposing the dissociation of school administration from municipal politics that diminished the chances workers had to shape their children's schools.

I

ONE might suppose that an approach stressing the needs of capital or the wishes of business as the key to understanding the politics of school reform would be exempt from the charge of inattention to the working class. Alas, such is not the case. Even where its advocates seek to identify the agents who intentionally act to secure the proposed relationship between capitalism and schooling, the working class is treated only as the passive client of an imposed system of education.

Like its main competitor, which focuses on the links between democracy and schooling, this perspective presents a plausible account of the available data. The broad argument that capitalist development needs a certain level of schooling to underpin the process of capital accumulation is consistent with the economic and educational histories of Chicago and San Francisco. Chicago was a boom city between 1900 and 1930. In just this span its population virtually doubled to 3,400,000; and the value of the products its industrial sector produced more than quadrupled to nearly $4 billion per annum. This dramatic growth was accompanied by the now familiar characteristics of the second industrial revolution: the extension of the corporate form of ownership, the "deskilling" of much of the work force (with the concomitant emergence of the new dominant category of semi-skilled workers), the concentration and centralization of capital, and the intensification of the labor process as a result of mechanization.[4]

San Francisco's population also virtually doubled in these years to just under 635,000, but its place in the national economy was rather less an industrial than a commercial one when compared to Chicago. Manufacturing grew at a steady but relatively modest pace. Competition from Los Angeles, which was beginning its industrial expansion just at the moment of the 1906 earthquake and fire, retarded industrial expansion in San Francisco. San Francisco's economy modernized mainly on the basis of its rapid expansion as a center for banking and shipping and for the processing of agricultural products.

The theoretical position focusing on capital's needs stresses that key features of reform in the schools of both cities mirrored important facets of industrial change. The governance of school systems imitated the corporate form of policymaking boards and management by experts. The organization and the rhetoric of factory life permeated the schools. "Scientific" educational testing tracked students for future careers. Authority patterns within individual schools, as well as the system as a whole, were rationalized on the bases of merit and efficiency.

Other evidence for this view is the significant role of business leaders and their groups in the politics of school expansion and reform. Arguing in this vein, Frances Fox Piven and Richard Cloward observe that "whatever the posture of working class groups, it does seem clear that, at crucial historical junctures, business elites played a very large role initiating, expanding, and reforming the schools. . . . The role of business elites is particularly evident in the century-long effort to centralize control of the proliferating schools, placing them under the control of small, elite boards and committees, the better to ensure that all schools conformed with the new educational procedures they were developing." Capitalists took educational initiatives, Piven and Cloward argue, because they experienced working-class defiance in other spheres of life and sought to find mechanisms to subdue workers and "to enforce their subservience to the requirements of the new industrial order."[5]

Whatever their precise motives or self-conscious designs, business elites did in fact play leading roles in the promotion of school reform in San Francisco and Chicago. In San Francisco the Chamber of Commerce and the Merchants Association, the two most important and stable business groups of this period, were key supporters of school reform. Together with the city's other major business and elite civic organizations—including the Commonwealth Club, the San Francisco Center of the California Civic League, the San Francisco Real Estate Board, the Association of Collegiate Alumnae, and the City Federation of Women's Clubs —these groups propagated the notion that government and its schools should be run like a corporation, on business principles. It was the Chamber of Commerce and the San Francisco Public School Society that invited and raised the funds for a report on the city's schools by U.S. commissioner of education Philander Claxton, whose report became the main text of the school reformers. These organizations were also crucial to the success of the reform campaign in 1920 to pass a charter amendment that abolished an elective school superintendency.

Business groups in Chicago, if anything, were even more well organized and central to the reform process. The Civic Federation, a "nonpartisan" organization dominated by businesspeople interested in tax and charter reform, regularly wrote, introduced, and promoted bills in the state legislature to reform the administrative structure of Chicago's schools. The Merchants Club, an organization of successful businesspeople under the age of forty-five, took charge of writing the provisions for Chicago's public education system in a proposed reform city charter in 1907. Businesspeople also supported the efforts of politicians who sought to discipline reform opponents. For example, in 1915 the Illinois Manufacturers Association indicated its support for the Loeb Rule, which prevented teachers from joining unions. Moreover, business leaders were generally well positioned to influence school policy. From its founding in 1904 the Chicago Association of Commerce (CAC) had an average of three to four members on the board of education. During Mayor William Dever's tenure in the mid-1920s five of the eleven board members, including its president, were members of the CAC. They were instrumental in the selection of reform superintendent William McAndrew, who, in turn, asked the CAC in 1925 to inspect the public schools and report their appraisal to him.[6]

The leading competitor of the view that capitalism or capitalists lay behind school reforms is the older and more common claim that democratic imperatives were central to the reform of the public schools. The crux of this view is the argument that democratic politics and society require a mass school system to support the larger democratic order. The evidence adduced focuses on the population served by the school system; the open, permeable process of school reform; the democratic impulses of reformers; and changes in the period's modes of representation.

The schools of Chicago and San Francisco, like American public schools more generally, were mass institutions. Their growth took place at a rate greater than the increase in the cities' populations. From an enrollment of 48,000 in 1900, San Francisco schools reached an enrollment of just under 109,000 by 1930. In Chicago, enrollment increased from 256,000 in 1900 to 535,000 in 1930[7] (see table 4.1). The schools were open to virtually all children irrespective of their class, neighborhood, race, ethnicity, or sex. Enrollment reflected this diversity. In terms of ethnicity, for example, Chicago was extraordinarily polyglot, with some two-thirds of its population foreign-born or composed of first-generation immigrant children from Ireland, Poland, Germany, Czechoslovakia, Russia, Scandinavia, Italy, and numerous other countries. Even in spite of San Francisco's distance from Europe, the majority of its population throughout the period was either born abroad or the offspring of foreign-born parents, mainly from Ireland, Italy, Germany, and Scandinavia.

For the democracy-oriented interpretation the most important characteristic of this population was their status as citizens who could participate in democratic politics. Diane Ravitch, one of the most polemical advocates of this position, has summarized it this way:

> Whatever the issue at hand, reformers had to take into account the necessity of persuading others to agree with them. In other nations, the schools were controlled by the established church or by a powerful centralized state agency. Popular control in the United States meant that school politics was an extension of democratic politics. . . . But the process of decision-making—the impact of public opinion, the necessity of discussion and agreement, the negotiations

TABLE 4.1

Expansion of Chicago and San Francisco Public Schools, 1900–1930

	Chicago				San Francisco			
	1900	1910	1920	1930	1900	1910	1920	1930
Average Daily Attendance	208,841	231,484	306,209	438,170	35,004	36,774	48,740	65,503
Total Current Expenditures	6,050,345	8,484,128	21,173,559	48,608,994	1,274,495	3,308,924	4,117,418	8,480,800

SOURCES: San Francisco, Board of Education, *Annual Report*, 1900, 1910, 1920, 1930; Chicago, Board of Education, *Annual Report*, 1900, 1910, 1920, 1930; Kenneth Wong, "Fiscal Strain of the Chicago Public School System 1890–1925" (MS, University of Chicago, 1980).

among different constituencies, the constraints of law and the judi-
ciary—is democratic.[8]

This perspective puts relatively less stress on the outcome and
more on the process of educational decision making. It finds
support in the drawn-out legislative battles leading up to the Otis
Act of 1917, which reformed Chicago's schools, and the two
referenda of 1918 and 1920 in San Francisco. There was a *politics* of education apparently at odds with a simple view that
reform was imposed from above by capital. The politics of reform
mobilized a host of concerned groups not defined exclusively by
class interest or identification. School reform and curricular expansion thus appear as the product of a democratic process of
political competition and persuasion.

There can be little question that advocates of the Harper and
Claxton reforms emphasized these democratic intentions as well
as the efficiency criteria that underscored their affinity with capital. Although, as Cremin has emphasized, urban reforms took the
factory system and its diffusion to government for granted, they
tried to create conditions for a more egalitarian and humane
society.[9]

Finally, the explanations that point to the democratic process
stress that political life in the reform era actually became more,
not less, democratic. The key to this development was the proliferation of interest groups. This explosion of associations produced a diversification of political life and a decline in the monopoly enjoyed by political parties in the representation of
interests.[10] This new pattern of interest intermediation arguably
was more, rather than less, democratic than the old party system.
Martin Schiesl, a leading student of municipal reform, suggests
that reformed government "enabled both inner-city ethnic
groups and suburban middle classes to exert more effective pressure on municipal officials without the continual intervention of
a party leader." One result, he claims, was an extension of the role
of government in education and social policy in ways "that
served the needs and wants of all social classes in the city."[11] This
triumph of citizenship over class, he reminds us, was ratified at
the polls. By 1920 progressivism as a movement was receiving the

bulk of its electoral support from immigrant and working-class voters.[12]

This view is entirely consistent with the history of reform in our two cities, which consisted of a series of issues fought out in open legislative and electoral arenas. But it should also be said that the assimilation of the working class into the general category of citizens obscures critical dimensions of the actual politics of school reform, including such vital matters as the formation of alliances and coalitions of which workers as labor or as ethnic group members played a vital part. The existing literature emphasizing the democratic impetus of reform tends to make the unfortunate mistake of identifying class analysis only with the adversary view that finds capital at the root of school reform. It has too frequently argued, in an effort to play down the significance of the division between businesspeople and workers, that virtually every available form of political identification but that of class has dominated the politics of reform. This empirical claim, as we shall demonstrate, is wrong.

The debate between economic and political functionalism has been the centerpiece of the historiography on the period of reform. With all their differences, these two positions share the formulation that the organizational development of urban school systems was the result of factors external to the schools. There is a third view, however, which has at least as much plausibility: an "organization logic" arguing that educational change was the result of forces *interior* to school systems as bureaucracies. In this perspective, organizations must expand in relatively predictable ways (the creation of hierarchies, rules, and career paths) to deal with inherent problems of uncertainty, limits on information, and difficulties in identifying and obtaining optimal solutions in market terms. Organizations try to maximize prospects for their durability and achievement of goals. They spawn reforms in order to achieve these goals. Evidence of school expansion before and after reform makes a plausible case for an "organizational" explanation: reform was needed to cope with the growth of public education, and once the administrative modifications were in place, schools could accommodate even more rapid growth.

There is a curious dichotomy in the literature on educational history. Recent events, especially concerning black social movements of the 1960s and early 1970s, have often been interpreted in these organizational terms, as reactions to insular and highly bureaucratized school systems. David Rogers's and Marilyn Gittel's treatments of decentralization struggles, for example, take the results of organizational reform as the starting point of their analyses.[13] In contrast, the literature on the origins of modern complex school organizations has paid rather less attention to organizational imperatives in the belief that the break with past forms of school organization in the early twentieth century was so radical as to rule out autonomous causes of school reform.[14]

The two main arguments, stressing capital and democracy, not only overlook this possibility but also tend to ignore professional school administrators as agents of reform. Advocates of economic functionalism tend to collapse these professionals into a larger elite dominated by businesspeople. Proponents of political functionalism treat school professionals either as citizens or as only one group among many. Both perspectives are misleading because school administrators have worldviews and interests that cannot readily be collapsed into those of other actors. Moreover, their central role made them pivotal actors in the school reform effort. The Claxton Survey and the Harper Commission set the terms and defined the options for debate about school reform. These initiatives, whatever their external sponsorship, were expressions of people with professional organizational claims to expertise and autonomy.

In broad outline the history of educational expansion in San Francisco and Chicago is consistent with this organizational perspective. The growth of San Francisco's public school system from 1900 to 1930 occurred in four stages. Largely as a result of the 1906 earthquake, the public school system grew very slowly in the first eight years of the century. While the annual average rate of the city's population growth was 1.5 percent, the corresponding rate of school enrollment growth was only 0.45 percent. Between 1900 and 1910 only 140 teachers were added to the teaching force. The next four or five years constituted a period of rebuilding. As San Francisco recovered from the 1908–09 financial panic and began to restore essential public services, it turned its attention to the schools, which received a relatively massive infusion of funds. Per-pupil expenditure, which had gone virtually unchanged between 1900 and 1906, increased from $36 to $93 between 1906 and 1912. Teacher hiring also accelerated, reducing average class size from 38 in 1906 to 31 in 1912. However, enrollment in 1912 was still well below the 1906 figure.

This period was followed by several years of steady expansion. Thus, while per-pupil expenditures leveled off during the teens, enrollment expanded and the teacher-pupil ratio continued to decline. With the installation of the reformist school administration in the early 1920s, San Francisco's public school system experienced unprecedented expansion. Per-pupil expenditure increased by over 70 percent between 1920 and 1922, when it reached a level of $143. After a temporary decline in 1924, school spending rose rapidly during the next three years. This was also a period of expansion in high school enrollment. By 1929 one in seven of San Francisco's public school pupils attended high school.[15]

Chicago's schools grew at a steady rate in the first two decades of the twentieth century. After 1920 the pace quickened, with significant increases in the numbers of pupils, teachers, and expenditures. Starting with an average daily attendance of little over 200,000 in 1900, the schools came to serve an additional 30,000 pupils ten years later. By 1925 nearly 400,000 children attended Chicago's public schools. Accompanying this influx of pupils were significant additions to the teaching force, particularly after 1920. In 1920 Chicago employed 8,447 teachers, nearly 3,000 more than in 1900. But over the next five years alone, the schools hired over 3,000 additional teachers, bringing the total to 11,672 in 1925. The growth of the teaching staff outpaced the increase in the student body. In the early years of the century, the average teacher taught between thirty-five and forty students, but after 1917 the number of students per teacher steadily declined, to the low thirties.

Expenditures grew dramatically in this period. Between 1900 and 1915, spending doubled from $6 million to $12 million. In just the next ten years they nearly tripled to $34.5 million by 1925, well outstripping the increase in enrollment. From 1900 to

1925, the amount spent on each student increased from about $29 to $89. As in San Francisco, high school enrollment played a significant role in school expansion. Only about 4 percent of students attending school in 1900 were in high school; by 1925 high school students accounted for 17 percent of all students.[16]

Troen's analysis of the St. Louis schools from an organizational perspective illustrates just how difficult it is to accept the dominant terms of educational debate. In presenting an organizational view, Troen also presents considerable empirical justification for the other two perspectives. He shows how the city's reform achievements borrowed from the business corporation and how reformed schools taught students "the many specialized skills demanded in a modern, industrial society. In terms of programs this entailed the introduction of vocational instruction, a doubling of the period of schooling, and a broader concern for the welfare of urban youth."[17] The last of these policy orientations may be understood partly in economic terms, partly as a social control attempt to regiment future workers, and partly as an extension of substantive democracy in English social analyst T. H. Marshall's sense of social citizenship. Reform, Troen also shows, promoted procedural democracy by providing interest groups with direct access to the schools. Such groups were now able to present their views free of the "tyranny of the ward." As this example indicates, it is silly to decide once and for all whether one or another of these claims is correct. It makes more sense to see their relationship as contingent, with the precise mix between them to be decided on the basis of an examination of cases. The literature on school reform, in our view, makes the mistake of being structured along fault lines of choice between the three (mainly the first two) perspectives, as if only one or another were logically and empirically plausible.

Workers appear implicitly in each of the three accounts. In the explanations that stress the role of capitalism, workers appear as adversaries of the capitalist class. In accounts that emphasize the democratic aspects of reform, workers are the bulk of citizen-voters. And in the organizational perspective, workers are the clients of a large service bureaucracy. In none of these perspectives does the working class appear as an independent and active participant. In the first, workers are the determined objects of the social structure. In the second, they disappear as a distinctive entity into the mass of the electorate. And in the third, they appear as individuals in families linked to the state in a single, specific policy domain.

Missing, in short, is a real working class, formed in a distinctive way and with its own traditions of collective values and practices. This omission is not trivial. Without a working class (other than a theoretically imputed one) the perspective emphasizing the role of capital is preoccupied with "the way in which elite-created institutions force people into acquiescent conformity with the requirements of industrial capitalism." The cost of such an argument, Piven and Cloward have shrewdly suggested, is the loss of the dialectical idea "that specific institutional arrangements emerge through a process of group and class conflict in the first place, and that once subject to particular institutional arrangements, people continue to react against them."[18] Without a working class, accounts that point to the importance of democracy dissolve into a pluralism without the capacity to differentiate important from less significant bases of conflict and social change. And without a working class, the organizational interpretation develops an insular form of analysis closed to the environment in which school bureaucracies are located. As a result, it misses the possibility of seeing the working class as a major source of organizational uncertainty and as a goad to professional administrators to make their organizations more permeable.

II

THE working class has not been entirely absent from scholarship on the reform of public education. Recently, important empirical work by several scholars has tried quite self-consciously to explore the relationship between the working class and educational reform. These contributions are limited, however, by their selective treatments of working people either as laborers or as community residents.[19] Because they reflect the dominant cultural understanding that working-class life is starkly divided between the realms of work and off-work, these scholars have found it difficult to identify the significance of this separation for the politics of education. Why, for example, did the Chicago working class in the heyday of reform pay attention to school issues as organized labor although in San Francisco religion and ethnicity, rooted in neighborhood and community, were common bases of school conflicts? To be able to explain variations of this kind it is necessary to treat the multiple identities that workers had and the reasons that particular identities were mobilized at various moments in different settings. The literature on schooling and the working class makes this task difficult.

Consider the illuminating exchange between Frances Fox Piven and Richard Cloward, who treat working-class resistance to educational authorities as part of a larger theory of deviance, and Julia Wrigley, who has done the most to treat the working class seriously as an actor in school politics. Piven and Cloward adopt a variant of the perspective that highlights the role of capital. Faced with a recalcitrant, undersocialized working class, businesspeople sought, with ultimate success, to create a reformed school system capable of controlling working-class defiance and "to enforce their subservience to the requirements of the new industrial order." Reformed schools, in Piven and Cloward's view, were more capable than their less well organized predecessors in undermining indigenous belief systems, in eroding the autonomy of working people, and in shifting the burden for failures of the occupational order onto workers themselves and away from the capitalist industrial system. This pattern of imposition and social control, however, was not a complete success. Working people "continued to react against the conditions which shaped their lives, but under the influence of the public schools, these reactions themselves were transformed." Collective protest, Piven and Cloward argue, was channeled by the reformed educational systems away from a broader-based class politics to a very limited, issue-specific school politics and to "individualized and self-destructive protest" that pinned responsibility for failure on students and their families.[20]

In this treatment the working class appears twice: as the motivating force compelling elites to create mass schooling and as the actor most likely to resist the imposition of schooling. School reform was "prompted in part by crime, vagrancy, fighting gangs, mass protests, and strikes—by working class defiance." In this view, schooling is an indirect and unintended result of working-class action. Once schools are created, Piven and Cloward go on to assert, workers fight back. But the forms of their protest are externally determined. They now must struggle within the "reformed" bureaucratic structure; their behavior is atomized as they become clients, and the politics of schooling is disconnected from any larger political battles. Workers in this account are virtually nonconscious actors. They have no interested, direct effect on the creation of the public schools or on educational reform. Nor is the working class shaped by education except in culturally destructive ways. School politics becomes the politics of working-class disorganization. The possibility that the arena of public education might under some circumstances enhance effective collective action by workers is not considered.

These points are the main ones made by Wrigley in her brief critique of Piven and Cloward's article. Drawing on the excellent research in her book *Class Politics and Public Schools: Chicago, 1900–1950,* Wrigley argues that the labor movement was supportive of public education and that "there were sustained and bitter conflicts in Chicago over the control, funding, and curriculum of the public schools, and the issues involved were posed in broad, class-related terms." She seeks to establish "that conflicts between the classes have been dynamic forces in historical change." She presents evidence to show how workers in Chicago, organized as labor, opposed the business community with respect to reform and curricular expansion; and she argues that the working class was an independent actor with a distinctive viewpoint, capable of shaping the outcomes of public policy disputes. She cautions, persuasively, that it is important to treat working-class participation and effectiveness as variables. The position and degree of mobilization of the Chicago labor movement varied considerably over time; these changes must be accounted for. "To assume in advance a pattern of no significant variability is to foreclose the possibility of addressing the question of why social movements arise or decline."[21]

We have learned much from Wrigley's empirical research and from her theoretical contributions. Nevertheless, we find that the manner in which she inserts the working class into political analysis has a number of limitations, perhaps inherent in her theoretical project and her focus on Chicago. At the theoretical level she is most interested in debunking the position that the working class had no free will. At this she succeeds very well, countering the expectations of revisionist scholars who assert the primacy of capital in their explanation. But she succeeds too well, because in showing that the working class was deeply implicated in school politics, she fails to focus enough on the contingent character of its participation. In Chicago the working class uncontestedly appeared in school politics as labor. In Wrigley's work the antithesis is nonparticipation. But surely this is not the only possible alternative. In San Francisco, for example, working people also engaged in school politics but principally on ethnic or religious terms. The identities were assumed, the language they used, and the institutions they mobilized were very different. For Wrigley, it was important to establish the reality of an active working class. We share this broad view, but we think it also important to understand the basis for alternative *terms* of working-class activity and the *impact* these alternatives had on policy outcomes.

Part of the problem is the difficulty of a one-case analysis. We are struck that the significant general history of schooling by David Tyack, *The One Best System,* draws a broad portrait of working-class activity in the period of reform very different from both Wrigley's *and* the revisionists'. For Tyack, the working class enters the story mainly as ethnic groups seeking to preserve local control of schooling against elitist attempts at centralization and reform. In this view, locality-based democracy sustained the local ethnic cultures that centralization threatened. "In almost every city where the population was heterogeneous, contests erupted in educational politics. Although there were sometimes overtones of class assertion or resentment in such conflict, the issues were not normally phrased in class terms but in the cross-cutting cultural categories of race, religion, ethnicity, neighborhood loyalties, and partisan politics."[22] He bases this finding on four case studies of centralization: New York, Philadelphia, St. Louis, and San Francisco. Our own research amply confirms the ethnic orientation of working-class educational politics in San Francisco (just as it confirms, with Wrigley, the importance of Chicago's labor participation). But the omission of Chicago from Tyack's discussion of reform leads him to underplay the conditional quality of working-class political interventions.

Where Wrigley sees the working class as labor and Tyack stresses ethnicity, we embed our treatment of the politics of schooling within the distinctive landscape of American working-class formation. We argue, contra Piven and Cloward, that the working class was a highly self-conscious actor in early-twentieth-century school politics—but an actor of a special kind. The participation of working people drew on and reinforced the distinctively American pattern of class formation. Workers were mobilized either as labor *or* as ethnics in school disputes, not as a working class in a more holistic sense.

Workers concerned themselves with reform as it affected issues of labor (as in the relationship of schoolteachers to unions in Chicago) or issues of ethnicity (as in questions of patronage for San Francisco Catholics). The selection of an identity with which to enter the fray of school disputes was not wholly voluntary. Workers mobilized one or the other of the available bases of action within the American tradition of class mainly as a response to how others sought to define the issues of reform.

III

THE most important group affecting working-class positions and activity regarding educational reform was the teachers. Teachers were pivotal in determining the shape of coalitions supporting or opposing reform and, more particularly, in shaping the identities that workers assumed in school disputes. Likewise, the identities with which teachers participated in school politics were affected by the institutions, language, and practical orientations of the working class as well as by the nature of their ties with the educational administration in each city.

In Chicago, teachers aligned themselves with the labor movement and consistently provided the force behind labor's opposition to reform. In contrast, San Francisco's teachers, bound to an ethnic-based patronage relationship with the school administration, shunned ties with organized labor. There, teachers joined with the educational establishment to fight reform while labor unions retained a muted opposition to some aspects of reform and eventually split on the question. Because reform proposals either implicitly undercut teachers' power or explicitly infringed on their current prerogatives, teachers provided the core for anti-reform forces in both cities.

Teachers may assume multiple identities. As we have seen, they may consider themselves professionals or workers, each identity implying quite different coalitional alignments. Yet because schools are not only workplaces but service organizations embedded in a structure of politics, a third choice exists. Teachers may view themselves as recipients of political patronage, bound to their benefactors by ethnic and political ties. While these three possibilities cover the main bases of identification, a subsidiary source of identity existed that could combine with one of the others, namely, teachers as women. This source of identity was particularly important in the opening decades of the 1900s, when the teaching force was overwhelmingly female and the struggle for women's suffrage was emergent. In Chicago, teachers aligned themselves with labor under the vigorous leadership of two women who embraced teachers as workers and as women and sought to defend both sets of interests. In San Francisco teachers acted on the ethnic-patronage dimension, fighting alongside educational administrators to protect existing arrangements. Unlike those of the Chicago movement, the leaders of San Francisco's movement were male administrators, and the teachers' organization, too, was dominated by a small number of male teachers.

In Chicago the problems teachers confronted, the organization of the school department, and the growing animosity of the business community all led teachers to identify with labor. Struggles over pensions, salaries, and reform set up a division of interest within the school department, pitting the administration against rank-and-file teachers and, consequently, men against women. The pension issue, which first spurred teachers to organize, set the tone for future conflicts. Disgruntled by provisions of the 1895 pension law that seemed to favor women, male principals launched an attack against the law. In defense, teachers, at a mass meeting attended by two thousand persons, voted to organize.[23]

The new group, the Chicago Teachers Federation (CTF), prohibited principals and other supervisors from joining, leaving an organization composed almost exclusively of women. The leadership of the CTF was drawn from grade school teachers. Most prominent were Catherine Goggin and Margaret Haley, both of whom had considerable political experience. Goggin had been active in organizing teachers since 1892, had helped lead the struggle for the pension law, and was the first elected teacher representative on the pension board in 1896. Haley's ties ranged even farther. She was active in the Referendum League, was an official of the Municipal Ownership League, and was a leader of the Illinois women's suffrage movement. The two women, not surprisingly, shared a vision of teachers' organizations that extended beyond narrow concerns for immediate benefits. Yet they also had the political experience to recognize that their claims could not be realized without strategic political connections, particularly since their disenfranchised membership could exert little direct political pressure.

Thus, in their struggle to secure higher salaries and to fight against administrative reform, Haley and Goggin enlisted the support of organized labor and sought solutions compatible with labor's interest. The Chicago Federation of Labor (CFL) backed the teachers' demands for higher pay and applauded Haley's efforts to increase business contributions to the school coffers.[24] The shape of the reform package, too, provided a basis for teacher-labor unity. Although the various reform proposals differed, they all contained elements that encroached on the power of teachers and decreased their job security. Reform combined this attack with provisions for an appointed board of education, a proposal that organized labor also opposed.[25] Cooperation with labor had proven so useful that by 1902 Goggin and Haley were able to persuade a somewhat hesitant membership to formally affiliate with the CFL.

The issues confronting teachers also reinforced their movement as part of the larger struggle of women for political power. The Harper Commission's recommendation that more men be hired in the elementary grades and be given higher salaries than women outraged the CTF, providing grounds for cooperation with women's groups that might otherwise have been more sympathetic toward reform.

Yet the nature of the issues alone need not have caused teachers to identify as labor; equally important was the way school administrators handled conflict. Throughout the early 1900s the schools were most often in the hands of reformers aligned with the business community. Along with their efforts to formally restructure schools, these administrators tried to reproduce the corporate model of schools with innovations that did not require legislation. Such plans invariably antagonized teachers by centralizing power at the top. Superintendent Edwin Cooley, a favorite of Chicago's business community, instituted reforms that broke any moderating influence that patronage ties might have had and that directly challenged teachers' autonomy.

Cooley sought to destroy competing bases of influence by blocking channels of political "pull." His earliest effort cut off the means by which board members and teachers established patronage relationships that could bypass the superintendent's control. Capitalizing on the atmosphere left by his predecessor's resignation, Cooley launched a campaign to "smoke the political pests out of the public school system."[26] He wrangled from the school board the power to appoint and promote teachers, a significant departure from the previous system, in which the board had retained control over personnel. Under Cooley's new system the superintendent made recommendations on the basis of merit. Written and oral communications from board members had to be made public. Other channels of political influence were closed as Cooley streamlined the committee system of the board, cutting the number of committees from a high of seventy-nine to four and reducing the number of district superintendents. Each of these reforms cut into the fragmented district-level centers of power and concentrated control at the top.[27] Cooley's innovations thus polarized conflict along teacher-worker versus board-superintendent-employer lines.

Business-aligned reformers did not consistently control Chicago's schools, however. In some periods forces more sympathetic to labor and teachers dominated the school board. At those times a less militant and more cooperative school politics proved possible, but only within limits. Cooley's merit-pay plan was briefly lifted in 1906 when Mayor Edward Dunne appointed a school board more receptive to teachers. This board sided with the teachers in bringing a suit against the *Chicago Tribune* in 1906. The litigation aimed to change provisions of the leases that granted the *Tribune* excessively low rents.[28] The courts upheld the *Tribune*'s lease, leaving a deep hostility between the CTF and the newspaper. During the tenure of Ella Flagg Young as superintendent (1909 to 1915), cooperation among teachers and administrators peaked. Young was attentive to teachers' interests and established the long-demanded Teachers' Councils to give teachers representation in administrative decisions. Despite her personal popularity among the staff, teachers' identity as workers was well established by this time, and Young's presence could only moderate the tone of their demands.

In contrast to Chicago, the leading foes of reform in San Francisco were primarily the city's Irish Catholics, who identified as an ethnic group. Ethnic divisions were latent in the first vote on school reform, but by the second round two years later ethnicity had emerged as the dominant issue. As in Chicago, San Francisco's teachers opposed reforms, but they did so under the leadership of the school board and the superintendent.[29] San Francisco teachers remained distant from the local labor movement. The main teachers' organization included school administrators who dominated its leadership. Instead of confronting one another as adversaries, board members and teachers were bound together in an informal network of political patronage. This relationship created a situation in which the dissatisfaction of teachers was dealt with on a one-by-one rather than a collective basis. This informal network contributed to the failure to develop a militant labor union of teachers in San Francisco. In Chicago, the business affiliations of board members was of central significance, but in San Francisco, Irish Catholicism was the hallmark of board membership. Further, many board members actually were school administrators.

Superintendents, too, differed. Whereas Chicago had a succession of reform-oriented professional superintendents who sought to restructure the school department by arrogating more power to themselves, San Francisco had a single elected superintendent, Alfred Roncovieri, from 1905 to 1921. A former member of the Union Labor Party, Roncovieri, though not Irish, had close ties to the Catholic community and was sensitive to the variety of ethnic demands made on the schools. San Francisco's school governance, based on a decentralized network of alliances, was the product of this board-and-superintendent relationship. The professional educators on the board were accessible to other educators and allowed them a great deal of local autonomy. Principals were given almost complete control over their schools, and teachers often looked to the board members, rather than the superintendent, for direction.

The effect of this pattern is evident in the types of teacher organizations that survived in San Francisco. The attempt in 1906 to form a teachers' union along the same lines as Chicago's met with decisive defeat.[30] This outcome was, in part, the result of factors outside the scope of school politics. The labor movement was in temporary disgrace after revelations that year of widespread graft and corruption in the Union Labor Party's city administration. Nevertheless, the aversion of teachers to labor-type organization was evident thirteen years later when only a tiny fraction of San Francisco's teachers joined a newly formed union. In sharp contrast to those of Chicago, the organization was composed primarily of male high school teachers. In the intervening years, a more professionally oriented Teachers' Association thrived in San Francisco. Formed in 1917, the association included both teachers and administrators but was dominated by administrators. The association did not seek material benefits by making demands on the board of education. Instead it attempted to induce city supervisors to funnel more resources, earmarked for teachers, to the board. Thus, the employer-worker mentality that characterized teachers and the board in Chicago and helped bind teachers to the labor movement there was replaced by a patronage-based network of mutual interest in San Francisco. Likewise, the male-female split that might have formed an alternative basis of organization did not exist. Women board members (often former principals or teachers) were just as likely to be patrons as were men. When San Francisco's business and elite women's groups began to push for reforms that would disrupt these relations, the overwhelming majority of teachers, not surprisingly, stood alongside school administrators in resistance.

The network of alliances among teachers and the board may account for the absence of a labor-teacher coalition fighting school reform, but it does not explain why the reform issue was fought out in ethnic terms. The answer must be found in the domination of the schools and of the city government itself by San Francisco's Irish Catholics.[31] Both incumbents and their challengers recognized that reform would undermine this hegemony. School reform had earlier been coupled with attacks on Catholics in the schools. In 1896 reform proposals would have prevented graduates of Catholic schools from teaching in public schools. Although the provision was deleted, the episode alerted Catholics to the Protestant bias of reform.[32] That the leading proponents of the current reform were members of Protestant and Jewish elites also did not go unnoticed.

In the absence of a strong push by teachers San Francisco's two major labor organizations, the Building Trades Council and the Labor Council, barely participated in the reform struggle. Like labor in Chicago, San Francisco's unions had consistently favored more democratic control of the schools in the form of elected boards of education. They consequently opposed reform, which, by instituting an appointed superintendent, would abolish the only elected office in the school department.[33] The labor groups, however, did not match their announced opposition to reform with organizational activism; the absence of teachers in the labor movement and the nature of the issues involved gave organized labor a relatively minor stake in the outcome. This low level of organizational commitment to the antireform coalition ultimately allowed the Labor Council to move into the reform camp when offered inducements on issues of more immediate concern.

IV

MOST of the important variation in the educational reform experience in different cities—the shape of the opposing coalitions, the course of the struggle, and the final reform package—can be understood in terms of the distinct identities workers assumed. In the process of gathering support for reform bargains were struck and compromises tendered, stamping each reform with features and consequences peculiar to each specific city.

In Chicago the repeated failures of business-backed reform measures to pass in the state legislature were directly attributable to the labor opposition, directed by the CTF. By itself, this alliance was potent enough, but CTF leaders were often able to secure allies by drawing in women's organizations who objected to the sex discrimination implicit in some versions of reform. This alignment defeated the Harper Commission's recommendations when they were first presented to the state legislature in 1899. Three subsequent attempts (in 1901, 1903, and 1905) likewise were crushed. The next attempt to reform school governance came in 1907 with the proposal for a new city charter. On this occasion labor and the CFT were joined by a wide assortment of allies who successfully sought to defeat the charter. Immigrant groups feared that it would close the city's bars on Sunday; realtors worried that it would raise property taxes.[34]

The repeated defeat of reform proposals at the hands of labor and the CTF provoked attempts to sever this alliance. In search of funds for salary increases, teachers probed business's contribution to school coffers, heightening business's antagonism to the CTF. Yet only in 1915, with the election of Republican mayor William "Big Bill" Thompson, did board members launch direct attacks on teachers. The alliance of Thompson Republicans and reformers proved short-lived. Thompson's appointees aimed at eliminating a competing source of power within the school department, not at clearing the way for school reform. These politicians nevertheless attracted the sympathy of some business groups anxious to quash the increasingly nettlesome inquiries of the CTF.

Their concerted effort to crush the CTF was first evidenced in 1915 in the committee appointed by the state senate to examine business aspects of Chicago's schools. The conservative chair, Percy Baldwin, quickly turned the proceedings into an attack on the CTF. School board member Jacob Loeb labeled the CTF a "curse to the school system" and asserted that Chicago had no need for "lady labor sluggers who fight with poisoned tongue and assassinate reputation." The committee refused to allow Margaret Haley to testify in defense of the union.[35]

In the context of this strongly anti-CTF atmosphere, the Chicago school board in 1915 forbade teachers to join any organization affiliated with trade unions or having paid business agents. Teachers and labor launched an all-out attack against this Loeb Rule, named after its sponsor. Although this question was primarily a labor concern, union leaders sought to cast a wider net of support, maintaining "the issue is clearly between organized labor and the common people on one side and the interests on the other and it will be fought on that basis."[36] Despite this ringing proclamation, the Loeb Rule controversy was fought as a labor issue in the courts, with very little participation by "the common people."

The CTF ultimately secured an injunction against the rule, but Loeb continued his attacks, turning next to undercut teacher tenure. After instituting new rules requiring annual teacher reappointment, Loeb led the board in a move to deny reappointment to sixty-eight teachers, among them thirty-eight CTF members, including all the union's officers and organizers. When the courts ruled the board "was free to contract with whoever it chooses," the teachers were left without recourse.[37]

Reformers' growing discontent with the corruption in the Thompson school board, however, drove a wedge through the reformer-business alliance. Reformers objected to the board's deletion of merit service clauses providing for teacher tenure after a probationary period. More broadly, reformers objected to the increasing political manipulation of the schools by Mayor Thompson's administration. The rift became institutionalized when reformers launched the Public Education Association (PEA) to contest Thompson's control. In response to the formation of the PEA, the Illinois Manufacturers' Association, which had no quarrel with Thompson's methods and did have an overriding interest in crushing the CTF, formed a competing organization, the Public School League (PSL). This group proclaimed that "any efforts to improve [the schools] materially . . . must be based on the entire elimination of the Teachers' Federation and its politico-labor activities."[38]

The next attempt to reform the schools engaged representatives of the CTF, the PEA, and the PSL. With this new pattern of participation, the deadlock that had stymied past reform efforts broke. The recasting of the issues had introduced more flexibility in group positions as the stakes and the dangers of refusal to compromise escalated. The city council reopened the reform issue in 1916 by appointing a subcommittee to present recommendations. Chaired by labor sympathizer Robert Buck, the committee drafted a bill providing for a seven-member board elected at large on a nonpartisan basis. Teachers were offered the right to prompt tenure. Teachers and labor found this bill attractive because of its provisions for tenure and an elected board. A second bill, more in line with reformers' wishes, was introduced by school board member Ralph Otis. His bill provided for an appointed school board and promised teachers tenure only after a three-year probationary period. It echoed the Harper Commission by calling for a division of executive authority but added a new element by splitting executive responsibility among a superintendent, business manager, and school attorney. The PEA also supported this bill. Yet a third bill representing the PSL position was also introduced. It maintained the current governing system but made no provision for teacher tenure.

Teachers and labor were thus faced with a tactical dilemma. They could stand firm on their support for the Buck bill, which promised popular control and tenure, and thus risk losing to the PSL, or they could abandon the popular control issue in favor of a sure win on the tenure question by supporting the Otis bill. They chose the latter course, in part to maximize their own most immediate interest and in part because they found attractive the Otis bill's division of executive authority.[39] The teachers hoped this split in executive power would reduce the absolute control of the superintendent. With the combined support of teachers, labor, and reformers, then, the bill passed in 1917.

Compromise did not end with the bill's passage, however. When the board of education rehired the dismissed CTF members, the union agreed to disaffiliate from organized labor. The struggle to reinstate these teachers had taken a heavy toll on the union's finances and support; over half the membership had left the CTF in 1915–16. Moreover, Loeb's reappointment to another five-year term on the board presented teachers with the prospect of a continuing battle if they did not compromise. In this context, CFL president John Fitzpatrick reportedly advised Haley to disaffiliate, arguing that the two organizations were close enough to work together without formal ties.[40]

As the next few years showed, however, reforming the structure of school governance could not guarantee the kind of education administration reformers envisioned. Soon after the passage of the Otis Law, Mayor Thompson appointed a new board, stacked with machine loyalists. Like his administration more generally, Thompson's schools were governed by patronage and corruption. In 1922 a grand jury indicted a former school board president and vice-president, the school board attorney, and forty other school officers. It charged that over one million dollars had been embezzled from the school treasury and that contractors had been extorted. With these revelations and after Thompson's subsequent defeat, the new superintendent William McAndrew proceeded with his mandate to "clean up the schools." Only during McAndrew's short-lived tenure did Chicago's reformers (in alliance with business) really control public education.[41]

In many ways, San Francisco represents a more "pure" case of educational reform than Chicago. In San Francisco, reformers scored a clear victory without compromising. They mobilized electoral support by exploiting simmering ethnic antagonisms and by prying the Labor Council away from the antireform coalition with promises of particularistic benefits. Thus, reform in San Francisco did not reflect the contradictions and concessions evident in Chicago's Otis Law. This consistency, however, helped create a large and powerful opposition that would later seize every opportunity to undermine school reform. Whereas in Chicago the reform measure changed the relationships among the forces on both sides, in San Francisco previous positions were hardened.

In the first vote on the Claxton proposals in 1918, ethnic conflicts remained largely unspoken. Voting reflected an elite-versus-working-class cleavage, a division overlapping but not identical to the Catholic-non-Catholic split. Supporters of the amendment included "the city's most prominent business and professional societies as well as elite women's organizations and well-to-do neighborhood clubs." Arrayed on the other side were the teachers' organizations, labor unions, and working-class neighborhood groups. The amendment was defeated by a vote of 1,713 to 888 (the light voter turnout was due to the flu epidemic that hit San Francisco that fall).[42]

Just two years later, under changed circumstances, the Claxton proposals were endorsed in a new referendum. This time the sponsors of reform, joined together in a group called the Educational Conference (which included most of the city's civic and business organizations) were aided by splits in the labor movement and between Catholic and Protestant workers.

Protestant working-class parents charged that the principal of the Polytechnic High School had been dismissed by Catholic board members because he was a Protestant. Catholics countered with claims that his firing had been warranted because the principal had dismissed seventy-one pupils for leaving the Polytechnic to attend religious schools.[43] The Teachers' Association and the Catholic Women's Professional Association passed a joint resolution favoring the principal's dismissal and vowed to work against the Claxton charter amendment. The association also sponsored a counter amendment that would have retained the elective superintendency. Protestants, in turn, formed the Public Schools' Defense Association (PSDA) to fight for reinstatement of the principal. This group soon announced support for the reform amendment. Reformers reciprocated with an endorsement of the PSDA. Once religion and ethnicity were injected into the conflict over reform, the division between the city's Protestants and Irish Catholics quickly overshadowed other issues. The Irish charged that reform would result in a purge of Catholic teachers and ultimately force all Catholic children to attend public schools. The Protestant rejoinder was to denounce Catholic control of the schools. Labor, formerly opposed to reform, now divided on the issue. The Building Trades Council (BTC) remained on the side of the opponents of reform. The BTC had embraced and benefited from an ethnic (largely Irish Catholic-dominated) machine style of politics since the turn of the century. When BTC leader P. H. McCarthy had served as mayor from 1909 to 1911, one of his first actions had been to dismiss the board of education appointed by his reform-minded predecessor. By blending labor into a patronage-based ethnic politics, which sought at the same time to defend the gains of union members, McCarthy charted a course between the assertive working-class rhetoric of the Union Labor Party and the reform backlash it engendered following the revelations of graft in 1905. The Labor Council, by contrast, became much more active in state-level reform politics and cooperated with Progressive Republicans to pass a variety of labor law reforms. Thus, the Labor Council's decision to join reformers in support of school reform engaged them in a coalition they had recently joined on other issues.[44]

Two additional, more immediate factors may have precipitated the shift in the Labor Council's position. The council recently had quarreled with the school department over its efforts to crush a newly formed local of the American Federation of Teachers (AFT), an affiliate of the council. This small group, largely male high school teachers, had denounced the patronage relationships that allowed the board of education a pervasive influence over teachers. The AFT's continual conflict with the school department certainly influenced the Labor Council's position on reform.[45] Further, the council apparently believed that under the reform proposal plans for vocational education would be more speedily introduced. The current board's failure to institute vocational education courses had frustrated the Labor Council for several years. Its support for reform may have been calculated to obtain some leverage on this issue with a newly appointed board.[46]

With the leadership of the labor movement split and the population torn by the Catholic issue, the forces favoring reform were able to win, if only narrowly (69,203 ballots were cast in favor, 66,660 against). A breakdown of the vote shows that the amendment lost in "every working class district and was passed in every middle and upper class district." Yet those precincts with large concentrations of foreign-born Catholics contained higher percentages of "no" votes than did working-class districts with mainly native-born voters.[47]

Although sizable opposition to reform remained, Mayor James Rolph's astute appointments to the board of education forestalled immediate challenges. His balanced slate offered something to please most religious, labor, and business groups even as reform brought a decline in influence for educators and Catholics. Unlike Mayor Thompson of Chicago, Mayor Rolph allowed reformers to proceed with their agenda without interference from city hall. Not until charges of financial irregularity were leveled against the new superintendent, Edwin Gwinn, were the opponents of reform given the opportunity to challenge the new arrangements.

Once school systems were reformed in Chicago and San Francisco to eliminate politics, working-class capacities eroded. By 1930 broad working-class influence over public education had significantly diminished. In the next two decades, to which we now turn, it disappeared entirely.

5

Taming Class Conflict: Undoing and Redoing Reform

$\mathbf{M}$OST considerations of democracy are free of content. They deal with voting and political participation, with access to and influence over decision makers, but not with "the nature of the issues over which groups and elites have been struggling." The purposes of democratic participation are frequently neglected, in part because it is assumed "that elites will respond if parties are organized and people vote, and that the content of politics is much less important than the procedures and the process of electing representatives to office."[1]

This usual perspective misses a number of key points that are evoked by the history of school reform in the early years of this century. Dominant groups and classes often act to counter the results of electoral power and other forms of democratic political participation. Rather than responding to the demands of organized citizens, various elites seek to insulate themselves from such demands or to affect their content. One mechanism of insulation is the definition of spheres of activity and policy as beyond politics, as nonpartisan—as the domain of specialists acting in the public interest.

The organization of government and the content of its policies affect how various groups will direct their demands to the state by providing a mix "of incentives and disincentives to politicization, mobilization, and radicalization."[2] We have shown how early access to public education helped divide the collective and solidaristic strains of working-class culture into the spheres of labor and community. School reform in the early twentieth century not only engaged these spheres separately but also highlighted the most individualistic and instrumental aspects of working-class life.

The reforms succeeded. In the period spanning the Great Depression and World War II, when class divisions played so important a role in organizing national politics, class was virtually eliminated in both its labor and its ethnic aspects from the politics of education. Not that labor and ethnic attention to school issues ceased: by a ritualized allocation of school board seats to discrete ethnic, religious, and labor groups on the one hand and by a series of accommodations between organized labor and school administrators on the other, working-class participation had become domesticated by 1950.

The usual chronologies of school histories make this process difficult to understand. Students of school politics usually leap from the era of reform to the 1960s, when educational conflicts are understood to have been the product of the consolidation and growth of the reforming impulses of the Progressive Era. Characteristically, Diane Ravitch's treatment of "the great school wars" labels the 1930s and 1940s as "between the wars."[3] The disappearance of this historical period from most of the literature on schooling has had the unfortunate consequence of significantly understating the contested character of school organization and policy between 1930 and 1950, the changing role of working people in these school conflicts, and the meaning of the second wave of reform in the 1940s.

Writing from diverse points of view, the great majority of educational scholars concerned with the turmoil of the 1960s have agreed on a portrait of the public schools as highly centralized bureaucracies, and they have accounted for this feature as the evolutionary product of the reform movement after the turn of the century.[4] This linear, developmental history assumes (usually without argument or documentation) that the reforms, once enacted, persisted until challenged by the racial unrest and the neighborhood control movements of the 1960s.

This record of historical amnesia is objectionable as a distortion of reality. But it also has unfortunate consequences for the very questions that the schooling literature on the 1960s has sought to answer. One of that decade's most striking features was the racial, not class, basis of educational insurgency. Yet the struggles over school reform in the 1920s had been class-based. What had happened in the intervening decades to the role of class in school conflicts? We shall see that reform educators of the 1940s, quite unlike their predecessors two decades earlier, accommodated labor and white ethnic working-class concerns, so long as those concerns were understood in very narrow and instrumental ways. By the 1960s, labor and ethnic interests had been grafted onto centralized urban school systems.

The more general literature on urban politics has assumed a cast rather similar to that of the majority of works on public education. The conventional construction of urban political development tells a tale of competition between machine politicians and reformers in the predepression era, with the ultimate victory of the reformers assured by the 1930s. Thereafter, rationalized bureaucratic government, largely insulated from the electoral process, achieved hegemony over more participatory alternatives.[5] In this textbook version the 1930s and 1940s appear as a time when a trend already in motion was merely extended to the preordained conclusion of urban modernization.

The temptation to write the history of school reform as the story of conflicts that were resolved in the first three decades of the century overlooks a fundamental difference between reform and the urban party system. Writing about political reform in New York City, political scientist Theodore Lowi sought to account for its cyclical and ephemeral character.[6] He observed shrewdly that reform represents not only a competitive principle but a rejection of the party system itself and the creation of a nonparty channel for innovation in urban public policy. Reform coalitions tend to be held together by animosity to the party system and to the neighborhood-based ethnic order of which it is an expression. Reform itself, however, lacks an enduring political organizational arm. As a result, Lowi argued, reform as a political movement has had important problems of persistence.

In contrast, the party system has a compelling logic of continuity. Even when political parties themselves are much weakened, patronage politicians command traditional organizational, material, and cultural resources. The typically short duration of pure reform administrations and the lack of an organized political base to reform movements make the innovations of reformers vulnerable.

Such was the case with educational reform in Chicago and San Francisco in the early 1930s. Under the impact of economic depression and the severe fiscal crisis it engendered, the reform coalition of businesspeople and educators in Chicago came apart as its members divided over whether professionals or a business-dominated board of education should exercise primary control, and over the scope of school expenditures. In San Francisco, where the impact of the depression was significantly less severe, financial malfeasance in the administration of public schools provided new opportunities for the opponents of reform. While the particular reasons for the shaky quality of reform thus differed, both cities followed a common pattern: rifts within the reform coalition and changes in city government were succeeded by the reassertion of machine-style politics.

The part workers played in the rollback of reform in these two cities was indirect but important. In general, their activity was more narrowly instrumental than in earlier periods. By the end of this era, neither the labor nor the ethnic form of working-class political participation shaped the broad agenda of school politics. In Chicago workers as ethnic group members were incorporated into the newly dominant political machine. Severe social conflicts and the identities that could sustain them were downplayed in favor of an issue-free politics of ethnic loyalty, balanced tickets, and a normative emphasis on friendship, loyalty, and social harmony. As constituent elements of Chicago's machine, workers were incorporated into school politics as ethnic people, that is, as candidates for the material and symbolic satisfactions and the

instrumental and particularistic terms of participation characteristic of machine governance. Labor, like ethnic groups, was
granted a symbolic role in educational affairs with a labor seat on
the board of education as well as such particular payoffs as relatively high salaries for janitors and craft workers employed by
the school system. Especially after the alliance of teachers and the
labor movement broke apart, the range of issues actively engaged
by the trade unions contracted, and the teachers found themselves isolated from the labor movement.

A similar domestication of class took place in San Francisco.
The reform impulse and its base of support contracted in the
1930s. San Francisco ethnic groups regained influence in school
politics but on an elite basis. Catholic leaders were consulted on
such matters as appointments to the board of education. Labor in
San Francisco increasingly allied with machine politicians, who,
unlike their Chicago counterparts, resisted cuts in teacher salaries, school programs, and the construction of new school buildings. Labor's main thrust, however, was in the area of vocational
education, where it sought to assert an interest group veto over
school administrators.

In the 1940s the schools were reformed once again. It was this
second, much neglected moment of educational reform that
created the institutional arrangements so familiar to educational
scholars of the 1960s and 1970s. This time, reformers and educational professionals did not oppose the interests of labor and
ethnic groups. In a politically more realistic way reformers incorporated workers' concerns, now more narrowly conceived than in
the early decades of the century, into the reform program. As a
result, party politicians found it very difficult to resist the new
reform initiatives. Those who tried were shunted aside. More
typically, party politicians accommodated reform by withdraw-
ing from school politics and school conflicts. In return, they purchased a tacit guarantee of noninterference in their affairs by key
actors in the school system.

The period from 1930 to 1950 thus was not merely an educational interregnum. To be sure, in 1950, just as in 1930, reform
leadership and organizational structures controlled major urban
school systems, but only after intense conflicts, challenges to

reform, and efforts to reconstitute reform with new bases of support. Working-class participation changed in important ways in this era, so much so that distinctive working-class positions disappeared from educational politics. We argue in this chapter that the domestication of class and the depoliticization of reform went hand in hand. This long-neglected period thus poses these main questions: How did the reforms institutionalized in the 1920s break down in the 1930s? How were they re-created under the auspices of a more politically astute educational leadership in the 1940s? How did the relationship between schools and the working class alter so that by 1950 class had been shunted aside as a key basis of popular mobilization and collective action? By mid-century reform was virtually uncontested, and the working class had receded from school politics. It is this dual process we wish to explain.

I

THE achievements of the school reformers of the 1920s proved fragile. Many changes in governing structures were overturned in the 1930s, and the depoliticized spirit of reform was violated by assertive interjections of patronage into educational appointments.

Central to the breakdown of reform in San Francisco and Chicago was a splintering of the coalition of professional educators and business. New city regimes promoted a repoliticization of school governance by consolidating power through machine-style politics. The extent to which reforms were rolled back depended on both the character of the city administration and the political strength of the remaining reformers. In Chicago the isolation of reformers by Mayor Kelly's Democratic machine helped transform the schools into a political playground. In San Francisco, where politicians shared power with disillusioned reformers, old patronage routes were also reopened, but no single party group gained control over school politics.

The chief cause for reform's defeat in Chicago was business's decision to cooperate with the nascent Democratic machine in exchange for deep cuts in school expenditures. Business had based its support for mayoral candidate Anton Cermak in 1931 on his promises to restore the city's fiscal base after the excesses of former Republican mayor William ("Big Bill") Thompson.[7] Even before the Great Depression, Chicago's municipal finances were in precarious shape; the public schools were particularly hard hit because uninterrupted expansion and increased expenditures accompanying reform had produced a steeply mounting educational budget.[8] Since 1915 Chicago's schools had regularly spent more than they took in by selling tax anticipation warrants. In the short run this practice saved the schools from piling up deficits, but by 1927 Superintendent James McAndrew had to acknowledge that finances were reaching the "breaking point."[9]

The city budget was not in much better shape.[10] Alarmed business leaders joined with teachers to demand an overhaul of the corruption-ridden property tax system, the source of 90 percent of school revenues.[11] A joint Commission on Real Estate Valuation composed of "prominent businessmen and citizens" was appointed to assist county assessors in 1927 with the aim of cracking the "political tax system."[12] The commission, joined by the CTF, forced a reassessment of 1927 taxes. The results proved disastrous. Instead of increasing revenues, the revised estimate reduced valuations by 17 percent.[13] Moreover, the delay that the commission caused, together with a tax strike by local property owners, cut more deeply into the city's revenues each year. School finances received yet another blow when the state legislature reduced the educational fund tax rate in 1930.[14]

Despite these setbacks and the tightening grip of the nationwide economic depression, business leaders made one last attempt to salvage the schools before resorting to cuts. Silas Strawn, ex-president of the Commercial Club and the Industrial Club, headed a citizens' committee that raised $74 million to tide the city over until taxes were collected again.[15] The committee solicited contributions from taxpayers (many of whom had not paid taxes during the reassessment dispute of the previous two years) and deposited them in the "Cook County Taxpayers Warrant

Trust," where they earned interest.[16] The committee also sought a more permanent solution by backing legislation to authorize Chicago's local governments, including the school board, to issue bonds, even without public approval in referenda.[17] Responding to the Strawn Committee's recommendations, the governor convened a tax conference the following year that urged reorganized tax assessment procedures and a variety of new taxes, including a graduated income tax.[18] The conference also acknowledged the need to slow the rate of public expenditures.[19] Though several of the proposals passed the legislature, the state supreme court declared the income tax unconstitutional. This decision marked the final attempt to resolve municipal financial problems by raising more revenue. By 1931 most business groups had accepted retrenchment as the only real solution, a stance that precipitated a split in the educator-business coalition.

Led by Chicago and Northwestern Railroad president Fred Sargent, a group of prominent businesspeople closely tied to the city's banks formed a citizens' committee with the single purpose of reducing governmental expenditures.[20] The school board first felt the power of the new committee in July 1932, when bankers announced that they would not buy tax anticipation warrants unless the board complied with the Sargent Committee's recommendations.[21] This left the board little choice. As one member ruefully acknowledged, "We are in the clutches of the bankers."[22] At the board's invitation, Mayor Cermak and Fred Sargent, among others, participated in preparing the 1933 school budget. Expenditures were pared 17 percent to stay within the guidelines recommended by the Sargent Committee.[23]

Although the committee outlined overall budget aims, it generally allowed the school department itself to determine particular programmatic cuts.[24] However, the majority of school board members, holdovers from the Thompson era, did not relish the task thrust upon the board and only grudgingly agreed to trim the budget.[25] Coordinated action between business and school board politicians had to await a Democratic majority on the school board. It was not long in coming.

Before the alliance was cemented, however, the Democratic organization suffered a change in leadership that tested the durability of its ties with business. Mayor Cermak was assassinated in March 1933 as he greeted President-elect Roosevelt at a political rally in Miami. His successor, Edward J. Kelly, reassured business leaders that he would work closely with them to straighten out the city's finances—in effect committing himself to cut expenses.[26] The new mayor carried through on this pledge in May 1933 when he named five new members to the board of education, all of whom publicly supported retrenchment. These appointments were strictly political; allegiance to the Democratic organization, not prior experience or expertise in education, guided Kelly's choice.[27] Bankers signified their approval the same day by indicating their willingness to purchase $12.75 million of 1932 school tax anticipation warrants.[28]

By July 1933 Kelly's appointees constituted a majority on the board. If any doubts lingered about who controlled the schools, the economy package passed in July dispelled them. The ten board members favoring cuts isolated themselves from Superintendent Bogan and their lone opponent on the board in a closed-door session to hammer out the specifics of the program.[29] The educational program was stripped to the bare essentials; extracurricular athletic and music programs were terminated. "Frills" were altogether removed from the elementary grades and cut back in the high schools. All elementary physical education teachers were discharged, as were 15 percent of their high school colleagues. House arts and manual training were removed from the elementary curriculum. Schools and services that stretched beyond the basics were discontinued. The city's junior high schools were abolished, as were the Parental School for Delinquents, the Crane Junior College, and most continuation schools. Funds for kindergartens were cut in half. In all, fourteen hundred teachers lost their jobs. High school teachers had their loads increased, and elementary school principals were assigned to two schools.[30] The scaled-down curriculum represented a vision of public education fundamentally different from the progressive ideal of reform that had produced the enriched program. Yet it corresponded to that strand of reform rhetoric concerning efficiency which business had so enthusiastically embraced.

The retrenchment also represented the renewed subordination

of the schools to politics, this time with the acquiescence of the business community. Business leaders who monitored school affairs allowed politicians a free hand so long as they operated within the new budgetary restraints. The schools occupied an anomalous position in the Democratic machine. Because unionized teachers, antagonistic both to party politics and to the local business community, lacked the protection of political patronage, they provided an excellent target for the economies that business demanded.[31] Success in cutting costs—at the teachers' expense—assured the machine continuing business support even after the immediate crisis had eased.

The financial emergency had destroyed, in just two years, the coalition of business and professional educators that had labored for school reform for nearly twenty. The transition attested to the underlying differences in the reform visions animating business-people and professionals. When it proved impossible to reconcile reform with economy, Chicago's business leaders showed little hesitation in choosing between the two.

In San Francisco, too, progressive school reforms gave way under new pressure in the 1930s. There, however, the breakdown of reform stemmed from different causes. San Francisco's reform coalition did not crumble under the weight of the economic depression. New financing arrangements in California had eased the burden on localities by shifting much responsibility to the state. Instead, the renewed influence of powerful opponents undermined the durability of reform in San Francisco. School reformers had triumphed in 1920 without striking the compromises that their Chicago counterparts had. But the narrow margin of their victory left San Francisco reformers with a substantial and powerful opposition that included leading Catholic and labor figures. Unreconciled to defeat, these foes of reform waited for an opportunity to reassert their influence in school affairs. By 1932 two events had reopened that possibility. The first was the financial blunders that led to reform superintendent Edwin Gwinn's ouster and strengthened the case against reform. The second was the new city administration, which paid off its political debts to labor and Catholics with school board appointments. Along with the renewed influence of ethnic and labor representatives went a fracture within reform ranks. Gwinn's failings introduced tension and suspicion in the relations between professional educators and middle-class reformers that were compounded when the latter restricted educators' autonomy in financial affairs.

Nevertheless, the result was not a school system subordinated to the single-minded purposes of a political machine as in Chicago. No section of San Francisco's reform coalition switched sides. Moreover, the absence of political parties denied San Francisco's patronage politicians the centralized control that Chicago's Democrats were able to establish. Reform was not replaced; machine politicians shared power with reformers in an uneasy, quarrelsome alliance.

The most striking difference between school politics in San Francisco and Chicago in the 1930s was that the depression had only a minor influence on San Francisco schools. The small proportion of school-age population compared with the total city population was partially responsible.[32] But the chief cushioning effect was provided by an amendment to the state constitution shifting the burden of mandatory school funding from the county to the state. Legislators enacted a new state sales tax and state user and income taxes to finance the increased responsibilities.[33] The new arrangements actually allowed San Francisco schools to increase expenditures during the depression: in constant dollars San Francisco spent 33 percent more on schools in 1940 than in 1930.[34]

The element crucial to undoing reform in San Francisco was the large unreconciled opposition generated by the reform struggle. Led by the powerful Catholic establishment and its allies, labor's Building Trades Council, and teachers, this opposition commanded considerable popular support. It had successfully defeated the first attempt at reform in 1918 and had lost only by a narrow margin two years later. Reformers' exploitation of the religious issue in 1920 had left bitter feelings among San Francisco's Catholics. Superintendent Gwinn did little to soften this opposition. His strict adherence to principles of progressive education alienated conservative Catholics; his attempts to streamline administration and centralize control compounded this dissatisfaction. In fact, Gwinn's aloofness from outside pressures earned reform new enemies, including the San Francisco Labor Council.

This combined opposition demonstrated its strength in 1930 by proposing an amendment to institute an elective board of education. A loose coalition of civic groups backed the measure, as did the Building Trades Council and the Labor Council. Although the Catholic church maintained a low profile to avoid turning the issue into a religious debate, it was vitally interested in the measure and labored behind the scenes to secure its passage.[35] The campaign reenacted the arguments and alliances of twelve years earlier, when reform was first proposed. Labor and Catholics lined up against most of the city's business organizations and prestigious clubs, which vowed to "keep politics out of our schools."[36] The amendment lost by a narrow margin with 68,292 favoring the elective board and 70,778 opposed. As in the vote that first instituted school reform, the proposal for an elected board showed greatest strength in working-class neighborhoods.[37]

Superintendent Gwinn's financial blunders soon provided reform opponents with a new opportunity. An audit undertaken in 1929 revealed that a number of misclassified teachers had been substantially overpaid. News articles charged that the payroll classifications represented deliberate fraud by the superintendent.[38] Although the board of education launched an investigation, the grand jury decided to conduct its own study of the matter. The jury never made its proceedings public. Ultimately it decided not to indict, but enough leaks had escaped to severely damage Gwinn's reputation. Testimony directly charged Gwinn with responsibility for the illegal rating, and other minor accusations cropped up.[39] Finally, in September 1933, the grand jury recommended that Gwinn be ousted.[40] By that time his reputation had been so tarnished that he could not rally enough support to serve out the remaining term of his appointment.

The charges against Gwinn tapped a deep-seated opposition to the reform ideal and the methods of progressive education he had come to represent. The *Chronicle* maintained that the reasons for the ouster could be traced to the old dispute over reform. Gwinn himself believed that "his dismissal had been motivated by parochial, patronage and religious feelings."[41] His difficulties introduced new fissures in the old reform coalition. Gwinn's strongest supporters on the board now moved to assert their own control over school business affairs by appointing a comptroller responsible to the board.[42] They delegated the new official full power of audit and assigned him control over all department employees except the superintendent and his immediate staff. All business matters were likewise removed from the hands of the superintendent. These changes effectively destroyed the superintendent-centered system that had been recommended by the Claxton Survey. In its effort to ensure that future superintendents would adhere to its ideal of "efficiency" the board wrecked the very institutional arrangements once designed to achieve that goal.

This movement away from reform was clinched by the new mayor's appointments to the board. Angelo Rossi was chosen mayor in 1932 when his predecessor, James Rolph, was elected governor after having served for twenty years. Rossi faced the immediate problem of establishing a stable constituency and sought, like Rolph, to attract both labor and business support. Although San Francisco reformers had restructured the schools a decade earlier and had recently pushed through a new charter, they had never totally eradicated the loose grouping of businesspeople, labor leaders, and politicians who conducted the city's business on an informal patronage basis. Whereas Rolph had bowed to reformers in his appointment of school board members after the reform of 1922, Rossi took advantage of the disarray caused by Gwinn's resignation to reopen the schools to politics. Rossi's appointments tilted the balance away from reformers without overtly disavowing reform. Throughout Rossi's tenure, the board split, five to four, into two factions; the majority aligned with Rossi, and the minority attached itself to reform.[43] These changes did not constitute an outright repudiation of reform, but they were sufficient to reopen the old routes of influence that reformers had sought to block.

Rossi's machine, however, in no way approached the disciplined and centralized organization of Chicago's Democrats. San Francisco had neither the party structure nor the political institutions needed to consolidate such control. City elections had been conducted on a nonpartisan basis since 1913, when Progressives in the state legislature extended nonpartisanship to include all city and county elections.[44] Without party organizations, San Francisco politicians could not impose sanctions strong enough to discipline potential opponents. Their supporters retained considerable independence. Likewise, reformed municipal institutions, dividing power between a "chief administrative officer" and the mayor, encouraged the fragmentation characteristic of San Francisco politics.[45] School politics reflected this absence of central control. Board members who sided with reform controlled expenditures; new "machine" appointees concerned themselves with patronage; superintendents tried, without success, to assert authority. School politics became mired in power disputes that eluded resolution.

In neither San Francisco nor Chicago, then, did educational reform prove durable. In neither case, moreover, were the modifications opened up for public debate. Workers did not .play a leading role in this initial shift in elite understandings about public schooling, but a transformation of their relationship to public education proved integral to consolidating the new arrangements.

II

SOCIAL CLASS ceased to be a basis of mobilization in school politics in the 1930s. In the very decade when labor emerged as a mass interest group to be reckoned with at the national level, working-class self-images, political language, and assertions of interest with regard to education contracted. Without the sustained involvement of workers as ethnic groups or as labor a second wave of reform, unopposed by working-class organizations, was now possible. The culmination of this process virtually eliminated class—in both its labor and its ethnic aspects—from educational politics; and, in turn, this process virtually eliminated schooling as a key issue from the politics of class.

Because the rollback of reform had narrowed the circle of influence in Chicago, it engendered considerable opposition from such newly excluded groups as teachers and middle-class advocates of reform. Workers had to define their position in this divisive context. Their choices reflected the political limits introduced by the Democratic machine. In San Francisco, by contrast, the breakdown of reform reopened the schools to the influence of formerly excluded groups without entirely supplanting the reformers. Unlike Chicago, then, San Francisco had little opposition outside the system. Instead, conflict was built into school politics as each faction exercised some small share of influence. Because contests over schooling did not challenge this arrangement, educational conflict in San Francisco rarely concerned fundamental, substantive issues. Throughout the 1930s labor unions and ethnic groups negotiated their way through this thicket, eventually establishing regularized paths of influence. In both cities, workers tested the limits of their power and emerged at the end of the period with a more narrowly defined but officially sanctioned participation. Not only had the scope of participation narrowed, but the circle of participants had been tightened as well. Workers were represented by officials drawn from the upper ranks of firmly established organizations; the mass base no longer participated in educational politics.

As a city famed for its ethnic diversity, Chicago presents something of a paradox: throughout this period, ethnicity occupied no prominent position in school disputes. In fact, ethnic issues had not played a contentious role in Chicago's schools since the late nineteenth century, when Germans had fought to have their language included in the school curriculum. Ethnic groups as such had little reason to complain about public school policy. Many enrolled their children in Catholic schools.[46]

The church's support for school economies thus reflected a common interest of the machine and Chicago's ethnic groups.[47] Cermak, moreover, had initially been elected as a champion of ethnic groups, and his organization carefully cultivated their support.[48] In school politics this meant, above all, symbolic recognition by appointment to the school board. Representatives of the Irish, Polish, and Czech communities were among Mayor Kelly's first appointees in 1933.[49] Ethnic groups were thus impervious to the appeals of the Citizens' Schools Committee (CSC), the main organizer of opposition to the cutbacks. The committee's efforts to solicit support through foreign-language newspapers aroused no interest. No Polish, German, Italian, Russian, Austrian, Lithuanian, or Czech organization sent representatives to the CSC Organizational Conference, which aimed to encourage participation by community organizations.[50]

If workers' ethnic groups had little trouble consenting to the Democrats' new regime for the schools, unions found the matter considerably more complex. Labor's ties with teachers stretched back some thirty years, and unions had defined their positions on school issues based on that alliance. Chicago teachers expressed no ambivalence about the new economy measures. As soon as the cuts were announced, the large number of competing teachers' organizations in the city coalesced into a Steering Committee of Teacher Welfare Organizations to fight the new program. They immediately allied with a group of more than forty women's and professional organizations to found the Citizens' Save Our Schools Committee (later the Citizens' School Committee) to oppose retrenchment.[51] This new alliance of teachers and reformers (once their antagonists), together with subsequent Democratic overtures to the trade unions, muddied the terrain of educational politics for organized labor.

When business leaders first proposed retrenchment, labor backed teachers' efforts to boost school revenues instead. The CFL publicly supported the reassessment drive in 1927 and passed resolutions demanding tax reform. Likewise, it denounced the various business committees that had seized control of school politics.[52] In a resolution lambasting the Sargent Committee the CFL declared that committee members had "set themselves up as a sort of super-government and were attempting to dictate policies to the duly elected and appointed representatives of the people."[53]

Ironically, labor's efforts to fight the Sargent Committee provided Democratic politicians with an opening wedge to neutralize labor's impact on school issues. In May 1933 the CFL passed a resolution asking for five seats on the board of education to protect the schools from business-backed cuts. Mayor Kelly responded by naming one labor representative—Charles W. Fry, president of the Machinists Union—out of the seven he appointed. Fry quickly established cooperative relationships with board president James McCahey and participated in drafting the economy measures that had provoked such vehement teacher opposition. The CFL's leadership faced a delicate choice: repudiate one of their most prominent members or acquiesce in supporting the economies demanded by the business community. Their response reflected these conflicting pulls. The federation lent its rhetoric to those denouncing the cuts but refrained from publicly criticizing Fry's actions.[54]

Labor became increasingly quiescent about school cuts. Even as they slashed educational expenditures, Democratic officials were careful to protect long-established privileges of the school's custodial staff. Chicago's unusually high expenditures for school operations and maintenance reflected the special treatment that custodial workers had enjoyed since the early 1920s.[55] Labor found itself in opposition to the Citizens' School Committee (CSC) when the reformers targeted custodial salaries as a better source of economies than teacher salaries or instructional expenses. As early as July 1933, Superintendent Bogan had recommended cuts in maintenance costs as an acceptable way of reducing school expenses.[56] The CSC picked up this theme, making it a central issue in its campaign against cutbacks, corruption, and patronage in the schools.

For the CFL there was no question of compromise. Custodial and janitorial workers were members of the building service trades, one of the most powerful components of the local labor movement. The CFL harshly criticized any attempt to attack union positions.[57] By pitting a narrow labor issue against broader concerns, the Democrats succeeded in breaking up the long-standing teacher-labor alliance that had advanced a distinctive labor position on most issues on the educational agenda.

By the end of the 1930s labor's organizational engagement in school politics had been pared down to the protection of custodial workers and to monitoring developments in vocational education. Union leaders had traded positions on general issues for influence on matters that directly concerned their members' in-

terests *as labor.* The choice was not one that labor had welcomed;
it had been thrust upon the unions by the economic depression
and the rise of the Democratic organization. In part, labor's re-
orientation reflected the dearth of alternatives open by that time:
to oppose the machine was to be cut off from political influence.
Identification with Democrats grew easier over time as the national administration's liberal policies brought labor solidly into
the national Democratic party. The growing bonds between Chicago's Democrats and President Roosevelt further reinforced the
logic of these connections at the local level.

Labor's incorporation into the machine, however, was less than
wholehearted. After all, labor occupied a subordinate status in
the new organization, whose alliance with business was more
central. Throughout the depression, labor exercised at least a
rhetorical independence in school politics by continuing to criti-
cize the cuts.[58] New relations with the Democratic organization,
however, kept organized labor from joining the CSC's crusade
against city politicians.

In San Francisco, ethnic and religious concerns had been central
to the conflict over school reform. Superintendent Gwinn's dismissal and the partial undoing of reform were a triumph for the
majority of Irish Catholics who had opposed Claxton's reform
recommendations and had supported the amendment for an
elected board in 1930. Yet the terms on which ethnic interests
were incorporated into the new organization of school politics did
not grant the mass of workers more influence over school affairs.
Instead, they secured the allegiance of the Catholic hierarchy.
The archbishop was consulted about school board appointments
and proposed changes in the structure of school governance.[59]
Moreover, fears that Catholics would be excluded from teaching
in public schools were dispelled. Board members aligned with
Rossi opened up the old patronage channels for teacher hiring,
assuring Catholics positions. Characteristic of San Francisco's decentralized patronage system, each teacher generally owed loyalty to a single board member. At the same time, they were
mobilized as a corporate group into the California Teachers' Association, denounced by the rival Teachers' Federation as a company union.[60] Superintendents, too, continually battled board

members over teacher hiring. On this issue, however, the board repeatedly outmaneuvered them, blocking efforts to return authority over personnel to the superintendent.[61]

In this way, a style of politics emerged that benefited both the church and school board members anxious to build up a base of power. Apparently satisfied that its enemies had been checked, the church accepted the exchange and dropped efforts to restructure the school administration. But the resurgence of ethnic influence in the schools took on quite a narrow meaning. It now related specifically to the concerns of the Catholic hierarchy and did not address broader issues that challenged the relations of the schools to diverse ethnic and cultural traditions. Along with this narrowing went a shrinkage in the base of participation. Now only the highest levels of the Catholic hierarchy took part in school politics directly.

San Francisco's labor movement had never played a prominent role in school politics comparable to that of Chicago's unions. Although the San Francisco Labor Council had drawn away from reformers during the 1920s, this estrangement did not signify a corresponding attachment to any coherent opposition. The decentralized "issueless" politics characteristic of San Francisco freed labor to pursue its own agenda, which was, in any case, a quite restricted one. Throughout the 1930s, close relations with the San Francisco Federation of Teachers guided the bulk of labor's participation in school affairs. In addition to its activities on behalf of teacher salaries and economic security, unions also strove to maintain a minimum labor presence on the school board. As the 1930s drew to a close, however, vocational education supplanted teachers' concerns as the prime issue on labor's educational agenda.

Labor's defense of the San Francisco Federation of Teachers was similar to the constituency-bound patronage politics practiced by other actors in school politics. Although the federation sought to speak for all teachers, its small unrepresentative membership challenged this aim. Despite a membership drive in 1930, the organization had grown little since its formation eleven years earlier. Male high school teachers constituted the core membership.[62] Repeated efforts to penetrate the web of alliances and patronage that bound most elementary teachers to the rival California Teachers' Association proved unsuccessful.[63] A separate local attempted, for a short time, to draw in elementary teachers, but it soon disbanded.[64] Even after the 1937 board of education rule allowing teachers to join the organization of their choice and banning coercion or pressure by principals, the federation failed to attract significant numbers of new adherents.[65]

It was under the prodding of this small group, then, that labor defined its priorities in educational politics. The Federation of Teachers formally affiliated with the Labor Council and dominated its educational committee. Unions took a leading role in struggles over teachers' salaries and tenure. The Labor Council spearheaded the successful 1928 drive to raise teachers' income.[66] Over the next two decades, unions consistently defended teachers against pay cuts. Although the depression's impact was minor compared with its effects in Chicago, the tightening of the municipal budget forced teachers to fight to defend their salaries. Annual increments were suspended in 1932, but teachers, led by the Labor Council, successfully forestalled large pay reductions. The council argued that if retrenchment were necessary, administrative expenses should be cut along with "emergency schools and classes that serve the few rather than impair the education of the masses of our school children."[67] Again in 1938 the council actively supported teachers' efforts to win back their salary increments.

The other school issues in which labor participated likewise reflected the narrow scope of its interests. Unions, for example, defended their right to representation on the board of education. In 1935, when Mayor Rossi proposed to fill a board vacancy with a nonlabor representative, the unions smothered him with an "avalanche of protest" and threatened to run an opposition candidate in the mayoral election.[68] Rossi retreated and nominated a local union leader for the post. On another occasion, the Labor Council proposed to meet with the curriculum committee of the board to introduce courses on the "purposes and ideals of organized labor" in the public schools.[69]

Vocational education was the other main educational issue that concerned the entire labor movement. Superintendent Edwin Lee

(1933–36) acknowledged the validity of this interest in a 1934 address to the Labor Council. Outlining his plan to expand adult education and vocational education, Lee promised that labor would be "satisfied that its educational interest will be promoted" under his administration.[70] The establishment of the Samuel Gompers Trades School in 1937 and the subsequent influx of funds for wartime training pushed vocational training to the top of labor's educational agenda.

With labor and ethnic participation thus routinized and restricted, Chicago and San Francisco politicians deprived reformers of support that might have helped build a strong popular movement to fight cutbacks. Instead, defenders of progressive reforms found themselves reduced to a core of educational and middle-class professionals. Despite concerted efforts, Chicago's Citizens' Schools Committee failed to attract a mass base. In San Francisco, the superintendents serving during this period raised the lone protest against the school administration. In both cases, reformers were outnumbered and outflanked. The CSC retreated to the role of watchdog, monitoring and publicizing school affairs. Two of San Francisco's superintendents resigned in frustration after being unable to attract support.

III

WITH the retreat of the working class from school politics, opposition to educational reform was limited mainly to diehard patronage politicians. The contrast is stark between the noise of the school disputes of the 1920s and the consensual quality of the second wave of reform in the early 1940s. Without a recognition of the changed role of the working class it is also rather puzzling. The narrow terms of working-class identity and participation made new alignments possible, just as it made reform initiatives very difficult for politicians to resist. The security of the patronage-based school administrations proved illusory. Because they rested on particular economic and political conditions, changed circumstances undermined the agreements and understandings forged in the earlier period and set the stage for reform. This time, the restructuring of school administration involved relatively little conflict. Although the politicians whose power had depended on patronage arrangements did not welcome such changes, they were unable to generate the kind of mass mobilization that had occurred twenty years earlier.

This difference reflected the modifications wrought in school politics during the 1930s. Previous opponents of reform were now reconciled to new structural arrangements so long as their narrow interests were protected. Similarly, the educational progressives whose monopoly over the definition of education had been integral to the first reform were now willing to accommodate a variety of local interests. Their political eclipse in the 1930s had alerted educational professionals to the need to pacify potential enemies by granting them influence over matters that directly concerned them. But educators did not relinquish their responsibility for setting educational standards. In fact, this prerogative proved central to reestablishing reform. Their professional voice lent legitimacy to reformers' charges against machine rule.

In Chicago, the CSC's threats of electoral reprisal induced Mayor Kelly to appoint a citizens' committee to advise him on school affairs in 1939. After the election, however, Kelly ignored the committee's recommendations. Likewise, the CSC's endorsement of the Republican mayoral candidate in 1943 had little effect on the race: Kelly scored an easy victory.[71]

Although the financial emergency that initially had allowed the machine to control the schools by now had passed, Democrats still held a firm grip on the Chicago school department. Having exhausted local resources, the CSC turned to outside groups to apply pressure for reform. Following the 1943 elections, the CSC, along with the teachers and several other civic organizations, enlisted the aid of the National Education Association, which agreed to investigate the long list of charges the CSC had been accumulating against the Chicago schools. The NEA's report, published in May 1945, confirmed the CSC accusation that politicians were using the schools for their own advantage. It warned that such bad personnel practices would "cause a progressive degeneration of the Chicago schools which [would] mark and handicap them for many years."[72]

The report recommended amending the Otis Law to create the office of general superintendent, to whom the business manager and the school board attorney would report. In this way, school governance would return to the corporate model of education that reformers had first envisioned. Opportunities for political tampering would be reduced by establishing an independent and tenured board of examiners (for teacher selection) and an elected board of education. The report also sought to enlist the aid of state authorities by calling on the governor or the state legislature to "conduct a thorough investigation of the operation of the schools during the past twelve years."[73]

The NEA's report paved the way for reform's triumph. Superintendent William Johnson, the school board, and Mayor Kelly initially attempted to disregard the outburst of publicity that followed publication of the report in the hope that the crisis would soon pass. It did not. Protest escalated when hearings held by Kelly loyalists on a city council subcommittee concluded that the charges against the board could not be sustained.[74]

In an unprecedented move, the NEA voted to expel Johnson for unethical conduct. Further outside pressure was applied by the North Central Association of Schools and Colleges (NCA), which issued a report in March 1946, warning that it would withdraw accreditation of Chicago's schools unless a thoroughly independent school board were set up and an office of general superintendent established.[75] With reluctance, Mayor Kelly responded by appointing a citizens' advisory committee to recommend procedures for selecting school board members. He asked the presidents of six local universities to serve on the new Heald Committee (named after its chair, Henry T. Heald, president of the Illinois Institute of Technology).[76]

The commission requested and the mayor was forced to grant permission to investigate all aspects of school administration.[77] The Heald Report, published in 1946, endorsed much of the NEA program of reform: a general superintendent and a reformed board of examiners. Instead of an elected board of education, however, the Heald Committee suggested that the appointed board be retained, supplemented by an independent committee composed of members of prominent organizations making recommendations for appointments.[78] The Heald Committee also demanded that the current superintendent and members of the board of education resign.

Recognizing the futility of further struggle, Superintendent Johnson stepped down the day the report was issued. Soon afterward, Mayor Kelly appointed an advisory committee for school board nominations. By September 1946 the new committee had helped select a majority of school board members. The new board of education prepared an amendment to the Otis Law, establishing the office of general superintendent with "executive responsibility for carrying out all phases of the school program."[79]

Anxious to prevent any backsliding, the NCA kept up pressure in its November 1946 progress report by again threatening to withdraw accreditation.[80] The association charged that the school board could not qualify as a nonpolitical body until the advisory committee had approved all its members and noted that the office of general superintendent still had not been established. Despite Mayor Kelly's displeasure with this report, he could not resist it. The school issue had proved so politically costly and had loomed so large in Kelly's declining popularity that he announced in December that he would not run for reelection the following spring. Hours later, James McCahey gave notice of his retirement from the board of education effective April 1947.[81]

With the major actors responsible for subordinating Chicago schools to the needs of the Democratic organization in disarray, the CSC and the CTU pushed for structural reforms to safeguard their victory. Backed by the CSC and the CTU, a bill to establish the office of general superintendent received the endorsement of the board of education in November 1946. Initially, the greatest source of opposition was the Chicago Federation of Labor.[82] The school janitors, engineer custodians, and other building service employees pressured the central labor federation to oppose the bill despite the appeals of the teachers' union. Even after Kelly's decision not to seek reelection, the CFL could not be persuaded to back the legislation.[83] Although labor had been drawn into the fold reluctantly, its suspicion of the CSC now bound the unions to the Democratic organization for protection.

But the Democrats, anxious to prevent reformers' success on the school issue from spreading to other areas of city administration, were staging a strategic retreat from the field of school politics. In April 1947 the new mayor, Martin Kennelly, called a meeting in which CTU representatives, nonteaching school unions, and other concerned groups conciliated their differences. After this session, labor agreed to support an amended version of the bill.

Reformers consolidated their victory in June with the appointment of Herold C. Hunt as superintendent. Arriving with a national reputation as a sound reform administrator, Hunt had the freedom to be more flexible than his earlier counterparts. The organization of teachers was an established fact; labor influence, too, had been institutionalized in areas such as vocational education and the salaries of custodial personnel. With their interests satisfied in this way, these groups, once opposed to reform, now accommodated to it.

World War II provided the critical backdrop to reform in San Francisco. The city's strategic location made it a hub of war transport and production. Business complained that Mayor Rossi's lethargic administration failed to provide the infrastructure necessary to take advantage of the new opportunities. They faulted Rossi for not getting city planning underway, for not solving problems of traffic control, for failing to lower water rates, and for myriad other shortcomings. Among these was a complaint that the schools were not turning out students prepared for the job market. These businesspeople were concerned not so much with vocational education as with basic skills (the "three Rs") vital to San Francisco's economy.[84] Labor, also, had begun to stray from Rossi's camp. More liberal elements in the labor movement had supported a rival candidate in 1939, and by 1943 most unions had shifted their support to an explicitly prolabor candidate.[85]

The split between patronage politician Rossi and labor candidate George Reilly made possible the election of Roger Lapham, the candidate of San Francisco employers. As head of the Waterfront Employers Council, Lapham had served for years as a spokesman for San Francisco business. Pledged to "get the city moving again," Lapham sought to increase business participation in city politics.[86] His administration promised major reform in all branches of city government, including the schools, which were to "get rid of politics" and be put "on a business and a rational basis."[87]

Criticism of the inefficiency and secrecy involved in the operation of the public schools had been mounting since the early 1940s. In 1942 Superintendent Nourse sent the board a series of recommendations designed to "curb . . . board interference with the superintendent's administrative authority."[88] Most of the recommendations gave the superintendent more control over personnel, a prerogative that the board guarded most jealously. The board's refusal to consider Nourse's recommendations seriously exacerbated existing frictions and prompted Nourse's resignation in 1943.

His departure and the subsequent appointment of Curtis Warren as superintendent marked the beginning of widespread dissatisfaction with the school department. Suspicions about Warren's progressive educational philosophy, the secrecy surrounding his selection, and charges that Nourse had been forced to resign all contributed to the controversy. The *Examiner* published an editorial condemning the board for its "contemptuous attitude toward the public" and urged that its members never be reappointed. The editorial also recommended that the board of education be made an elective body.[89]

After the immediate uproar had subsided, little more was heard of the plans to institute an elective board. In the November elections, however, voters not only rejected Mayor Rossi but failed to confirm one of his school board appointees. This was the first instance since the establishment of the appointed board that voters had rejected a mayor's nominee. According to the *Examiner,* the vote represented a "revolt against the board's policies as a whole, particularly the custom of holding secret sessions and its refusal to permit the superintendent of schools to be more than an office boy." Specific practices of the board that the paper cited included

. . . the injection by board members of personal and petty politics into the administration of school affairs, the attempt of some board members to find havens for relatives on school payrolls, the repeated interference of board members in purely educational matters as distinct from administrative affairs, the board's insistence upon relegating the superintendent to a subordinate role and, finally, the board's gradual assumption of an attitude that it was not responsible to the public.[90]

The change in political leadership accomplished what years of superintendents' complaints could not. By introducing uncertainty about reappointment to the board, Lapham upset the alignment of its internal factions, in the process somewhat loosening the board's grip on the school department. In the midst of this uncertainty, the board was called upon to publicly announce its position on the publication of the Hill Report, a survey of San Francisco schools conducted in 1944. The board had authorized the report in October 1943, allotting money for a "postwar educational survey in the city schools."[91] The report's recommendations echoed those made by superintendents for the previous fifteen years: divest the board of education of its executive responsibilities and authority over personnel and make the superintendent the executive officer of the board.[92] With the spotlight focused on them, the majority of board members voted to adopt the basic principles of the Hill Report.

Despite the board's approval of an administrative code formalizing the reform, school directors refused to relinquish executive and administrative power. The major stumbling block was Superintendent Warren's political and educational philosophy of progressivism. In many ways, Warren was a transitional figure. His professional credentials endeared him to the minority of reformers on the board, and his lack of a power base in the city made him acceptable to most of the other board members. Labor's representatives on the board, however, had initially opposed him as an outsider, and most of the city's politicians and media had rallied against him.[93] Warren's few public supporters outside the board were prominent middle-class reform organizations, including the San Francisco Center, the League of Women Voters, and the Public Education Society.[94] Their vision of reform differed from that of Lapham's business-oriented appointees, who were avowed enemies of progressive education and who, moreover, mistrusted Warren's liberal and labor ties outside of the city.[95]

In the course of Warren's term, Lapham's appointees swayed the balance on the board away from the new superintendent. By 1945 a majority of members had renounced progressive education in favor of a "proper drilling in the three R's."[96] They also developed a deep-seated mistrust of Warren, who used "important labor figures and left-of-center politicians to put pressure on some of the more conservative members."[97] Labor, in contrast, grew closer to Warren as he strengthened his ties with local union leaders.

The probusiness climate of Lapham's administration was not congenial to Warren's political survival. In 1947 the board denied his reappointment. The labor representative and a prominent liberal businessman were his only supporters left on the board.[98] The subsequent appointment of Herbert Clish as superintendent finally cleared the path for reform. As a conservative Roman Catholic with impeccable administrative credentials, Clish was an ideal compromise candidate. The new superintendent announced his attachment to education that stressed fundamentals and indicated his willingness to listen to the business community's complaints about San Francisco's educational system.[99] The board demonstrated its trust in Clish by finally relinquishing executive and personnel responsibilities, making him the first superintendent to exercise full administrative control over the schools since Gwinn was dismissed more than fifteen years earlier. Clish reciprocated by promising "no sudden shakeup in the schools' administrative staff" and pledging to fill vacancies with insiders.[100]

By blending reform structures with a conservative content, San Francisco had finally solved the dilemma that had crippled earlier reform efforts. No longer did an influential minority stand outside the new arrangements. Reformers, business, and the Catholic hierarchy all had a voice in the new arrangements presided over by a professional educator. Even labor, whose political fortunes were at a low ebb, was not excluded. Its influence over vocational education went unchallenged, and labor participation in teachers' affairs expanded as the teachers' union grew. As in Chicago, however, Catholics and labor secured their share of influence by trading in an older version of schooling that had called for mass participation. Schools would now be more receptive to the church's and labor's most narrow organizational objectives within a reform structure that granted professionals ultimate control over schooling.

The postwar educational reform in San Francisco and Chicago, like earlier reforms, aimed to shelter schools from politics. By the late 1940s, however, this goal was tempered by the knowledge that schools operated within a political context and that durable reform would have to make accommodations to local interests previously opposed to reform. Such deviations from the traditional stance of reformers, who self-consciously had opposed politics as usual, were complemented by the new basis on which labor and ethnic groups, former opponents of reform, were now incorporated into school affairs. The most narrow organizational interests, which had been met by patronage politicians in the 1930s, continued to be satisfied. Labor influenced teachers' issues and vocational education, and church concerns about curriculum and school board appointments were considered. In exchange, class mobilization, the chief tactic of labor and ethnic leaders prior to the 1930s, was dropped. With these new roles and understandings forged in the 1930s, the second wave of school reform was institutionalized with little controversy and generated scant opposition until the racial upheavals of the 1960s.

6

Training for the Workplace

IN the nineteenth century the issue of high schools galvanized working-class organizations to fight, on a class basis, for the vision of common schooling for all. In the first half of the twentieth century vocational education stood out as a similar issue, with the capacity to mobilize not just a labor politics but a working-class defense of democratic values. Ironically, the terms of this struggle and the victories that unions secured contributed to the domestication of class as a basis of educational conflict.

More than any other educational issue, vocational education touched directly on the concerns of American workers organized as labor. Unions perforce took the lead in shaping a working-class response to the issue. There was considerable variation, however, in the union position in different cities; the stance of local unions depended on the context in which the issue arose and the scope of choice it afforded to working-class children.

Overall, however, there was an underlying consistency to the trade union position. Vocational education was not intrinsically desirable or undesirable. Workers almost never took a position that flatly opposed the concept of such schooling. Rather, what was important was how vocational offerings were incorporated into the school curriculum and whether they would become tools, controlled by employers, to undercut union power.

In fighting against business control, the trade unions invoked the traditional republican justifications of schooling for all. But once this danger passed and unions established their right to exercise influence in this area of school policy, the rhetoric of the issue changed. Unions no longer emerged to defend a broad working-class interest in schooling for all. The conflicts over vocational education thus proved to be the last site where a class-based battle was fought over whether the ideal of the common school would be replaced by a highly stratified and differentiated system of public education.

For a moment, as unions sought to protect their own interests, they emerged, along with educators, as the chief defenders of the vision of common schooling. But once unions secured their immediate interests they refrained from invoking these larger questions. The resolution of the vocational issue thus helped tame and ritualize working-class participation in school politics.

I

BUSINESSPEOPLE and industrialists, joined by a handful of educators, were the first to advocate the introduction of vocational training into the public schools during the early decades of the twentieth century.[1] In opposition to the nineteenth-century concept of "manual training," which bore little relation to workplace activities, many of the new proponents of vocational education envisioned more practical trade training designed to prepare workers for industry.[2] Yet among these supporters of vocational education there were significant differences as to the appropriate range of instruction; industrialists tended to favor more narrow training, whereas educators supported a broader vision of training that would be applicable to a variety of specific jobs.

Despite such differences over the precise content of vocational training, enthusiasm for strengthening the ties between schools and the labor market joined a broad coalition of support for vocational education in the first decade of the twentieth century. In 1906 these businessmen and educators formed a national organization, the National Society for the Promotion of Industrial Education (NSPIE), to develop and publicize the case for vocational education on a nationwide scale.[3] The association monitored the progress of state-level initiatives to introduce vocational education and devoted itself to securing federal funding to encourage these state systems.

Preferring a limited and gradual introduction of vocational training into the public schools, organized labor remained aloof from the early activities of these enthusiasts. Fears that vocational training could be used by employers to undercut labor power in the marketplace made organized labor skeptical of the new movement. However, faced with a growing movement initiated by business leaders and social reformers, the American Federation of Labor revised its earlier ambivalence toward vocational education in order to achieve some influence over how vocational courses would be introduced into the schools. As one AFL member put it, "We cannot stop the trend in the direction of this kind of education in the school; but we can, if we cooperate with the educators, have it come our way."[4]

In response to the formation of the NSPIE, the AFL took a closer look at the problems of apprenticeship and trade schools. The 1910 report of the Committee on Industrial Education of the AFL backed public industrial training. The report cited the dangers that private trade schools posed to the labor movement by turning out nonunionized competition.[5] In the face of such a threat, organized labor's primary objective in the debate over vocational education was to ensure that any vocational educational programs that were established would remain within the jurisdiction of public education and would not be part of a separate system, as some industrialists were urging. In a 1912 report endorsing vocational education and again in its congressional testimony on federal funding for vocational education in 1914, the AFL underscored its position that industrial education should "be conducted by the State and not by any private interests."[6]

On the local level, too, strong business advocacy of a separate system of vocational education pushed labor into supporting public vocational schooling. Where significant business pressure for vocational education existed, as in Chicago, labor took a more positive stand on vocational education in the public schools than when business pressure was weak, as in San Francisco. In Chicago, business leaders strongly pressed for a separate system of vocational education, prompting labor to come out solidly in favor of vocational education—but within the existing public school system. By contrast, in San Francisco, where business leaders showed little interest in expanding vocational education beyond the few privately funded vocational schools in the city, neither school officials nor organized labor showed much interest in vocational training until 1917, when labor began to fear employer attempts to control apprentice training.

Chief among the arguments advanced by business proponents of vocational education was that public high schools, as they were constituted, were geared to college-bound students and consequently failed to serve adequately the greater part of the student body, whose numbers were increasing faster than those of the college-bound. Although the number of pupils attending high schools still accounted for a small percentage of those enrolling in public school, the numbers attending high schools grew dramatically in the first three decades of the 1900s. In Chicago, 10,201 pupils, only 4 percent of the total school population, attended high school in 1900; by 1920 this number had more than tripled, and by 1930 the number of high school students had increased more than tenfold to constitute 23 percent of the total school enrollment.[7] In San Francisco as well, high school enrollment grew significantly during this period, although not quite so dramatically as in Chicago. In 1900 San Francisco's public schools enrolled 1,934 high school students, 4 percent of the total enrollment. That figure had tripled by 1920, when high school students numbered 6,703, or 9.5 percent of the total school population; by 1930 the number had jumped to 13,881, over 18 percent of the total school enrollment.[8]

Behind these numbers lay important transformations in the composition of the schools. As numbers expanded, the children of working-class parents, many of them immigrants, increasingly sat alongside upper and middle-class children who had previously dominated the high schools. Vocational education was aimed at these newcomers, most of whom would not go on to college. This was the argument made by the Commission on National Aid to Vocational Education in 1914. In the commission's language, vocational education could extend "equal opportunity to all to prepare for their life's work . . . by recognizing different tastes and abilities."[9]

Without adjustments in the curriculum, advocates reasoned, the majority of children would not be able to take advantage of the public schools even though they were theoretically open to all. Indeed, it was as much for the greater numbers who dropped out after elementary school as for the new entrants to the high schools that proponents of vocational education recommended new educational programs. In San Francisco the Junior Chamber of Commerce and the City and County Federation of Women's Clubs presented the board of education with a proposal for two vocational junior high schools in 1930. Supporters of the proposal maintained that such education would attract certain pupils who otherwise would end their schooling at the junior high stage "and who might just be persuaded to continue if they could be taught a trade instead of being required to continue with a classical education."[10]

In this they echoed the concerns that the elite City Club of Chicago had expressed nearly two decades earlier. The club's extensive report documenting the need for vocational education in Chicago centered its argument on the large numbers who left school before completing eight years. Such students left, the report maintained, not for financial reasons but because "the instruction in the lower grades is not suited to the abilities and interests of the average child."[11] The report pointed to the substantial enrollment in private commercial and industrial schools —19,800 in all—as evidence of the demand for vocational education.[12] In a survey of 205 boys, 75 percent told investigators that they would have stayed in school had trade training been available.

Unions held considerably more guarded opinions of public education. The City Club's report, for example, noted that 82 percent of Chicago's unions answering a questionnaire about vocational education registered their approval of public trade training but stressed that the goal should not be to produce skilled workers ready for the labor market.[13] A leading Chicago unionist stated these reservations more bluntly when he expressed his fears that vocational schools would turn into "scab factories" used by employers to crank out cheap labor.[14]

San Francisco's unions were likewise wary of trade schools. In a poll conducted by the Commonwealth Club in 1909 the "prevailing opinion" among unionists was that trade schools "are calculated if not designed to turn out ill-trained workers who may be used to defeat the objects of organized labor."[15]

Despite these reservations, unions did not unilaterally oppose vocational education in the public schools. The Chicago Federation of Labor, for example, took a generally positive attitude toward vocational education in the early 1900s, although it did not see such education as a major topic of concern. The CFL counseled its committee on schools to cooperate with the board of education on plans for vocational education, and in 1908 the CFL offered to work with the board in developing industrial and commercial education. Although the board turned this proposal down, the CFL joined the Association of Commerce and the Industrial Club of Chicago to advise the school board on vocational education the following year.[16] It was to the unions' advantage to participate in the debate over vocational education. If labor could secure at least some control over vocational programs, they could be a positive addition to the public education for workers. Organized labor did not have the resources to establish its own system of industrial schools, and a public system that workers could influence was certainly preferable to one dominated by employers. Moreover, as educational historian David Hogan has argued, by the early 1900s workers were faced with the deterioration of the traditional forms of apprenticeship by which skills were passed on and intra-working-class mobility attained.[17] As mass production began to replace older craft work, the new organization of work undermined the instruction and close on-the-job supervision that had characterized the earlier arrangements. Employers, moreover, found it less profitable to

employ apprentices. The need for broad knowledge of the production process, which had been the objective of apprentice
training and the three- to five-year course of study it required,
was less defensible in the context of mass production.[18] The
school offered a potential substitute for defending the need for
broad knowledge and training skilled workers, but unions approached the topic cautiously and slowly. Before 1910 Chicago
unions approved of introducing vocational education into the
public schools but, as Julia Wrigley points out, only in a "limited
and controlled manner."[19] In San Francisco, unions indicated that
vocational schools, if not "used by industry for exploitation purposes," would benefit workers and their children.[20]

Yet workers could not dictate the circumstances under which
the debate over vocational educational would be held, nor could
they control the pace of events, which hastened the introduction
of vocational education into the public schools. The controversy
over the Cooley bill in Chicago sharply demonstrates the way
labor was drawn into supporting vocational education in the
public schools to fend off a separate business-dominated system.
In the process of protecting their organizational interests, the
unions emerged as the defenders of a broader working-class interest in common schooling.

The conflict over the Cooley bill also demonstrated that business was not concerned simply with extending the benefits of
higher schooling to the working class, as much of its rhetoric
suggested. Debate over how vocational education would be organized within the public school system revealed a strong business
desire to control vocational training to ensure that the results
corresponded with business's needs.

Although business leaders had been instrumental in establishing several private trade schools in Chicago, these institutions
could not guarantee a sufficient supply of skilled labor. For over
a decade, the public schools had been gradually adding vocational
courses to their curriculum. In 1908 the board of education, with
the advice of the Chicago Association of Commerce, established
four "continuation schools," designed to provide five to ten hours
of vocational training to those who had dropped out of school to
work. Two years later, commercial courses were introduced into

the last two years of high school. The public schools also operated three technical high schools for boys and one for girls, schools that were geared to produce an elite segment of the work force, including foremen, superintendents, and engineers as well as skilled workers.[21]

Business leaders, however, had found these efforts insufficient to meet industry's needs for a trained work force. In 1909 the Chicago Association of Commerce, the city's largest employer group, issued a study that urged expanding industrial and commercial education in Chicago. As presently conducted, the report argued, Chicago's schools would never fulfill society's needs for trained workers. As a remedy the report endorsed vocational training as a means of attaining "social efficiency."[22] Responses to the City Club's survey of 1912 found that 74.4 percent of the firms questioned complained about shortages of skilled employees; 88 percent suggested that industrial schools for children between the ages of fourteen and sixteen might provide a solution.[23] Such continuation schools formed a central component of the plan proposed by the prestigious Commercial Club in 1912.

The Commercial Club, which had made the expansion of vocational education a chief objective, hired former Superintendent of Schools Edwin Cooley (1900–1909) in 1911 to draft legislation proposing a comprehensive system of vocational education. As superintendent, Cooley had established warm relations with business leaders, impressing them with his concern for efficiency.[24]

The club financed Cooley's trip to investigate vocational education in Europe, particularly in Germany, whose highly stratified educational system was credited with having produced the skilled labor that contributed heavily to Germany's preeminence in international markets. Cooley and his backers in the Commercial Club saw continuation schools as a means of achieving similar results in the American context. Their proposal envisioned a wholly vocational curriculum in which children over fourteen would be compelled to attend some hours of school in addition to working.[25] Labor objected strenuously to the continuation schools as a substitute for raising the compulsory attendance age to sixteen. In the union's eyes, continuation schools for fourteen-year-old children were merely a way to sanction child labor, whose cheaper rates undercut the unions.

However, the continuation schools did not prove to be the most controversial aspect of the entire package proposed by the Commercial Club. Even more troubling to unions and, importantly, to school officials, was the provision that vocational education be provided in a separately administered system.[26] A separate state board for vocational education and local boards composed of the superintendent of schools, two employers, and two skilled employees would be responsible for running the system. This arrangement was meant to ensure that "practical men," not educators, would be responsible for vocational education policy.[27] The bill proposed that the new system be financed by boosting local property taxes.[28]

Despite the provision for employee participation on the separate vocational boards, labor swiftly denounced the proposal, charging that employers would inevitably come to dominate them.[29] The Illinois State Federation of Labor branded dual administration "a menace" that would trap working class youth in an inferior dead-end educational program.[30]

Defense of the common school tradition, which promised to place working-class youth on equal footing with their middle-class counterparts, dovetailed nicely with unions' organizational interests in preventing employer control of vocational training. Such control would, of course, allow employers to exercise increased influence over their future work forces and undermine new workers' receptivity to unions. Nonetheless, organized labor at the same time affirmed its support for vocational and technical training if it were conducted within the public school system and administered by public school authorities. In this way, unions reasoned, students in vocational courses would also be assured of the general education that labor deemed "the best system to . . . educate our children for their future activities as citizens and workers."[31]

Hostile as unions were to the Cooley bill, their active opposition within the state legislature was somewhat less energetic than that of professional educators, for whom the plan posed a major organizational threat. Charging that a dual system would sever the links between democracy and education, educators, including the University of Chicago's John Dewey, urged that vocational training be integrated into the general curriculum to make the schools less academic and remote from practical concerns.[32] Chicago's superintendent, Ella Flagg Young, likewise condemned the plan, defending the unitary system as the superior organizational principle and charging that Cooley's proposal would effectively "train the young to belong to a lower industrial class."[33]

When the battle reached the state legislature in 1913, 1915, and again in 1917, both organized labor and educators were poised to strike out against the business backers of the Cooley bill. As was typical on educational issues, Chicago Federation of Teachers head Margaret Haley led the battle for organized labor. Educators made their influence felt through the City Club of Chicago, whose educational committee they dominated. With professionals comprising the bulk of its membership, the City Club did not share the manufacturers' interest in controlling the industrial work force and tended to sympathize with the arguments of educators about the relation between education and citizenship. The City Club offered its own proposal for expanding vocational education within a unitary system but failed to win over advocates of the Cooley plan. Joining labor and professionals in opposition were the state's bankers, who favored vocational education, particularly agricultural education, but feared the effects of tax increases on heavily mortgaged farm properties.[34] Led by Illinois Bankers Association president B. F. Harris, the bankers backed a conference in which the differing factions would come together to formulate a bill they could all support. But, like the City Club's bill, the unitary system that emerged from the conference proved unattractive to the proponents of dual administration.[35]

With the Commercial Club unwilling to compromise and with a wide coalition of educators, professionals, labor, and bankers arrayed against it, the Cooley bill's failure to pass in three sessions of the state legislature is unsurprising. The most vigorous lobbying efforts of leading industrialists associated with the Commercial Club were no match for this broad coalition opposing the dual system.[36] Industrialists finally dropped their campaign for a separate system in 1917, consoling themselves that the passage of the Smith-Hughes Act by the federal government that year would provide the expanded vocational training they had sought.[37]

The culmination of the efforts of the NSPIE, business groups, and labor at the national level, the Smith-Hughes Act provided federal moneys for state systems of vocational education that complied with federal guidelines. The new law did encourage the growth of vocational training in Chicago but in a form quite unlike that advocated by the Commercial Club. Safely located within the organizational purview of the public schools, the vocational education program solicited the advice of employers and workers, but public school officials remained responsible for the ultimate shape of the program. Thus, the initial impact of Smith-Hughes corresponded more to the educators' conception of vocational education than to the industrialists' vision: vocational offerings within the comprehensive high schools multiplied. There was little immediate increase in separate trade training programs, although all non-high school graduates were required to attend continuation schools for one day a week in 1918–19.[38] Although the new arrangements were far removed from the labor-dominated apprentice system that the unions would have preferred, labor was satisfied with the outcome, having blocked potentially disastrous business control.

The way vocational education was framed as an issue in the dispute over the Cooley bill allowed unions to defend a broader working-class interest while safeguarding their own narrow organizational security. The challenge thus afforded the labor movement the opportunity to reaffirm its commitment to a more general working-class interest and to acknowledge the centrality of the public school system in guarding that interest. Labor remained skeptical about vocational education so long as it suspected that industrial training would be used by employers to undercut union wages or to deprive working-class children of access to equal education. Once the overt challenges posed by business proposals for a separate vocational school system had been defeated, however, organized labor's attention to the issues of educational differentiation and equity diminished. Despite the

American Federation of Labor's position that education should prepare children not only for employment but also for leadership, local unions were ill equipped to monitor the impact that the increased diversity in the secondary school curriculum had on the ideals of common schooling.

II

AS the issue of vocational education developed in San Francisco, labor had little occasion to represent a broader working-class interest, as it had in Chicago. San Francisco businesspeople attempted to control the supply of skilled labor by setting up apprentice schools, but proponents of a dual system of education, such as that envisioned in the Cooley bill, attracted little support. In San Francisco, business advocates of vocational education thus posed a direct threat to organized labor but not to the common school. In contrast to Chicago, where labor and educators fought business efforts to control vocational education, San Francisco unions found themselves in conflict with local educators, who sought to introduce vocational education at a slower pace and in a more diffuse form than labor wanted. In the absence of a powerful movement to establish a dual system, San Francisco educators had little incentive to push ahead with vocational education.

In the context of San Francisco's tightly organized labor movement, which was strong enough to enforce the closed shop in many trades, and its comparatively unorganized employers, vocational education remained off the educational agenda until 1920. But with a major employer offensive that was organized in 1916 and culminated with the establishment of the open shop in the building trades in the early 1920s, unions began to fear employer attempts to control the supply of labor. In an effort to head off employer-dominated training, San Francisco unions dropped their earlier skepticism regarding public trade training and began to pressure school authorities to take advantage of the new federal funds provided by the Smith-Hughes Act. With the federal law assuring that publicly funded vocational training would not be overseen by a separate administration, unions viewed public vocational education as a way of retaining some control over the supply of skilled labor.

Before 1917 there was little sustained pressure for vocational education from any sector of San Francisco society. Compared with Chicago, business was strikingly quiescent. Although employers responding to a Commonwealth Club survey in 1910 declared themselves generally in favor of trade schools, they undertook little activity to expand trade training.[39] Two central factors help to account for the contrast between the two cities: the differences in the organization of their labor and business communities and the difference in the shape of their economic bases. San Francisco's business community was less well organized than its counterpart in Chicago and had had little success in preventing the establishment of the closed shop in many leading trades.[40] Any serious effort to control vocational training would mean breaking strict union rules limiting the numbers of apprentices. Prior to 1916 San Francisco's business community lacked the capacity to challenge the unions on such a fundamental issue. Contributing to the disorganization and weakness of the business community was its diversity. The phenomenal growth of Chicago's manufacturing industry in the early decades of the 1900s had no counterpart in San Francisco where the industrial base shrank in relative importance as commercial and financial activities took off. Shortages of appropriately skilled labor were consequently a less widespread problem in San Francisco than in Chicago. San Francisco's Commercial High School had long prepared students for clerical and commercial posts, and several privately endowed trade training schools turned out skilled workers. Many business leaders consequently showed more concern with the costs of new educational endeavors.[41] As the Hill Report noted in 1944, "The traditional viewpoint that the city was primarily a cultural and financial center was strong as the belief existed that people could find their own jobs and hold them if they were given regular academic schooling."[42]

A more broadly drawn segment of San Francisco's civic elite evinced an interest in vocational education, but, again, both its activities and its proposals paled in comparison with the vigorous advocacy of the business-oriented proposal backed by Chicago's Commercial Club. The coterie of elite women's groups that conducted the School Survey of the Collegiate Alumnae Association, for example, criticized the lack of trade schools in San Francisco in its 1914 survey. However, the association subsequently threw its energies into administrative reform of the schools rather than pursuing trade training as a priority.

The Commonwealth Club of California, whose membership included business leaders and professionals as well as labor leaders and educators, issued a report on a survey of vocational education conducted by its committee on education. Like those of the women's clubs, the report declared that "the problem of getting an efficient common school education for all of the children of the nation is even a more pressing one that that of improved vocational education."[43] It denounced the "German" model, which slotted pupils for particular vocations as early as age twelve, and urged that vocational training be provided only after the individual student had discovered his or her own needs for training.[44] Nonetheless, the report did go on to recommend the establishment of industrial training schools controlled by a separate board composed of employers, employees, and the superintendent of schools, much as the Cooley bill had.[45] It was, however, more circumspect than the Cooley plan with regard to the establishment and financing of these programs, opposing a statewide system whose costs would be borne by the state. Instead, the club urged that schools be established only where demands for them arose and recommended that localities assume the costs.[46] The club's committee worked the following year with the state commissioner of vocational education to draw up a bill based on the committee's report. The measure that was ultimately proposed abandoned the notion of a dual system and instead provided vocational education within a unitary public school system. Although the state legislature passed the measure, the governor's pocket veto—due to insufficient funds—kept the provision of vocational education a strictly local prerogative.[47]

Educators demonstrated some interest in increasing the vocational offerings in the public schools. In 1908 San Francisco Su-

perintendent of Schools Alfred Roncovieri toured Europe studying the school systems with particular attention to industrial
training.[48] Unlike Cooley's, Roncovieri's visit concentrated on
Britain and France. His recommendations upon his return were
considerably less sweeping than Cooley's. Roncovieri carefully
distinguished between vocational education, designed to turn out
trained workers, and industrial education, which taught the
scientific principles underlying a variety of trades. It was the
latter that San Francisco schools needed to expand, according to
Roncovieri.[49] In a presentation before the State Building Trades
Council, the superintendent outlined the advantages of broad
technical training in a rapidly evolving industrial setting and
reassured his audience that increasing technical training in the
public schools would not result in a "production line of apprentices."[50] Despite his avowed enthusiasm for a more extensive
industrial curriculum, Roncovieri took few concrete actions to
promote these ideas. He did not associate himself with the Commonwealth Club bill, nor did he propose any dramatic restructuring. Apart from floating a bond in 1909 to equip the Polytechnic
High School, San Francisco did very little to expand vocational
education in the public schools.

San Francisco labor unions feared the effect of employer-
dominated trade schools on the labor movement and on the quality of labor. But until the direct offensive by business was
launched in 1916, San Francisco unions showed little concern
over this potential threat and scant interest in publicly funded
vocational education.[51] After 1916, however, labor looked on
public vocational education with increasing favor. In 1917 the
San Francisco Labor Council's *Labor Clarion* praised the vocational
training bill that had passed the California legislature and
watched hopefully for developments at the national level. It
noted the particular benefits that vocational training might extend to skilled workers and the training that it would give children.[52] Tempering this general approval was only the caution that
vocational education legislation must be watched to ensure that
employers did not turn it to their own advantage.[53] The chief way
to guard against employer encroachment was to keep vocational
education under the supervision of the school authorities with

advice by committees of employers and employees.[54] *The Labor Clarion* applauded the passage of the Smith-Hughes Act in 1917 and carefully monitored efforts to comply with its provisions in California.[55] It praised industrial education as a perfect way for skilled workers to keep abreast of the developments in their trade and urged workers to consider employment as vocational education teachers.[56] The council declared that expansion of the vocational curriculum would remedy the inadequacies of the public school system by giving "every boy and girl over 14 years of age a chance to learn his or her trade or vocation."[57]

However, the paper noted ruefully that San Francisco would not receive any of the first moneys disbursed in California under Smith-Hughes because the board of education had not attempted to comply with the law's requirements.[58] Although many other California cities had established day trade classes after the passage of the bill, San Francisco limited its new offerings to trade extension classes in the evening. These classes aimed to supplement the training of skilled workers who practiced their trade during the day; an example was the Evening Navigation School conducted for shipyard workers in conjunction with a local employer.[59]

The Labor Council requested meetings with the board of education to investigate the Smith-Hughes provisions so that vocational education in San Francisco could be strengthened.[60] By 1920 the council had grown impatient with the school department and publicly charged that San Francisco educators opposed vocational education.[61] To underscore its dissatisfaction with the school department, the council announced that it would support the proposed Claxton reforms, believing that reform would facilitate the extension of vocational education. While the provisions of the proposed reform would have had little bearing on vocational education, the issue was one that permitted labor some political leverage over the school department, which it could not otherwise budge on this issue.[62] Despite Roncovieri's protests that the school department did support vocational education and that the proposed reform had nothing to do with the issue, the Labor Council could not be swayed from siding with reformers.

The trade-off between vocational education and administrative reform confronting the Labor Council was unusual. For the most part, labor in San Francisco (as in Chicago) had retreated from issues of predominantly ethnic concern, and, as we have shown, the conflict over school reform in San Francisco was charged with ethnic and religious antagonisms.[63] In the first round of voting on the issue, the Labor Council had sided with the school department against the reformers, a position that election results confirmed to be the stand taken by the majority of working-class voters.[64] With the failure of the current school department to take advantage of the new resources freed by the Smith-Hughes Act, despite the repeated requests by the Labor Council, the unions resolved to join the foes of the department who intimated that vocational courses would be more readily implemented once administrative reforms had been enacted.[65] In taking this step, the council had weighed the broader working-class interest in a popularly elected superintendent and the anticorporate model of school governance associated with it against labor's interest in vocational courses. Its choice indicated a triumph of a narrow corporate interest over a more general, though ethnically determined, working-class position.[66]

Once reform was implemented, however, no major expansion of public vocational offerings took place. Seven thousand sixteen- to eighteen-year-olds were now enrolled in continuation classes, and more evening trade classes had been established.[67] But these classes were intended to supplement the training of adults who were actively engaged in a skilled trade during the day and who wanted to improve themselves in the evenings.[68] The notion of progressive education that animated the new administration, while not hostile to technical education, promoted an "overall development" approach to educational philosophy that was at odds with the more specific technical education that labor desired. Thus, just as the administrative reforms enacted in 1917 represented a triumph of the professional educator, so, too, did the kind of public vocational education stressed in the 1920s reflect the educator's vision of vocational training.[69] Frustrated with the public schools' approach to vocational education and finding itself more shut out of influence over school policy than it had been prior to reform, labor turned against the new administration and backed proposals to establish an elected board in 1930.

In the interim, labor's fears about employer-controlled vocational training had materialized. After the triumph of the open-shop campaign in 1921 employers, through their central organization, the Industrial Association, moved to assert control over the supply of labor. Their chief vehicle was the newly established private vocational schools, which trained workers in a fraction of the time that apprentice-controlled training had.[70] The schools were, as labor had feared, strongly antiunion. As the Industrial Association noted, the schools strongly encouraged each apprentice to "maintain undivided loyalty to his employer who was offering him an opportunity to gain a place in the trade."[71] And as labor had anticipated, the schools served to produce strikebreakers during 1923, when bricklayers, plasterers, and plumbers were trying to reestablish the closed shop. Unions had effectively lost control over apprentice training in the building trades; five employers and two members of the Industrial Association now presided over the apprenticeship program.[72] By 1925, however, a flooded local labor market had forced the schools to cut back considerably.

In the early efforts to establish vocational education, then, labor's particular interest made it the key working-class participant in both Chicago and San Francisco. Yet the nature of labor participation and its relation to a wider working-class interest hinged on the structure of the conflict in each city. Where business efforts to control vocational education were expressed in support for a dual system of education, as in Chicago, labor joined with educators to defend the broad working-class interest in the common school. In San Francisco, where employers were not strong enough to press seriously for a dual system, unions defended their more narrow organizational interest against private employer-controlled vocational programs. In neither city did the most vocal proponents of public vocational education achieve their aims: in each case educators (in alliance with labor in Chicago and with business quiescence in San Francisco) deflected pressure to shape vocational education according to the wishes of either labor or business. Educators' success in shielding vocational education from strong business or labor influence set the stage for a new round of struggles later; in an area of such vital concern to industrialists and unionists alike, both groups continued to search for ways to shape vocational training to their own specifications.

III

BY the 1930s, after over a decade of federal involvement with vocational education, both employers and employees were criticizing the way vocational programs had been implemented. The Metal Trades Department of the AFL, for example, charged that many of the trade schools were biased in favor of employers' needs, neglecting employees' welfare, and that they were causing overcrowding in some trades.[73] These complaints were documented in the 1938 Russell Report commissioned by President Roosevelt to reexamine vocational training in the public schools.[74] Employers, on the other hand, faulted the schools for restricting the scope of the offerings and for failing to produce workers with sufficient training.[75] For educators, the 1930s presented the new challenge of defining the role of vocational education in a severely depressed economy as the rise of unemployment sparked renewed interest in vocational training as a potential remedy for youth unemployment.[76]

This renewed interest set off disputes about vocational education in different localities, arguments whose contours reflected the terms of the earlier debates in each city. In each case, the nature of vocational education—that is, whether training would be narrowly focused on the acquisition of a specific skill or viewed as a part of general education—and its scope became targets of controversy. In Chicago, for example, a short-lived scheme to vocationalize most secondary education formed the focal point of debates about vocational education. In San Francisco, the renewed strength of labor was evidenced in the unions' push to establish a public trade school in the city as a means of reasserting and institutionalizing labor control over apprentice training. In both cities, the shape of vocational education by the end of the 1940s reflected an accommodation among educators, employers, and unions, although in a balance specific to each city. In both cases, however, official recognition of labor's right to influence decisions about vocational education was a vital component of the domestication of labor's participation in school politics. With labor's role thus narrowed, unions concentrated on guarding their organizational interests, lacking both the framework and the impetus to speak for a more broadly defined working-class interest.

The defeat of the Cooley plan ended business efforts to establish direct control over vocational education in Chicago, but it by no means signaled a halt in the expansion of vocational training in the public schools. By 1930 three technical high schools prepared pupils with a general technical background as well as more specific training in a particular trade. The course of study was not, however, equivalent to apprenticeship training, which was provided only in the Washburne Trade School, a training school initially established to rehabilitate disabled war veterans. The school department's decision to establish such apprentice training programs was greeted with skepticism by labor and employers. Unions feared a glut of ill-trained workers, while employers balked at releasing young workers for a day each week to receive training. Yet public school authorities solicitously courted both unions and employers, granting the former a voice in deciding the number of apprentices to be trained and persuading the latter that the benefits of an adequately trained work force would compensate for time lost in training.[77] These two-day programs were supplemented by a variety of evening vocational classes, some of which were held in private plants around the city.[78]

Although vocational education had thus expanded considerably in the decade since the controversy over Cooley's bill, the majority of children still attended general high schools, not specifically aimed at establishing links with the workplace. The high school curriculum was geared, as it had been two decades earlier, to general education, although it was now considerably more stratified by the introduction of testing, guidance, and tracking as well as vocational courses. Fitted into this framework, vocational courses were seen as primarily contributing to the overall development of the student. The former principal of Lane Technical School, Superintendent William Bogan (1928–36) was an ardent supporter of vocational education but viewed it, as did progressive educators, as part of a general preparation for life. Even specifically technical courses he saw as laying the foundation of general knowledge rather than as imparting a particular skill.[79]

With Bogan's death in 1936 and his replacement by William Johnson, this progressive conception of vocational education was challenged by a much narrower employment-linked orientation. As the choice of the Democratic machine's board of education, Johnson exhibited little of the professional independence that had poisoned relations between Bogan and the board. Johnson's views on vocational education were akin to those of Cooley. Johnson scoffed at Bogan's emphasis on the general benefits of vocational education and called for a more "practical" program that would equip students with the skills to enter industry immediately after leaving school.[80] Board president James McCahey concurred with Johnson's judgment, faulting the public high schools for overemphasizing college preparation and paying insufficient attention to training students for work.[81]

Although this move did not provoke much controversy, a much more sweeping plan proposed a year later did. An article published by the *Chicago Daily News* claimed that Superintendent Johnson planned to restructure Chicago's high schools so that 80 percent of the courses would be vocational. The proposal was consistent with Johnson's earlier observations that the present curriculum did not serve the needs of the vast majority of high school students who would not go on to college.[82]

Public reaction to the plan was immediate and re-created the arguments of two decades earlier. The Chicago Federation of Labor again argued that the schools' purpose was to "develop good citizens" and denounced the proposed plan as "inimical" to workers' interests and to the social and economic mobility of their children.[83] The Chicago Teachers' Union worried that the plan was a ploy to replace current teachers and to turn teacher hiring over to patronage concerns.[84] Labor and teachers were joined by the middle-class reformers who dominated the Citizens' Schools Committee. The committee summarily rejected the plan and actively worked against it, sponsoring a conference at which leading educators and even some industrialists denounced Johnson's scheme.[85]

The plan aroused so much furor that Johnson disclaimed responsibility for it only a month later. At a conference among school administrators, labor officials, and teacher representatives, the superintendent maintained that he had not planned any major changes in the school curriculum and reassured teachers that their positions were secure. Although Johnson promised to work with labor and teachers on future modifications in the vocational education program, he rarely did so, defending his actions on the grounds that only businesspeople really knew the needs of the labor market.[86]

In this episode, Chicago's labor movement once again defended a broad working-class interest in general education at the same time that it guarded a corporate interest in regulating the supply of skilled labor. This time, however, the attack on general education did not come directly from business, as it had twenty years earlier. Instead, the close relationship between the business community and the Democratic machine found expression in a superintendent who took his cues from business leaders. Public pressure, spearheaded by labor and teachers, forced Superintendent Johnson to back down from his most audacious plans. But they could not break Johnson's close ties with business, nor could they block his less sweeping efforts to introduce the business vision of vocational education into Chicago's public schools. During Johnson's tenure, vocational offerings expanded considerably. A new commercial high school designed to turn out clerical and secretarial employees was established in 1939. The following year, the Washburne Trade School was expanded and rehabilitated. In 1941 a new vocational high school opened, providing specialized training for its pupils and "with no intent to meet college entrance requirements."[87]

By the 1930s pressure for expanding vocational education in San Francisco had mounted. Educators expressed concern about the growing numbers of youth out of school and unable to find work. Elite women's groups proposed that the board of education establish two vocational junior high schools.[88] Labor, too, renewed its efforts to expand vocational education in the public schools. Noting that "the collapse of the apprenticeship system in many industrial trades . . . and the restriction of immigration quotas [had] decreased the number of skilled tradesmen coming from the Old World," the unions began to cooperate with the board of education in designing plans to institute vocational education.[89] The notable exceptions to this rising interest in vocational education were San Francisco employers, who remained aloof from the discussion over revitalizing vocational education in San Francisco.

The issue of how expansion would take place was ultimately settled largely in accordance with labor's preferences. The women's clubs' proposal was swiftly rejected by the board and Superintendent Gwinn, who opposed vocational schools at the junior high level.[90] Instead, a very selective trade school geared toward high school graduates and a limited number of older high school students was established. Opened in 1937, the Samuel Gompers Trades School provided both day and evening trade classes. Apprentice courses were "developed by committees in each trade consisting of representatives of employers and union representatives of the specific trades. . . . a representative of [the school department sat] in as advisor only."[91] New courses were added at the request of these labor-employer committees.

The decision to establish the school was hailed by the City and County Federation of Women's Clubs as a "big step in the prevention of delinquency for those students not 'bookminded.' " The federation noted that the school would need the constant backing of all citizens and declared, "Women's clubs can do much to insure its success."[92] For labor groups, however, the school was to be not a repository for potential delinquents but a relatively exclusive training ground for future craftsmen. While acknowledging the "urgent necessity for apprentice training," *The Labor Clarion* was careful to note that the school would offer only "limited instruction."[93] Enrollment in the day section was small; an average of 244 students attended in 1939–40, suggesting that, at least initially, the school conformed more to the ideal of labor than to that of the women's clubs.[94]

The issue of control over vocational education provoked two major controversies. The first dispute centered on the dismissal in 1940 of Edgar Anderson, principal of the Gompers Trades School, whose independence rankled both labor and the board of education. Anderson's efforts to control school activities soured his relations with labor. Local political columnist Arthur Caylor maintained that Anderson had been fired because "certain labor leaders didn't like the way he was turning Samuel Gompers—a place where householders used the facilities to fix the kitchen sink—into a school where students actually learned trades."[95] The board of education appeared to have its own purpose in dismissing Anderson: a desire to undermine the school whose control by labor was viewed as a challenge by board of education members.[96]

The board's actions a year later underscored its ambivalence toward the Gompers school. Because of its strategic location, San Francisco had became a vital center of war production by the early 1940s. As part of the war effort, the school department received substantial amounts of federal funds for defense training programs aimed at mobilizing adequately trained manpower. These increased demands threw the vocational training wing of the school department into disarray as new programs were established and authority delegated. Amid this confusion, the board discontinued the day classes for high school students at Gompers and turned the school over to national defense classes for full-time use.[97]

Unions denounced the discontinuation of the day classes as "very unfair" and voiced concern over whether the classes would ever be reestablished. Superintendent Nourse assured critics that the move was only temporary and promised that the trade school would be reopened and refurbished after the war. He went on to note that the department "had intended a very definite reorganization of the Samuel Gompers Trades School, combining all the trades, revising and reorganizing the entire industrial and vocational work in all schools of San Francisco."[98] Despite Nourse's reassurances about the future of the trade school, there was speculation that the demise of the Gompers school in its current form was precisely what the school department had wanted.[99]

Unions were generally in favor of the trade training classes established under the auspices of national defense and often complained that training programs were not being set up fast enough.[100] Because of the acute labor shortages, the classes did not threaten to produce enough newly trained workers to glut the market. Moreover, the classes provided an excellent opportunity for the unions to recruit new members, since they were organized outside of the schools and labor had considerable control over them.[101]

In contrast to this favorable attitude toward defense training, labor remained hostile to any efforts to increase the scope of vocational training in the public schools. In the early 1940s, the Navy Department and shipyard officials began to pressure the school board to dispense with industrial arts instruction in the senior high school. They pointed to the great need for producing trained workers and complained that "industrial arts are hardly more practical than 'gadget and trinket making.' "[102] Within the school department, the director of vocational training and the supervisor of national defense training classes tended to support extension of vocational education; Superintendent Nourse, most principals, and many teachers, on the other hand, preferred industrial arts.[103] Labor unions likewise opposed extending trade training classes to the high schools, fearing that such a move would institutionalize a vocational education program beyond the reach of labor's influence.[104]

When the director of vocational education attempted to turn Samuel Gompers into a trade school with high school accreditation and simultaneously to reduce labor influence, a three-way dispute between the director, the principal of Gompers, and the superintendent created an impasse in the attempts to upgrade training. Labor joined in the dispute as well. J. G. Ennis, chair of the trade advisory committee governing apprenticeship programs in San Francisco, sent the board a letter "upholding the apprenticeship training program and condemning efforts to compel apprentices to produce goods in competition with industry and labor."[105] At the same time, he derided the vocational classes as "boondoggling" that would never prepare students for industrial jobs.

The lack of coordination and the infighting that characterized the administration of vocational education in San Francisco was a central criticism of the Hill Report, the survey of San Francisco schools conducted in 1944. The report recommended that a single administration be appointed to oversee all vocational education programs. But administrative restructuring would solve little unless school officials possessed a clear vision of what kind of vocational program the public schools would provide. By the mid-1940s, union opposition to trade training at the secondary level and the ambivalence of the school department to specialized vocational training set limits on the direction that vocational education would take. Most specific vocational training courses were upgraded to the junior college level as the city college system expanded in the postwar era. In addition, unions received city funds to supervise apprentice-training courses.[106] At the secondary level, the public schools concentrated on industrial arts classes with a much more general orientation than vocational training offered by the city colleges. These arrangements provided labor unions with adequate assurance that the public schools would not flood the local labor market with competition.

Although business had little to say on the question of trade training, it was more vocal on the failure of the schools' vocational program to train students for sales and clerical posts. Proclaiming a "new era of cooperation with local business," the board in 1945 announced a new distributive education program in response to business complaints.[107] Yet, as with industrial training, the preponderance of specific career preparation in the commercial and clerical fields moved into the city colleges with elementary and secondary schools devoted primarily to providing general education.

IV

BY the postwar era, then, with the shape of vocational education determined and the channels for business and labor participation established, the struggles that had animated earlier decades were subsiding. In each city, the shape of previous conflicts bestowed different administrative arrangements for providing vocational education. In Chicago, business influenced sympathetic school administrators to establish numerous vocational schools at the secondary level during the 1930s. But labor participation kept specific vocational training confined to these specialized schools, whose small enrollment posed little threat of competition. In San Francisco, labor did not succeed in its more audacious goal of controlling a secondary-level trade school, but labor opposition to any such school not under its control contributed to the move to concentrate vocational education at the junior college level.

Despite these different outcomes, the cities underwent a common process in the 1930s and 1940s in which business and labor successfully challenged the attempts of earlier educators to exert preeminent control over vocational education. In both cases, educators acknowledged the rights of labor and business to influence the content, delivery and reach of vocational education. The political process of accommodating these interests, together with the emergence of vocational educators as a profession seeking to establish some autonomy, gave the United States a hybrid system of vocational education by the end of World War II. Secondary education in the postwar era resembled neither the sharply stratified European model admired by early proponents of vocational education nor the common school ideal of nineteenth-century American educators. Substantial differentiation within the secondary curriculum created a stratified system of education without turning to large-scale trade training that established direct ties with the labor market.

Organized labor, which had struggled earlier against a dual system of education, voiced few objections to this growing differentiation of public education. As labor secured its organizational objectives to prevent the use of vocational schools to challenge unions, the labor movement's role in educational politics was transformed. In exchange for official recognition in the sphere of vocational education, labor effectively agreed to participate in a framework of educational administration incapable of processing the demands of unorganized workers.[108] With attempts at business control thwarted, labor now primarily represented its own organizational concerns as it participated in decisions about vocational education. As organized labor reached accommodation with city governments and business leaders on the local level in the postwar era, those concerns grew increasingly distant from the interests of nonunion workers, many of them minorities. Labor's victory in securing influence over vocational education was thus a crucial element in quieting class-based struggles over educational policy and in setting the stage for the racial conflicts that dominated the 1960s and 1970s.

7

The Significance of Race

THE STORY of American education that we have told thus far rests on the presumption that the right to schooling was not contested. The early establishment of a public school system open to the children of all white citizens went hand in hand with the formation of the distinctively American pattern of working-class participation in educational politics. From the beginning, white workers entered school conflicts with a fragmented identity, emphasizing either ethnic or labor concerns and only rarely bridging the two. As we have shown, this pattern of participation led to the eventual domestication of class in disputes over public education.

Yet the presumption of access to schools which underlies this entire history applies only to white workers. For nonwhites, a radically different relationship to public education created an educational experience quite distinct from that of whites. This chapter examines the politics of education when citizenship is challenged and the right to schooling questioned. It is largely a story of black Americans but at times has also included Asians. In contrast to the fragmented character of white working-class participation, nonwhites engaged in school politics with a single identity forged in response to policies that denied them access to public education or relegated them to a separate and inferior position within that policy domain. For minorities, the divisions between work and off-work were less relevant than for whites because the condition of nonwhites has generally been a total one, spanning both realms. At work, as in residence communities, the chief factor shaping the experiences of minorities was race. And when blacks, and excluded Asians, entered school politics to challenge the unequal status accorded them, they were united on the basis of color.

In such cases, where the right to access was questioned, the politics of schooling in the United States resembled the struggles of the working class in western Europe more than those of white workers in the United States. The parallels between the American minority experience and those of European workers are striking. Consider the relationship of exclusion and working-class participation in nineteenth-century England. Before the passage of the Education Act of 1870, no national system of primary schools assuring schooling to working-class children existed in Britain. Workers were excluded, and unlike the dominant classes they were incapable of providing satisfactory "private" solutions, though they made many attempts to do so. As a consequence, their exclusion helped shape their formation as a class in action to demand state education. After the 1870 act ushered in mass schooling in England, the working class was incorporated in a manner that reproduced class inequalities in explicit ways, especially but not only at the level of secondary education.[1] Workers continued to pose curricular and other demands in class terms through the institutions of an organized working class that, in part, had been formed in opposition to the earlier exclusion of working-class families from access to mass schooling. Working-class capacity to affect school policy was tied intimately from the outset to the larger battles fought by the labor movement. The class basis of demands by school movements in England in the 1960s for the provision of comprehensive secondary schooling is at least partially comprehensible in these terms.

In a similar fashion, the history of exclusion and the subsequent unequal incorporation of blacks (and sometimes Asians) into the American public school system and into the American political system forged racial unity and created a set of demands for improved or equal access to public schooling. For blacks, most

educational issues became infused with a racial content as they
sought to attain the schooling benefits that white workers had
taken for granted. As in England, the struggle for equal schooling
was linked to a broader agenda of social change sought by the
movement's leaders.

I

IN the 1960s, bolstered by the support of federal courts and
emboldened by the civil rights movement, blacks launched a
major challenge to the unequal access to schooling permitted
them. The ensuing turmoil placed racial conflict at the center of
American school politics in a period when class—in either its
ethnic or its labor incarnations—had ceased to provide a main
fault line of school disputes. Indeed, the absence of class was as
striking as the presence of race at the center of American urban
school movements in the 1960s.

   Black educational demands created unprecedented turmoil because they implicitly reached beyond the range of school politics
as usual to evoke fundamental issues of citizenship. Equal education and integration were central pillars of the black effort to
participate in American social and political life on the same terms
as whites. Black educational demands were linked to a whole set
of issues that challenged white dominance on many different
fronts. In the South education emerged along with voting rights
as the key to equal participation in social and political life. In the
North, where citizenship rights were not so flagrantly violated,
educational movements sought to end the more subtle forms of
inequality that incorporated blacks into social and political life on
unequal terms.

   The historical exclusion of blacks from mainstream school services and policymaking created conditions for demands that, by
their nature and tactics, radically challenged the status quo. These
demands for integration, community control, and equal provision
threatened to disrupt established practices of educational policy-

making and to destroy long-standing features of American public school organization. Demands for integration endangered the existence of the neighborhood school, the cornerstone of local public school organization and a powerful symbol of popular control of public education. Community control promised to leave the neighborhood school intact but jeopardized the hard-won gains of teachers' unions and challenged the prerogatives of the central educational administration. Black demands for equal education entailed changes too fundamental to be incorporated into school politics as usual.

In spite of local variations, we have observed a similar politics of race and education in Chicago and San Francisco. Black demands, even when initially raised in modest form, proved threatening to a wide array of whites: neighborhood residents who feared racial integration and its expected consequences; politicians who feared the loss of traditional constituents as a result of population change; and school officials who sought to preserve time-worn patterns of organization, definitions of school issues, and personal political ties. With varying degrees of articulate consciousness, whites also understood that the black attack on the exclusionary policies of the public schools was part of a broader effort to achieve social, economic, and political equality. Thus the targets of black demands felt all the more imperiled because, contrary to the fragmentary, issue-specific character of school politics as usual, black school struggles were linked to a wider, more global set of concerns. The view of most Americans that education was the key to opportunity (a belief shared by blacks, who placed a high priority on schooling) underscored this relationship and raised the stakes even higher.[2]

The result was a dialectic of white resistance and intensified black activity that became increasingly unruly (and that, in some cities, included a change from a focus on integration to community control). Ordinary patterns of dispute resolution were utterly incapable of managing conflict with this content, meaning, and intensity. The shift of the arena of school politics from school boards, bureaucracies, city halls, and city councils to the courts is an indicator of both the disruptive capacity of black school movements and the search for a "nonpolitical" forum to manage school politics and restore order. As both Robert Dahl and Richard Funston have demonstrated in their work on the Supreme Court, courts tend to take a more activist role when the legitimacy of public policies is under severe strain and when conditions of crisis prevail.[3]

It was the Supreme Court itself, of course, in the landmark case *Brown* v. *Board of Education* of 1954 that made possible the reopening of fundamental questions of race and schooling. In the South, where segregation was mandated by law, *Brown* shifted black demands from pleas for improved facilities within Jim Crow to calls for the total abolition of the dual school system.[4] Although *Brown* did not immediately precipitate challenges to school policy in the North—it did not clearly apply to cities like Chicago and San Francisco, where school segregation resulted mainly from residential patterns—the demonstration effects of the southern civil rights movement stimulated by *Brown* helped produce northern school movements that tried to define the issues of segregation, access, and the terms of access to education in ways appropriate to northern cities.

As in the South, fundamental assumptions about race relations were questioned. In southern cities the challenge was to a policy of overt separatism, in the North to one officially color-blind—but in both to the ideological assumptions and basic practices of local politicians and school officials. Even when the influence of black power ideology created a rupture between integrationists and separatists in the black community, all the movement actors understood that the processing of racial issues required fundamental departures from school politics as usual. In Chicago and San Francisco, even ordinary issues—about curriculum, personnel, governance, school location, and so on—became increasingly contentious as they were tinged with racial overtones.

Local school districts lacked the capacity or, in many instances, the will to respond to calls for such profound changes, and extraordinary tactics were required before the full force of black demands was acknowledged. In Chicago and San Francisco, the absence of early court precedents dealing with de facto segregation and the political heritage of both cities led to group mobilization and virulent conflict. Blacks took their demands to the streets, especially in the early 1960s when boycotts, picketing, sit-ins, marches, and other confrontational tactics were greeted with the adamant opposition of tradition-minded educators.

In San Francisco, the rapid growth of the black community in the postwar period (from 0.8 percent of the population in 1940 to 10 percent in 1960) encouraged the development of a diverse array of black political groups.[5] The relatively fluid organizational environment that resulted helped to foster a substantial willingness to use protest as a political tool despite the objections of moderate blacks who preferred to rely on legislation and litigation.[6] This tendency to rely on activist techniques was reinforced by the questionable utility of litigation and by the initially cool reception of school officials to black demands.

San Francisco's school officials in the late 1950s and early 1960s proudly maintained that segregation was not a problem in the city's schools despite claims to the contrary by civil rights leaders.[7] By the early 1960s these groups began to press for an end to de facto segregation, urging the board at least to undertake studies of the problem. Superintendent Harold Spears dismissed these requests, maintaining that enforced integration would destroy the neighborhood school.[8] Spears's steadfast defense of an officially color-blind school policy antagonized civil rights groups, creating a climate in which protest would flourish. The environment grew increasingly polarized in the early 1960s as new schools were subjected to racial scrutiny and as white opponents of the civil rights groups mobilized.[9] A 1962 board of education report favoring action to reduce racial imbalance in the schools temporarily defused tensions, but the extremely conservative implementation of the board's recommendations signaled that the controversy had not been resolved, only postponed.[10] The potential for conflict was heightened by a power struggle in the local National Association for the Advancement of Colored People (NAACP) in 1964 from which militants emerged as the victors.[11]

Frustrated by the lack of progress in moving toward integration, the NAACP took the lead in forming a Committee for Direct Action, filed complaints with the U.S. Department of Health, Education, and Welfare and the state board of education, picketed the local board of education, and planned a school boycott for September. Despite the release of a school census that many observers regarded as proof that segregation was not as serious as civil rights groups contended, the NAACP continued to maintain that segregation was a major problem in San Francisco schools and vowed to build a "community-wide organization" whose direct-action techniques would "grow in size, significance, and drama."[12] Protest activity never reached this ambitious scope, but considerable unruliness and scattered protest erupted over issues at particular schools. Pressure from civil rights groups had moved the school board from a position of recognizing de facto segregation to one of endorsing integration, but the critical problem of how this goal could be achieved had yet to be resolved.

In Chicago, the Democratic machine's tight hold on local political power discouraged early independent black protest over school segregation, despite the fact that residential patterns and school board policy had combined to make Chicago one of the most segregated school systems of any large American city in the North, and despite the fact that Chicago had a large black population comprising 22.9 percent of the city's population in 1960.[13] Soon after *Brown,* the Chicago branch of the NAACP began to collect information about schooling patterns for black children in Chicago. Convinced that blacks were being systematically shortchanged, they protested to the board of education. However, the potential for developing a movement around these issues was headed off by the Democratic machine, which infiltrated the local NAACP and ensured the election of moderate leadership for the organization.[14]

By 1961 the expectations and excitement provoked by the southern civil rights movement and the possibility for litigation had loosened the machine's grip on black activism. Black parents whose children attended overcrowded schools with double shifts participated in the NAACP's "Operation Transfer," in which they tried to enroll their children in nearby underenrolled white schools. When Superintendent Benjamin Willis refused to allow the transfers, the NAACP filed a suit accusing the board of gerrymandering the school boundaries.[15] As in San Francisco, the superintendent interpreted black demands as a challenge to the neighborhood school, and, much as his colleague in San Francisco had done, Willis defended the neighborhood school as the organizing principle of American public education. The most tangible result of the renewed agitation was a number of studies of the Chicago school system seeking to document black claims of inequality.

The emphasis on studies and litigation finally gave way to the confrontational tactics of boycotts and sit-ins in 1963. In the context of national strife over civil rights and of Chicago's own highly segregated racial arrangements, the confrontation between black protest and white resistance became fierce. A small-scale transfer plan allowing some blacks to attend less crowded white schools provoked vicious backlash from white parents.[16] Superintendent Willis responded to these protests by stalling on the transfers, and, when challenged, he resigned. The ensuing white outcry was instrumental in his rehiring. Superintendent Willis's adamant refusal to approve any policies that might have improved the racial balance of the schools made him a particular target of protest and a national symbol of white resistance to black educational demands.[17] The school board, however, appeared impervious to black pressure and actually rehired Willis even though he was slated to retire that year.

As the depth of black grievances became apparent in the mid-1960s, local officials looked for ways to deflect or to placate some of the demands raised by black protests. Aware of the explosive potential of racial issues and unwilling to antagonize their white electoral bases, officials in both cities launched time-consuming studies and introduced a variety of desegregation proposals that relied on voluntary action. Nowhere were white politicians eager to introduce sweeping reforms that would carry the risk of substantial upheaval. School conflicts concerning race could no more be accommodated within the political bounds of northern cities than they could in the South. Ultimately, comprehensive responses to black demands for desegregation were achieved only with the prodding of federal courts, as in the South. Where such intervention was missing, as in Chicago, only minimal steps toward desegregation were undertaken.

In San Francisco, comprehensive studies were the first major effort to address black demands. The Stanford Research Institute (SRI) was commissioned to produce a massive series of reports on racial problems in the city's schools. In 1967, however, newly appointed prointegration members of the school board and the new superintendent, Robert Jenkins, sought to sidestep the technical questions of busing discussed in the SRI reports and instead promoted a plan to use federal funds for integrated educational complexes requiring minimal student busing.[18] In this way they hoped to avoid emotionally charged public debates about busing and the neighborhood school. Jenkins also aimed to defuse criticism by holding community meetings around the city to establish an open decision-making process. Both efforts failed. The community forums provided a context for mobilizing antibusing groups, considerably raising the temperature of the debate, and the complexes came under attack by opponents of busing and integration.[19] The militant opposition of white neighborhood groups, encouraged by Mayor Joseph Alioto, undermined these plans, which were largely abandoned when the school department failed to raise the necessary funds (at least partially because of the local opposition).[20]

With the school department paralyzed and the mayor abetting busing foes, the NAACP despaired of reaching a local solution and turned to the federal courts for relief. Although the merits of their suit remained questionable when measured against the de jure standard that had been applied in previous cases, the Supreme Court's ruling approving busing in *Swann* v. *Charlotte-Mecklenberg* induced Judge Stanley A. Weigel to issue a desegregation order for San Francisco's elementary schools. With this ruling San Francisco became the first northern city to undergo citywide busing to achieve racial balance in its schools.[21]

In Chicago, local civil rights groups, fed up with the intransigence of both Superintendent Willis and the school board, also looked to federal intervention for relief. Because the court's jurisdiction over northern cities was still uncertain in 1965, dissident blacks instead turned to Title VI of the newly passed Civil Rights Act of 1964, which would withhold funds from the school district for violating provisions against discrimination. To the shock and dismay of Chicago's white political establishment, the Department of Health, Education, and Welfare (HEW) initially acceded to these arguments and denied the school district its first funds under the Elementary and Secondary Education Act. However, within a week, heavy pressure from the Justice Department and the president had induced HEW to reverse its decision.[22] National Democratic leaders had little to gain by alienating Chicago's influential Democratic machine, especially when the legal bases for HEW's decision were still uncertain. This early test of the willingness of nonjudicial government agencies to involve themselves in racial school issues set the pattern for government action: in the North, as in the South, the courts would have to forge the way.[23]

Yet each time Chicago's blacks turned to the courts, a solution short of major reorganization of the school system was worked out. Unlike that of San Francisco, where militant independent black organizations flourished in the decentralized political environment, Chicago's black leadership was not sufficiently well organized independent of the machine to press for the judicial remedies sought in many other cities. Although Superintendent Willis's successor, James Redmond, initially sought to implement a small-scale busing program, bitter protest by white parents induced the board of education to substitute a voluntary plan. Not surprisingly, this approach did little to modify existing racial patterns of school attendance.[24] Chicago's schools remained highly segregated, and local school officials seemed immobilized in the face of the conflicting demands of white and black groups and the ever-present threat of federal sanctions or an unfavorable court ruling.

In both San Francisco and Chicago, black school movements precipitated a crisis for local government. The entry of this previously excluded group into the political arena challenged the long history of racial segregation and unequal provision of education that had been a central feature of American public education. It also appeared to challenge the concept of the neighborhood school, which had formed the basis of American public education. The white resistance and political stalemate that ensued undermined the institutions of local school governance. And as blacks sought redress from authorities beyond the local jurisdiction, federal agencies and especially the federal courts became the key conflict managers.

In the long run, however, the failure of conflict resolution at the local level took its toll. In San Francisco, the decision mandating busing was only the beginning of a protracted battle. The process of defining an acceptable plan proved to be a time-consuming task for which the city was ill prepared. Moreover, the prospect of busing activated San Francisco's ethnic and language minorities (chiefly Chinese and Spanish-speaking residents), who fought to defend neighborhood schools, which they regarded as their own.[25] The busing plan was implemented in 1971 despite Chinese protest. A Chinese boycott kept one thousand children out of the public schools for a year, and scattered protest by whites marred the opening weeks of school. School officials ultimately succeeded in luring Chinese pupils back into the public schools by permitting them to remain in their neighborhood schools.[26] The desegregation plan represented the culmination of civil rights groups' struggles for over a decade, yet many questioned the fruits of desegregation soon after it was implemented. Changing residential patterns rapidly resegregated many schools. The small proportion of whites remaining in the district limited the scope of possible integration, and the quality of education showed little improvement as the district grappled with the administrative aspects of desegregation.[27] Although demands for community control were never prominent in San Francisco, some disillusioned black parents began to indicate a preference for neighborhood schools by the early 1970s.[28]

Mounting dissatisfaction led to another NAACP suit against the school district in 1978. A final settlement was not reached until 1982, when the NAACP and the school department agreed on a plan that combined voluntary busing and enriched education of schools in black neighborhoods. But the ultimate meaning of this victory remained in doubt: the drop in white enrollment to 16.9 percent by 1982 had made integration an elusive goal, and the plan to upgrade minority schools hinged on substantial state funding in a period of fiscal austerity.[29]

In Chicago the absence of a court order permitted local officials to evade the issue of school desegregation with less overt contention than in San Francisco. However, in 1975 Chicago was denied nearly eight million dollars in special funds administered by HEW for continued failure to show progress on desegregation.[30] Bargaining over voluntary busing dragged on until 1977, when a program of magnet schools and voluntary busing was agreed on. By this time, Chicago's white school population had dropped to under 25 percent of the total enrollment.[31] As in San Francisco, neither desegregation nor newer concerns about the quality of black and minority schooling had been resolved after decades of strife and litigation. In both cities black grievances, white resistance, and the political incapacity of local districts had left racial issues unassimilated into routine school policy.

II

IN the United States, where the white working class had been incorporated into the public schools fully and equally without struggle, the politics of education concerned issues that assumed inclusion in a system of elementary schooling and the provision of a minimum standard of instruction. Because white male workers in the United States were also citizens in the full sense of possessing the right to vote and because they were mobilized as voters into the political process by mass political parties, they possessed the ability to influence the contours of urban school systems. The American pattern presumed that working people were incorporated fully and equally with a capacity based on political participation to affect school policy.

For blacks (and for Asians in San Francisco), however, the situation was conspicuously different. Immediately after the Civil War blacks were confronted with attempts to exclude them from mass schooling; and after they were included, they were linked to the various urban school systems in structurally subordinate ways with very limited capacities to influence what the schools did. Even where blacks were concerned with other issues of school politics they were at the same time concerned with securing and maintaining a tenous access to education and with questions of *de jure* or *de facto* segregation.

Nowhere were these patterns more pronounced than in the American South. There, rigid prohibitions against racial mixing dictated that blacks would be confined to their own schools. The white monopoly of local political institutions meant that blacks would have a limited—and diminishing—capacity to improve the schools allotted them, and that the possibility of challenging their subordinate status within that system would be even more remote. But because it identified education as central to the larger effort for full and equal membership in American society, the black community tirelessly searched for new ways to influence school policy. The struggle for schooling was central in bringing blacks together as a group with particular political demands and a distinct history of political practice centered around educational issues.

The formation of a black politics of schooling can only be understood by studying the black experience in the South. In the nineteenth and the early twentieth century only the South contained enough blacks to make race a major issue in school politics. Until World War I, blacks were a negligible proportion of the population in Chicago, and not until World War II would San Francisco's black population rise above a tiny minority of the city's population. But in Atlanta, a major southern city, blacks accounted for some 40 percent of the city's population in 1872, when the public school system was founded.[32] Atlanta's white leaders, accordingly, confronted the problem of race at the inception of the public schools, and black leaders continually faced the challenge of securing adequate education for their children in a political and social system that denied them full partnership. We shall look closely at the case of Atlanta to understand the development of a black politics of schooling and the elaboration of a black tradition of political activism on educational issues.

Despite a constitution that granted political rights and acknowledged the state's responsibility for educating blacks, Atlanta's newly formed board of education ignored blacks when it met in 1869 to design a public school system. To obtain even the

legal minimum, Atlanta's black community had to place organized and persistent pressure on public officials.[33] Once schools
had been established, the board of education's continuing neglect
of black educational needs handed blacks an issue around which
to organize. Early black elementary schools were markedly inferior to those for whites and were grossly overcrowded. By the
end of 1883 there were three black grammar schools, only one
more than when the school system had begun. The combined
capacity of the three new schools was woefully inadequate; the
1883 superintendent's report noted that only half of the black
children who wanted schooling could be accommodated.[34] New
facilities were opened only after considerable prodding by black
leaders. Moreover, no secondary education was available to
blacks, and the board of education refused to yield to numerous
petitions requesting a black high school. Until the 1920s black
students desiring a high school education were required to pay
tuition at Atlanta University.[35]

Although black leaders actively pressured school officials and
mobilized their community, the demands and tactics that they
formulated did not fundamentally challenge the Jim Crow framework of public education in the South. In the earliest efforts to
obtain better schools, black spokespeople were solicitous of
white officials, persistently requesting public funds but at the
same time accepting inferior facilities for fear of being denied
schooling altogether. Blacks also accepted a much greater share
of the burden of providing public education than did whites. For
example, ministers who led the initial movement for schools
offered their churches for sale or rent to the school board, which
was reluctant to construct new buildings for blacks.[36]

So long as blacks were confronted with a united white electorate, they had little hope for substantial change. However, when
disputes ruptured white unity, blacks enjoyed rare opportunities
for improving their schools. On two occasions in the nineteenth
century, in 1888 and in 1891, Atlanta's white electorate split into
opposing camps, each attempting to lure black voters. In 1888 the
emergence of the white working class introduced sharp divisions
within the white electorate. Controversy over prohibition exacerbated white disunity. The elections that year were punctuated by

class-based appeals and the emotional fury stirred up by prohibition. Both parties directly appealed to black voters.[37] Black leaders were circumspect in their use of such infrequent opportunities
and ultimately opted for the more conservative party's firm commitment to build a new school rather than the vague promises for
representation in the school board offered by the competing
party.[38] The need for concrete improvements was so great and the
possibilities of successfully challenging the basic structure so
remote that black leaders defined the prudent course as the most
fruitful. In 1891 this scenario was replayed with blacks again
supporting the conservative ticket in exchange for the promise of
an additional school.[39]

These episodes were critical in the formation of a black political
identity and practice. The strategy of white politicians implicitly
defined blacks as a group with its own distinctive needs and
demands. Blacks were compelled to act as a *political* group because
the rare opportunity to win benefits through the use of political
power depended crucially on the ability to deliver votes as promised. In both instances blacks, led by an articulate, church-
based middle class, bargained to obtain the facilities they had
requested, further underscoring the importance of black political
cohesion.

Although the institution of the white primary in 1892 plunged
blacks into political oblivion, it paradoxically served to intensify
unity as blacks searched for new avenues to press their claims for
better educational facilities.[40] The dismal schooling provisions
for blacks began to stand out more clearly as white schools were
upgraded in the early twentieth century. Atlanta's school officials
further provoked blacks by attempting to augment the vocational
offerings in black schools due to the need for "more industrially
trained workers and fewer professionals among the Negro population."[41] When in 1916 the school board proposed to eliminate
the seventh grade from black primary schools, a new spirit was
evident in the reactions of some black leaders. Representatives of
Atlanta's growing middle-class black community demanded that
the board of education provide blacks with educational facilities
equal to those for whites.[42] When their demands were ignored
and the proceeds of the latest bond issue were allocated dispro-

portionately to white schools, black leaders began to search for new sources of leverage.

Although barred from selecting candidates for municipal office, blacks were still able to vote on citywide bond issues. The newly formed local of the NAACP launched a voter registration drive that proved a resounding success.[43] The black vote provided the margin to defeat a new bond issue submitted twice in 1919. In 1921 the city council, bowing to the power that blacks had shown on bond issues, promised improvements in black elementary schools as well as the construction of a black high school. Still the allocation of subsequent bond proceeds between black and white schools was nowhere near being equal. In 1939, and again in 1940, blacks were instrumental in voting down new bond issues.[44]

This tactic had required a high degree of organizational activity and group solidarity, and the repeated victories encouraged black leaders to take up more controversial issues. Many of the organizations that had participated in the bond campaigns, particularly the NAACP, were active in the 1941 struggle for equal salaries for black and white teachers, long an issue of contention.[45] As the first major campaign to use the federal courts, this movement presaged the later campaigns to establish educational equality by relying on the courts and other agencies outside the city to resolve local conflicts. Likewise, these organizations took the lead in extending the claims for equality and integration of educational facilities in the 1950s and 1960s.

Not until black demands were backed by the federal government and an emerging national civil rights movement did they challenge the structural subordination of blacks within Atlanta's public schools. Without sources of political leverage outside the local structure of power, blacks had played according to the rules of that structure, as they had to if they were to receive anything. With the backing of the federal courts, however, Atlanta's black leadership set about redefining the terms of school politics in Atlanta.

In the North, the absence of a history of strict racial segregation made the ways in which blacks would be bound to school systems more uncertain. In both Chicago and San Francisco early regulations mandating segregation were successfully challenged, so that blacks were incorporated into the public schools by 1875. Yet, because they constituted a negligible percentage of the population, northern blacks were powerless to affect school policy. Moreover, once their numbers increased, a pattern of de facto segregation took shape, effectively recasting the black relationship to schools by forging a new structurally subordinate linkage. As in Atlanta, the unending struggle to secure or retain equal participation in schools was a central force in uniting blacks as a group.

In San Francisco, where blacks accounted for less than 1 percent of the population throughout the nineteenth century, they were initially excluded from the public schools.[46] Only persistent petitioning persuaded the board of education to establish a "Colored School" several years after white schools had opened. Facilities for black children in San Francisco were inferior to those for whites, and their existence remained precarious, as a school board order arbitrarily closing two black schools in 1868 vividly demonstrated.[47]

Better schools constituted a chief goal of black activity from 1850 to 1875; black newspapers carefully monitored educational progress; black leaders used school issues to mobilize the community.[48] The very different position of blacks in the social and political environment of the American West opened the way for alternatives unthinkable in the South, most notably a demand for school integration.

Although the size of the black community precluded the use of electoral power (in 1880 there were probably fewer than 450 black voters in the city), the combination of strong political allies and the low salience of the issue for whites meant that the capacity of blacks to challenge their subordinate status was greater than that of their counterparts in Atlanta.[49] In 1871 the San Francisco-based black newspaper *Pacific Appeal* sponsored a statewide conference on black education. Calling for an end to "caste schools," the conference established a permanent committee, the Educational Executive Committee, to fight for educational reforms.[50]

However, after many community meetings, petitions to the board, introduction in the state assembly of a bill proposing school integration, and an 1872 test case in the supreme court of California, blacks still had not achieved their goal.[51] Only in 1875, when the San Francisco board found itself under severe financial strain, did it yield to the pressure, abolishing the "Colored School" and integrating blacks into white schools.[52] No incidents accompanied integration, and black school attendance rose substantially after integrated schools had been introduced.[53] Once segregated schooling was abolished, blacks disappeared from San Francisco school politics as a group with distinct demands until the post-World War II influx of blacks established a pattern of *de facto* segregation, recasting the contours of racial politics.

For Chicago's blacks a similar tale of exclusion and consequent emergence of specifically black demands can be told. As in San Francisco, blacks comprised only a tiny fraction of Chicago's population—1.8 percent in 1900—so that race was a relatively uncontroversial issue in school politics.[54] Chicago's public schools were integrated and remained so except for a brief period of segregation during the Civil War. Largely at the behest of Chicago's Irish community, the city council enacted a "Black School Law" in 1863 segregating blacks in separate schools. Yet the fervor over integrated schools was not sustained; black parents simply refused to remove their children from the "white" schools, and the law was quietly repealed two years later.[55]

As the black population of Chicago grew rapidly after the turn of the century, so did calls for formal resegregation. Rapid growth of the black community (an eightfold increase from 1900 to 1930) upset the established political and economic patterns that had sustained the earlier racial harmony.[56] As changes in school boundary lines and pupil transfers brought black pupils into previously all-white schools, whites responded with strong and occasionally violent protest.[57] Although school officials never seriously contemplated reinstituting segregation legally, they designed policies to prevent racial mixing, thus creating a parallel but inferior school system more like Atlanta's than San Francisco's.

Much of the segregation in Chicago's schools was the product of demographic trends and restrictive housing policies that resulted in extreme racial segregation; yet, as political scientist John Echeverri-Gent's research has shown, deliberate actions on the part of school officials reinforced segregation. In the 1930s an estimated 85 percent of the city's black population lived in the area known as the "black belt."[58] School officials exacerbated black isolation with a variety of devices including shifting district boundaries to conform to the changing racial composition of neighborhoods, establishing "branch high schools" to keep blacks in locations separate from white high school pupils, and issuing transfers to white students in predominantly black neighborhoods.[59]

Blacks were not only segregated, they were also allocated schools of markedly inferior quality. In 1931 a school survey found that 39.2 percent of the black schools were "so inferior . . . that it is not advisable to expend any considerable amount of money on them in an effort to make them acceptable plants."[60] Problems were exacerbated by severe overcrowding. By the end of the 1930s an estimated three-fourths of Chicago's black school children attended part-time sessions because there were insufficient facilities for black children.[61]

Unlike Atlanta's black community, Chicago's blacks were not disenfranchised. The black vote, if not harnessed, could disrupt the designs of Chicago's white politicians. In its consolidation in the 1930s, the Democratic machine successfully eliminated this possibility by including blacks but on unequal terms. Although black politicians provided a conduit through which Democrats funneled limited amounts of patronage into the black community, they were relegated to the periphery of machine affairs. Moreover, the kinds of benefits that blacks could receive were severely circumscribed by what was acceptable to the machine's white constituents. Thus, although black claims for better schools were more successful in Chicago than in Atlanta, in neither city were blacks able to transform the nature of their relationship to the schools.

Even so, the school issue was a potentially volatile one for Chicago's Democratic politicians: any suggestion of integration was apt to provoke violent white reaction, yet blacks continued to challenge the dismal schooling facilities allotted them. Evaluating the political weight of these conflicting claims, the school department sought to stave off potential political damage to the machine by devising token responses to black demands, at the same time sidestepping the fundamental underlying issue of segregated schools. In 1939 blacks won a seat on the school board; but the unequal terms on which blacks were incorporated into Chicago's Democratic machine rendered this representation primarily symbolic.[62]

Although they continued to press for an end to segregated schools, most black leaders recognized the obstacles to this goal and opted for improvement of black facilities at the expense of integrated schools. Their voting strength gave them power to extract more benefits than Atlanta's blacks, but Chicago's black community did not have the leverage to compel school officials to desegregate. Thus, even in the North, where segregation was not legally mandated and where blacks did demand integration, low political capacity handicapped blacks, preventing them from breaking out of their subordinate status within school policy. Blacks were citizens, and American citizenship guaranteed the right to free public schooling, but where white opposition prevented blacks from enjoying the full measure of their citizenship, the educational facilities available to blacks remained inferior to those for whites.

The link between citizenship and access to public schooling is highlighted by the experiences of Chinese and Japanese residents in San Francisco in the late nineteenth and early twentieth centuries. Bound by treaty laws that made them ineligible for citizenship, Asian immigrants' access to public education was vulnerable to shifting political currents that sought to segregate or altogether exclude Asians from the public schools. Only with the growth of an American-born Chinese population whose formal citizenship could not be challenged was the right to public schooling for Chinese-American children firmly established. For the Japanese community, access to public schooling was secured without formal citizenship but only after extraordinary intervention by the federal government.

The economic and social position of the Chinese in nineteenth-century San Francisco was in some respects analogous to that of

Chicago's blacks in the early decades of the 1900s. Like the northern black migrants, San Francisco's Chinese population constituted a growing segment of the population and of the labor market. Although they accounted for only 9 percent of the total population in 1880, the Chinese proportion of the work force was estimated at as high as 25 percent due to the predominance of single males.[63] This substantial presence and the Chinese economic role as cheap labor and strikebreakers threatened San Francisco's tightly organized craft unions, provoking extreme hostility among the white native and immigrant workers with whom they competed. Without the protection of citizenship, local policy toward the Chinese, including educational policy, reflected this unmediated social and economic antagonism as white politicians sought to appease their white constituents. Democratic politicians, in particular, sought to win political advantage by appealing to the growing anti-Chinese movement.[64]

Because most Chinese immigrants were male sojourners seeking work in the United States but not planning to settle permanently, children constituted only a tiny percentage of San Francisco's Chinese population in the 1870s and 1880s.[65] Yet Chinese workers did take advantage of public schools to gain minimal competence in English. The first Chinese school was established in 1859, before any organized or widespread opposition to the Chinese existed. Its closing three months later coincided with the election of Democrat James Denman as superintendent of schools. A night school opened several months later was the only educational facility open to the Chinese throughout the 1860s.[66] Even this facility was withdrawn in 1871 as anti-Chinese sentiment exploded.

Unlike Atlanta's blacks of the nineteenth century, the Chinese were totally powerless to resist these moves. In the year after the closing, several influential Chinese family organizations presented a petition to the board of education requesting the establishment of an evening school for Chinese boys. This request was ignored, as was a later petition for public schools.[67] In 1877 a petition signed by thirteen hundred California Chinese residents was sent to the state legislature requesting amendment of the state law to allow Chinese children to attend the public schools or "what we would prefer, that separate schools may be established for them."[68]

Submitted at the height of the anti-Chinese movement in California, the request was ignored. The only allies the Chinese had were American missionaries who defended the rights of Chinese residents to send their children to the public schools. However, the urgings of the Ministerial Union of San Francisco were rebuffed by the school board, which professed ignorance of any attempt by the Chinese to enter the public schools.[69] The intensity of the anti-Chinese movement led the Chinese to adopt a "wait and see" attitude toward public education. Its virulence dampened much of their interest in Americanization, making their exclusion from public schooling less important to San Francisco's Chinese residents.[70] In the meantime, a strong network of missionary schools operating in the Chinese community offered an attractive alternative to the public schools.

Once the foes of Chinese immigration had achieved their aim with the passage of the first set of Exclusion Acts in 1882 and 1884, the Chinese community directed its attention to the rights of American-born Chinese, including the right to public schooling.[71] In 1884 the exclusionary policies of the board were challenged in court by a Chinese family that had tried, unsuccessfully, to enroll its American-born daughter in the public schools. Both the municipal court and the state supreme court ruled that the child should be admitted to the public schools. San Francisco superintendent Andrew Moulder responded by rushing a bill through the state legislature to establish a segregated school for Chinese children.[72] With its passage, a separate Chinese School was set up in San Francisco, but attendance was sparse. In 1885, only 3.9 percent of school-age Chinese children attended the school; five years later the figure had climbed to only 8 percent.[73] Years of vicious attacks by white residents and repeated rebuffs by the school department had caused many Chinese parents to turn their backs on the public schools. Instead they sent their children to missionary schools and to private Chinese-language schools, where attendance figures were over four times greater than in the public schools.[74]

Once its right to exist had been secured by the courts, there were no further attempts to close the Chinese School, but segregation was strictly enforced, and Chinese pupils were not permitted to attend public high schools. No formal attempts were made to challenge segregation until 1902, when the father of two American-born Chinese children filed a legal complaint against the school board. The court upheld the segregation policy, but this outcome was short-lived.[75] Only three years later, Chinese parents threatened to boycott elementary schools if the board refused to admit Chinese pupils to the public high schools. Because such a boycott would have reduced the state's financial aid to San Francisco schools, the board reluctantly reversed its policy and opened the high schools to Chinese pupils.[76]

The formal abolition of a separate school for Chinese students did not occur until 1936. By that time, organized opposition to the Chinese presence had ended, Chinese workers had diminished as significant competitors in the labor market, and China had become an ally of the United States. Moreover, the abolition of the law calling for segregation did not produce a flood of Chinese children into previously all-white schools. Because of residential restrictions that remained in force until after World War II, most Chinese children continued to attend schools that were predominantly Chinese.[77]

Without the cloak of American citizenship, Chinese San Franciscans found themselves totally excluded from the public schools. But as an Americanized Chinese community emerged, Chinese parents sought support in the courts to guarantee the basic right to education, even if on a segregated basis. Once Chinese residents became American citizens, the issue of their right to public education could no longer be barred from the local political agenda. Even amid the vicious opposition to the Chinese in San Francisco, one school board member acknowledged the link between citizenship and schooling, remarking that "if the Chinese may sometime be allowed to vote, they certainly ought to be educated."[78]

Like the Chinese, Japanese immigrants in San Francisco were ineligible for citizenship. But because their numbers were so small (only 590 Japanese lived in San Francisco in 1890) the Japanese had not become a target of antagonism during the nineteenth century.[79] The few Japanese school-age children in the city attended public schools. In 1901, however, the Union Labor Party, a newly formed organization that hoped to become the party of labor, brought the issue of the Japanese in the city's schools to public attention by advocating the segregation of Japanese pupils.[80] Once in office, however, the party did not immediately pursue the issue.

But mounting anti-Japanese agitation by labor unions called attention to the Japanese presence in San Francisco in the early years of the twentieth century.[81] The board of education began to receive letters complaining about Japanese pupils in the public schools. Most protested the presence of older Japanese boys in the primary grades.[82] Finally, in May 1905, the board of education passed a resolution calling for separate schools for Japanese pupils. The resolution served a primarily rhetorical purpose, since the Chinese School was too crowded to admit Japanese pupils, and the school department lacked the money to establish a new segregated school.[83]

This deadlock was broken in April 1906 by the San Francisco earthquake and fire, which opened space in the Chinese School as many of its students left the city. Pressed by the Japanese and Korean Exclusion League, an organization composed of representatives of local labor unions, the board ordered Japanese pupils to attend the "Oriental" public school in October 1906.[84] Most Japanese parents flatly refused to send their children to the segregated institution. Instead they held numerous community meetings to formulate an organized response. After unsuccessfully appealing to the board, San Francisco's Japanese community publicized the issue in Japan, where it was widely discussed as a grave humiliation to national pride. Through its consul in Washington, Tokyo lodged a formal protest with the U.S. government.[85]

President Roosevelt valued highly the friendship of the Japanese government, as both a trading partner and a major naval power in the Pacific. Critical of the board's decision, he dispatched an emissary to gather information and to try to convince the board to open all its schools to the Japanese. When the board refused to budge, the federal government decided to press legal action. In December, 1906 the U.S. Attorney was instructed to prepare a test case against the San Francisco Board of Education.

The board initially stuck by its position that Japanese students should be segregated because they were keeping out white students and because, according to the school department, Japanese students were primarily overage men. A careful study by Roosevelt's emissary Victor Metcalf refuted both claims. In December 1906, he found that the ninety-three Japanese pupils in the San Francisco public schools accounted for only 0.3 percent of the total student population and that only six Japanese males over fifteen years old were in primary schools.[86]

After prolonged negotiations and considerable federal pressure, a compromise was worked out. The board agreed to rescind its decision forcing Japanese pupils to attend the Oriental School but retained a provision against overage pupils in the primary grades. Roosevelt, in return, committed himself to negotiate a "gentleman's agreement" with Japan to end immigration of Japanese laborers to the U.S. mainland. The legal action was dropped, and on 13 March 1907 the segregation order was rescinded.[87]

Although San Francisco's labor movement announced its displeasure with the compromise, the source of its discontent was not so much the fact that Japanese pupils would attend public schools but rather the anticipated ineffectiveness of the gentleman's agreement. Although the Japanese presence continued to grow as an issue in California after the "school board incident," in San Francisco it diminished in importance. Japanese pupils were peacefully integrated into the public schools, and in 1921, when a new state law allowed the segregation of Japanese pupils, San Francisco continued to allow Japanese pupils to attend integrated schools.[88]

Because of their small numbers and concentration in such occupations as domestics, gardeners, and small businesspeople serving their own community, the Japanese had never posed a serious threat to established social and political relations in San Francisco.[89] In the schools, their presence had gone unnoticed until the Union Labor Party, capitalizing on labor's fear of potential Japanese competition in the labor market, raised the issue. For Union Labor Party mayor Eugene Schmitz, the upheaval surrounding the school board's actions offered a way to deflect attention from the graft trials that were undermining his administration and the Union Labor Party.[90] Since the schools were one of the very few areas where Japanese life intersected with that of the white working class, they provided convenient grounds for attacking the Japanese presence. Moreover, because public education evoked the symbolism of citizenship, couching the Japanese issue in these terms held the promise of attracting wider public concern. Without the protection of citizenship, only the most unusual exercise of federal pressure, trespassing onto the jealously guarded local territory of public education, established the Japanese right to equal education.

The distinctive historical experiences of blacks, Chinese, and Japanese in the American public schools are joined by a common thread: either a full or partial denial of citizenship and the rights that accompany it. In every case where citizenship was less than full-fledged, the right to schooling on the same terms as white children was challenged. Exclusion and segregation helped to brand these minorities with distinctive identities that bound each group together. However, only when minorities challenged the terms on which they had been incorporated into the public schools did bitter strife erupt. Neither Chinese nor Japanese San Franciscans confronted the challenge faced by blacks in the 1960s. Federal intervention had facilitated the peaceful integration of the Japanese by the early twentieth century; Chinese residents, bound by ties of language and culture, showed little interest in altering the patterns of de facto segregation that persisted long after formal segregation was dropped. Only blacks attempted to challenge long-standing patterns of educational organization that were deeply rooted in the structure of local political power. The turmoil of the 1960s was the consequence of this challenge.

III

THE global character and the intensity of the black school movements of the 1960s stand in sharp contrast to the fragmented and partial nature of white working-class involvement in educational issues, even in its most intense periods. When modern school systems were first established in the years before the Civil War, workers and their families did not have to struggle for mass schooling. Their inclusion was a part of what was understood by a wide array of social groups and classes to be the minimum state responsibility for free mass education. This early and relatively painless inclusion affected the basis and character of working-class school demands. They were made not by a class demanding inclusion but by groups that varied from issue to issue. Only on occasion were school concerns articulated and understood in class terms.

Once included in a policy domain of the state, groups are linked to it in one of four broad ways that structure transactions across the boundaries of state and civil society. First, the group may be incorporated fully and equally and may possess the capacity to affect the contours of the policy. Second, the group may be incorporated fully and equally in the policy arena but be relatively incapable to affect it. Third, the group may be incorporated in partial or structurally subordinate ways, yet it may possess the capacity, at least at some moments, to influence the state's policy activities. And fourth, the group may be structurally subordinate in the policy arena and without resources to affect what the state does.

In the United States, the relevant linkages tied blacks to the arena of public schooling (and, more broadly, to American political life) in subordinate ways. The American pattern of political incorporation thus muted class and highlighted race as bases of collective action. The state initially defined blacks as a target of exclusion from schooling; and even after blacks became clients of school systems the terms of their incorporation continually reproduced the group as a unit of society that was simultaneously economic, cultural, and political by linking them to school policy in structurally subordinate ways. Blacks could not participate in school politics on the same terms as whites; they lacked the capacity to shape educational policy except in very limited ways.

With the emergence of the civil rights movement in the 1950s and the entry of the federal government into local school politics, blacks moved to challenge the unequal character of their relationship with public education. Possessing, for the first time, substantial political resources to back their demands, black leaders sought to realize the promise of the common school that had been withheld from the black community for so long. But redrawing the links between educational policy and blacks meant disrupting established modes of decision making and violating the under-standings and ties that had bound whites to public education. Once activated, this challenge catapulted race to the center of urban school policy.

The increasing importance of race in this arena contrasts with what sociologist William J. Wilson argues is the "declining sig-nificance of race" in the period after World War II.[91] Wilson's argument centers on developments in the labor market. He argues that the relaxation of racial barriers in American industries in the postwar period created numerous opportunities for black ad-vancement, changing the position of blacks within the American political economy and creating internal class differentiations within the black community. According to Wilson, these devel-opments have dislodged race relations as a primary determinant of the black condition and have correspondingly increased the salience of class.

Though broadly sympathetic to Wilson's analysis of labor market trends in the postwar era, we are struck by the increasing importance of race as the defining feature of school politics in the 1960s. The centrality of race in school politics belies the sweeping generality implied in Wilson's title. It does, however, confirm his analysis of the displacement of racial conflict from the private sector to the public arena with the entry of the federal govern-ment as the guarantor of black rights. Wilson notes that in the postwar era, and particularly since the 1960s, "the traditional racial struggles for power and privilege are now concentrated in the socio-political order."[92] In the arena of educational politics, these struggles proved so explosive that they dominated the agenda of the public schooling for over two decades. In seeking to redefine common schooling in America to include blacks as equal participants, black school movements challenged the con-cept of the neighborhood school, which white workers had come to regard as the cornerstone of American public education. Bitter strife between these two groups stalemated efforts to meet black educational demands despite the continuing intervention of federal courts.

The relative quiescence of the past decade is no indication that black educational issues have been resolved. Rather, the absence of the unruly questioning of the 1960s signifies an impasse in the search for means to achieve equal education for blacks. As whites have retreated to the suburbs, it is obvious that citywide integration will not solve the problems of racial mixing, nor will it improve the quality of black education. The Supreme Court's refusal to back metropolitan busing has made the goal of integration impractical in many cities. As integration has receded as a chief objective, blacks have put increasing effort into improving the quality of black schools. However, the enormity of this task and the paucity of available resources make the chances for significant improvement remote. Three decades after *Brown,* the dream of equal schooling remains elusive for large numbers of blacks.

8

From Politics to
Markets in
Public Education

THE IMAGE of schooling for all has had a powerful hold on American political consciousness for more than a century and a half. Mass education has been the country's most important domestic social policy. From the early years of the Republic citizenship and public schooling were bound tightly together. For working-class Americans these connections constituted fundamental rights. When question of access to schooling were raised, as in conflicts about early high schools in the mid-nineteenth century, workers acted on a class basis to protect egalitarian rules of entry. For Americans of color, citizenship rights were limited, and so, too, was their entitlement to state-sponsored schooling. For them, struggles about citizenship and battles about schooling have been entangled to the point of being inseparable.

Schooling for all, in the sense of access to public education, nearly has been achieved in full. The democratization of education has been profound. In the 1980s three in four teenagers graduate from high school (compared to fewer than one in two at the end of World War II), and nearly half of these graduates attend college.

If access to public education was achieved for white children in the United States earlier and more fully than in any other western society, and if it has now been extended to all residents (including the children of undocumented aliens), the egalitarian qualities of schooling, nevertheless, have been more limited than many of the early advocates of mass primary education anticipated. The idea of schooling for all initially meant more than equal access. It signified a school experience common to all children. Such schooling was undercut by the social geography of American cities. Society divided in class ways; work and home separated; social classes lived in different residential communities. By the late nineteenth century neighborhood primary schools reflected the fragmented character of city space.

Schooling for all, in the sense of common schooling, is a goal very far from realization, facing more impediments today than a century or even just a decade or two ago. Most big-city schools have black and Hispanic majorities. Most suburban districts are overwhelmingly white. White working-class families have joined an exodus from city schools, and their organizations have stopped pressing for common schooling. The more segmented and segregated the schools become, the more uneven are their finances, their curricula, and the capacities of their teachers and administrators.

Consider an extreme instance. Four in ten of the residents of Sumter County, Georgia, are black; eight in ten of the schoolchildren are black. The school board is entirely white. The superintendent is white. The school attorney is white. None of these officials has children or grandchildren in the public schools; the superintendent's children attend the segregated Southland Academy, one of a number of private schools created since the county's public schools were desegregated in 1970. Since then public funds have been cut by two-thirds as white voters have tried to limit the local tax burden now that their children mostly attend private schools.[1]

Although it is atypical in its starkness, this case illustrates a more general trend. For a period from the early 1960s to the early 1970s southern schools were desegregating at a pace that made de facto segregation less of a problem there than in the North. But since then there has been a massive flight to segregated academies. In Georgia alone the numbers of students in such schools increased from 33,000 to 83,000 in the 1970s. More than 650,000 pupils now attend these all-white schools in the Deep South.[2]

Massive resistance to desegregation in the North and especially to school busing as a remedy has also been a key characteristic of this era. In Boston, where protests turned violent, white enrollment fell by half in the 1970s as private and parochial school registrations increased substantially. Overall, the segregation of big-city blacks has been increasing for the past fifteen years across the country, especially in the Northeast. There, in the 1970s, the percentage of students in predominantly black and Hispanic schools increased from two in three to four in five as the black urban population increased and whites moved to the suburbs.[3]

This period has also been one of demographic and fiscal hardship for the public schools, declining morale of teachers and administrators, and diminishing popular confidence. The forty-two million elementary and high school children in 1980 represented a shortfall of between ten and twenty million from the demographic estimates of 1960. The drop in students was most sharp in the public schools of the country's largest cities and oldest suburbs. These districts suffered declines in state aid tied to enrollment. Schools were closed (more frequently than not, in the poorest and politically least powerful neighborhoods), younger teachers fired, and compensatory programs cut back.[4]

These assualts on equality and standards were compounded by local fiscal revolts, state caps on expenditures, and federal cutbacks in the Reagan years. After the passage of Proposition 13 in California in 1978 fully half of San Francisco's schoolteachers received layoff notices. Results of these budgetary shocks were felt in very tangible fashion. Big-city schools had to teach and deal with social realities against great odds. New York City's Columbus High School—a multiethnic school with twenty-four hundred working-class students, half of whom are white and half black or Hispanic—was recently profiled as an "average" school:

> In a deteriorating building with paint peeling from the walls, in a city that has only recently extended the hope of a less stringent school budget than those of recent years, [school principal Grace

Rosa] sometimes seems to spend almost as much time worrying about basic survival: how to get the teachers' moonscape-like parking lot repaved, how to get the leaks in the roof repaired, how to get window shades for the classrooms, how to replenish a paper supply that is in constant danger of depletion, how to get a car—just one car—for driver education. "There is no money," Mrs. Rosa said. "I'm always trying to get something for nothing." This is education on a shoe-string, education in the trenches.[5]

Under the impact of retrenchment, public confidence in the schools continued to decline, and the morale of educational professionals declined severely. Teachers "had to work harder as support staff were fired and survivors were expected to do more with less."[6] The present mood is one of alarm and concern.

We argue that these difficulties and disparities have much less to do with educational issues per se than with an extension of the unbalanced qualities of geography, society, and politics in the four decades since World War II. Unfortunately, because scholars of education focus more narrowly on matters of educational policy, the ways in which they talk about schooling call attention to questions of secondary importance and to short-term changes rather than to more basic trends.

I

THE WAY we talk about schooling matters. Language neither simply precedes other human activities nor just reflects material realities. It is the hinge between social reality and social consciousness. Our conversations define possibilities and probabilities. They focus attention on some issues rather than others. The noise and silences of language shape our practical consciousness.[7] The public debates of the 1960s had this effect for educators, scholars, and citizens, and the work of a new group of analysts is having this effect today.

Published at the crest of the educational struggles of the 1960s, David Rogers's *110 Livingston Street* gave definition to the concerns of activists and critics. Focusing on the most complex school district in the country, that of New York City, Rogers stressed how the organization of the educational bureaucracy and the way it was embedded in the larger political structure made desegregation, educational equality, and popular control difficult to secure. The prevailing arrangements encouraged vacillation, delay, and ineffective planning. Authority was diffused and responsibility elusive. The system provided few incentives to educational excellence and experimentation. Rogers proposed decentralization backed by the political muscle of new urban coalitions as the appropriate response.[8]

Two years later, following a three-year study commissioned by the Carnegie Corporation, the journalist Charles Silberman published a best-seller, *Crisis in the Classroom.* Silberman castigated the schools of the "poor of every color, race, and ethnic background" for "failing in a way that middle-class schools are not." As a result, he said, they promote inequality: "Far from being 'the great equalizer' the schools help perpetuate the differences in condition, or at the very least, do little to reduce them.'"[9] Overall, the book focused on the lack of pedagogical imagination in the classroom and on the pathological concern of educators with order and docility. Silberman lauded the British model of the open, informal primary classroom as an available remedy.

Although their emphases varied, these two books, read together, summarize the prevailing tone and content of educational conversations in the late 1960s. Race was the focus (there are no references to class in the index of either book), bureaucracy the problem, and equality the goal. Radical changes were required. Reflecting the mood of the time, such new departures seemed possible.

The dominant conversational voice has become much more skeptical. The public mood is more cautious and conservative. The reform impulse has been stilled. Educational standards have supplanted equality as the focus of public discourse about schooling, and the proposals for decentralization and a new pedagogical informality have been overtaken by events. They now seem archaic in light of the current troubles of public education.

More than any other recent treatment, Diane Ravitch's *The Troubled Crusade: American Education 1945–1980* has captured and shaped the way we think about and act on the new situation of public education. She attributes the troubles of the public schools —which she identifies, as do a host of recent governmental and foundation reports, with a decline in qualitative standards— mainly to the passionate concern with equality in the postwar years. Reforms animated by the quest for desegregation, public participation in educational governance, and pedagogical equity caused schools to lose their élan. They became defensive, lowered expectations and requirements, and experimented with too many reforms that were often contradictory. Overall, public schools failed to solve the tension between those who "claimed that a democratic school system had to proceed through the willing consent of the governed" and those who "insisted that a democratic school system had to assure everyone a sound education or suffer the creation of differential elites and of intolerable popular ignorance."[10]

Today the most strident educational voices are raised in the name of standards and quality. A recent Twentieth Century Fund report warns of "disaster" unless we make a new commitment to "excellence." The word has been used so frequently that it is in danger of becoming a cliché. The federal government has sponsored a National Commission on Excellence in Education, and the Education Commission of the States has published a report called *Action for Excellence.* Learning is promoted neither for its own sake nor to secure a more equal and just society. Rather, schooling is seen as the key to economic competition on a global scale.[11]

The concern with standards and the decline in the fiscal constituency of schooling fit uneasily with each other. At a time when so many studies have assessed the standards of schooling only to find them wanting, there is little willingness to spend public moneys to reduce class size or improve the attractiveness of teaching as a calling. Instead standards are mandated by law, and pupils who cannot meet them are penalized by being left back.[12] It is not hard to see why David Tyack and his colleagues find that "it is easy to imagine a future in which public schools will become a declining industry, moving unsteadily from crisis to crisis, beset by scarcities and challenges known and un-known."[13]

Much has changed in tone and emphasis in educational con-versations between the late 1960s and 1980s, but these alterations should not mask that which has not changed. The critics of the 1960s and the 1980s share a common definition about the *terms* of the conversation as one of an emphasis on equality or on standards. In the 1960s there was a good deal of resistance to the thrust for equality in the name of educational quality, and today the cry for standards is answered by a more muffled plea to remember equity.[14]

We take issue with the basic terms of this conversation about educational policy even more than we object to the patently specious choice of equality as opposed to quality. Discussion cast in these terms masks key changes in the relationship of schooling and social space in the postwar years—changes that challenge common schooling and the capacity of democratic politics to shape the development of public education.[15]

Since World War II there have been fundamental alterations in the territorial distribution of the American population and in the ways in which political boundaries overlay the spatial patterning of class, race, and ethnicity. These ways include the massive resettlement of the American people in new kinds of residential communities and changes as a result of these shifts in the bound-aries of local political jurisdictions.

These developments have radically changed the contours and possibilities of public education by subordinating the politics of schooling to the imperatives of economic markets. Once we ac-knowledge these changes, our conversations about schooling must be adjusted and the issues that have dominated our public discussions recast. The current decline in confidence in public education's quality and in its capacity to affect the distribution of resources and opportunity in society, we argue, has much more to do with these shifts in American society than with the results of the educational reforms of the 1960s. The qualitative and quantitative issues of schooling for all are today less about schooling on its own terms than about fundamental, perhaps intractable, features of the American regime.

II

THE early vision of common schooling was embedded in republican understandings of citizenship. The most radical and egalitarian versions of republicanism, such as those of the Workingmen's parties of the 1820s and 1830s, were the most insistent on the links between public education and the rights of citizens, but their rhetoric reflected, rather than challenged, a more general cross-class agreement. To be sure, schooling for all was thought by the dominant classes to be a recipe for social order capable of withstanding the strains of capitalist industrialization and proletarianization. But virtually all Americans understood that this was a social order of citizens.

That common access to schooling was also thought to be access to common schooling, as if the relationship between the two were unproblematical, was the product of a transitional moment in the organization of urban space.

The preindustrial mercantile cities of the East Coast (Boston, New York, Philadelphia, Charleston, and other smaller centers) were jumbles without much spatial order. The social classes lived together in nonsegregated residential areas that contained many industrial and commercial workplaces. In these "walking cities" social distance between the classes was not underpinned by stark divisions in space.

Most people lived at or very near work. Many workshops were incorporated within the household. Many merchants and shopkeepers had businesses on the ground floor of their homes. Along with domestic servants employees often lived in the homes of their employers, in their own quarters. Other workers rented accommodations adjacent to their workplaces. These cities were divided into different zones of activity, such as shipping areas, and there was a degree of residential segregation dividing more from less desirable areas of living. But compared to the situation in the second half of the nineteenth century, these patterns of urban differentiation were very limited.[16]

Primary schools for all white children were founded just at the moment when this pattern was beginning to be transformed.

Firms grew too large to house their workers. Factories required space to expand. The population grew too rapidly for the older spatial system to contain its expansion. Transportation technology improved. Members of the dominant classes invested in houses on the periphery of cities in areas that were exclusively residential. Real estate investors, chasing opportunity, built tenements for the working classes, thus creating new, socially homogeneous neighborhoods.

Work, in short, began to divide from the home; residential areas began to be differentiated from factory areas; and the social classes came to live less and less with each other. Once these processes were set into motion they were reinforcing. Housing markets, differentiating areas by price and thus by the income of residents, and land-use markets, defining property values and areas as being appropriate to housing or commercial usage, in their ordinary operation began to divide the city into increasingly well defined districts.[17]

Mass public school systems were founded at the very beginning of these fundamental changes in social geography. As the morphology of cities changed in the second half of the nineteenth century and into the twentieth, the possibilities of genuinely common, cross-class, cross-ethnic schooling eroded. The confluence of industrialization, urbanization, immigration, and land-use markets created cities whose residential building blocks were neighborhoods distinguished by the income and the ethnicity of their residents.[18] Because children attended schools in their own neighborhoods, the social demography of schooling was a direct product of the distribution of the urban population in space.

Thus was the idea of the common school undercut by transformations in the organization of urban places. The divisions created by spatial growth and change were mitigated, however, by the fact that all the children in a given city attended schools that were part of a single school district in a single municipality. There was a local *politics* of education that provided a forum, as we have shown, for struggles about such critical issues as who should govern, what children should be taught, how much money should be invested, and how insulated educators should be from popular pressures. While markets divided social space and social groups, politics created a common forum of citizens. Much of this book has chronicled happenings on this ground.

This shared political forum has disappeared. The geography of the American urban system has changed in ways that have made the hegemony of the market over the public schools nearly complete. In so doing, the idea of schooling for all has been strained and its practice profoundly changed.

At the end of World War II the majority of Americans who did not live on farms lived in cities. No longer. Today the majority of people who do not live on farms reside in sprawling and complex suburban areas. This built-form rivals the great urbanization of the nineteenth century in scale. Its development has radically reshaped the spatial and political landscapes of America. Current problems and possibilities of schooling make sense only if this massive reorganization in space is understood.

The expansion and development of postwar suburbia has created brand-new regions that have become increasingly independent of adjacent central cities. More and more the new suburbs have been penetrated by national, rather than local, economic institutions. Their massive consumer markets are controlled largely by national retail chains, grouped at strips alongside major highways. Fast-food restaurants, gas stations, supermarkets, automobile dealerships, and massive department stores integrated into the national corporate economy and new, often mammoth factories and company headquarters are the dominant economic institutions. Spread out in a low-density sprawl, these regions have an economic role quite different from the traditional functions of bedroom communities.[19]

The spatial reorganization of metropolitan areas in the postwar years reflects basic changes in the national political economy in an era of unprecedented economic growth and innovation. Before World War II least-cost location considerations impelled most firms that expanded to do so within established urban areas. With the decline in the relative costs of transportation, especially after the construction of the federally funded interstate highway system, firms were much freer to locate at some distance from old manufacturing centers. Overall the result has been somewhat paradoxical: there has been a centralization and concentration of economic activity in the largest metropolitan areas, but within those regions there has been a decentralization and deconcentration of economic activity.

The underside of this growth and development has been disinvestment from older central cities, population loss, and demographic change. Norman and Susan Fainstein have summarized much research in the literature this way:

> Cities became poorer and blacker, albeit smaller, as middle and working class whites moved out to be replaced by minority households. Accompanying these well-known social changes was the relative economic decline of [central cities] unable to replace obsolete industries and the associated disinvestment from their built environments. On the whole, older American cities became vehicles for the encapsulation of minority groups and low-income whites in obsolete sectors of the economy and deteriorating physical environments.[20]

In the past two decades central-city employment and income have declined dramatically in relationship to those in surrounding suburban areas. One economist has estimated that whereas 56 percent of metropolitan-area jobs were located in central cities in 1962, that figure had declined to under 40 percent by the early 1980s.[21]

The pace and dimensions of the massive shifts in the political economies, populations, and spatial organization of metropolitan areas would not have been possible without key policies of the federal government. Tax deductions for homeowners, federal sponsorship of secondary mortgage markets, and, most important, the mortgage guarantee programs operated by the Federal Housing Administration have subsidized and protected the boom in suburban housing construction. Massive highway construction likewise has been a crucial element. By permitting a shift from rail to automobile transportation it has opened up formerly inaccessible property to housing, commercial, and industrial uses.

Within the suburbs, however, the role of local government has been a minor one. There, policies of government established a framework for various markets to operate, but within that frame-work housing and land-use markets have been free to operate with far greater freedom than in central cities.

The physical form of modern suburban America has been shaped by market processes operating relatively unconstrained by government and public planning. Much as in the cities of the early industrial revolution, when the dictates and imperatives of capital shaped city space, so in the suburbs land-use patterns are the products of market optimization. Government has been the helpmate of the market, but "the overall land-use pattern result-ing from this process is one that would broadly occur if there were no zoning at all." Investors, developers, speculators, bank-ers, politicians, and planners have joined together to make what appears to be an unplanned environment, but one disciplined by markets and profits.[22]

Suburban markets overwhelm politics in the shaping of the built-form. To be sure, suburban governments have very large land-use planning agencies, but those agencies utterly lack politi-cal power or sanction. As a result, their hortatory statements and glossy plans perform symbolic functions. The only meaningful planning is that of zoning in the hands of local politicians. But the zoning powers of these officials, who direct very weak town-ship governments to which residents usually pay little attention, are only rarely used to alter the plans of private developers. After all, housing development is the key to the local tax base. It has also proved the means for politicians and their political parties to profit handsomely, sometimes corruptly, from regional growth. Together, "the local political party and those businessmen in-volved in submetropolitan growth tend to merge into something of a land development corporation."[23]

The result of this process is easy to see: the creation of massive residential and commercial areas lacking in history, communal foci, and other boundaries. Land-use patterns in these spaces even more rigidly divide work and off-work sections from each other than has been the case in central cities; and, further, these new spaces starkly segment living and shopping quarters. Each function is in its own, clearly demarcated place.

So, too, with social groups. Residential areas in the suburbs are usually built by developers who create communities—single-family houses, streets, roads, sewers, and other necessary infrastructure—all at once. Built in tracts, houses in a given area are priced in the same range and marketed to the same clientele. Class in Max Weber's sense of the term, connoting shared capacity to consume in the marketplace and shared styles of life, dominates the selection and distribution of housing. Families who purchase homes at the same time purchase homogeneous residential communities, which are tailored to and protected by existing zoning arrangements. To buy a house is to purchase a community identity, social standing, neighbors with similar incomes and tastes, and a neighborhood all at once.

The differences between more and less affluent areas are defined by this process of building and marketing real estate. Homogeneous, developed communities are the building blocks of suburbia. They take the processes of segregation common to cities to uncontradicted extremes. Within a given suburban area such heterogeneity as exists is created by variations in zoning requirements over a large area. Areas with small plots of land are geared to populations rather different from those requiring one or more acres per house. Over time, open space and public amenities are replaced by this patchwork of microcommunities, planned by developers within the zoning codes and purchased by people seeking a particular style of life.

As a result of the combination of development and defensive zoning, residential segregation ineluctably increases. The desire to protect property values (the family's investment in a house, in most cases, is the most significant one it will ever make) joins the interests of homeowners to those of politicians who want to guarantee the stability of their constituencies and harness suburban development to political support.

In the big city, diversity in the social character, uses, and organization of space is tempered by shared government and a politics of the city as a whole. In the suburbs, political fragmentation overlaps social segregation. Lacking serious metropolitan or regional governments, political authority tends to be used to reinforce regional differentiation and segregation. The divisions between political communities, magnified by the desire to protect

favorable property values, create a much more complex and fragmented social order than the old-fashioned portrait of a homogeneous middle-class suburbia.

The most basic substate unit of government is the county. In
some states, counties are subdivided into townships, and in all
they are subdivided again into municipalities (villages, towns,
cities), which are incorporated and whose terms of activity are
defined by charter from the state. In addition, there are ad hoc
special districts, the most common of which are school districts.
There are more than eighty thousand units of local government
in the United States, many of them very small.

Because of the massive suburbanization of America there is
currently a great disparity between the political boundaries of
central cities and the extent of the metropolitan area of which
they are the center. The separate incorporation of suburban
municipalities has brought them many benefits, such as the exclusion of unwanted neighbors through exclusionary zoning,
control over land use, and the ability to limit the character of local
services. Although they have very great fiscal resources, they are
not used to contribute to the management of central-city problems, nor are they utilized in great measure for government services other than education. City residents pay far more of their
income in local taxes than do suburbanites. "These data," an
observant urban geographer has noted, "suggest very strongly
that the political geography of the American metropolitan area is
structured to place the greatest burden on those least able to
pay."[24]

The interaction between these factors has produced an exclusionary politics of education characterized by wide fiscal disparities between districts and by new patterns of segregation by race,
class, and ethnicity. Schools continue to be subject in a formal
way to public oversight. The politics of education, however, has
been overtaken as a result of weak and fragmented governments
as a determining factor by private housing markets protected by
defensive zoning. The neighborhood basis of schooling has long
challenged the idea of the common school. But the combination
of residential segregation and the fragmentation of political
boundaries is unprecedented.

III

UNLESS we talk about these issues and their consequences for education we shall be doomed to miss the point that the stark inequalities in American education that are now so deeply embedded in social geography and in the political economy raise new and fundamental questions about access and citizenship. Issues that in different form had long seemed resolved for the great majority of Americans now constitute the very core of meaningful conversation about public education.[25]

The critics of American education in the 1960s and in the 1980s have shared not only the terms of conversation—equality versus standards—but also, in spite of their laments for the present state of schooling, a persistent optimism about the possibilities of public education. School as the repository of hopes for a more equal social order was the constitutive idea of Charles Silberman's and David Rogers's analyses and proposals. But even the more skeptical and disenchanted recent treatments by Diane Ravitch and the group led by David Tyack maintain this faith. Ravitch reiterates the "naive" American view that "to believe in education is to believe in the future, to believe in what may be accomplished through the disciplined use of intelligence, allied with cooperation and good will." Tyack and his colleagues remind us that "American public education has survived hard times before, and an alternative future seems at least as plausible as one painted in . . . grim colors."[26]

We are less sanguine. Or, more precisely, we find it hard to be hopeful about the future of public education so long as the dialogue about it remains stuck between the poles of equality and standards. In light of major changes in American federalism and the social organization of space this debate is a superficial one. It defines a conversation that produces false dichotomies and much pain.

"Educational policy of a period," R. H. Tawney wrote on the eve of World War I, "reflects its conceptions of human society and of the proper object of human endeavor." The differentiation of education according to class, he argued, reveals a coarseness of spirit:

> Stripped of its decent draperies of convention, what it means is that there is a class of masters whose right it is to enter . . . on the knowledge which is the inheritance of the race, and a class of servants whose hands should be taught to labour but whose eyes should be on the furrow which is watered with their sweat, whose virtue is contentment, and whose ignorance is the safety of the . . . powers by whom their iron world is ruled.[27]

Seven decades later, on this side of the Atlantic, these words may seem outmoded. But in the face of the new inequalities of American society they remain a pertinent call to reason and to commitment.

Various postwar European social democratic attempts to reform education to minimize social differences, especially in Britain and Sweden, have revealed powerful tensions between the alleviation of ignorance and economic modernization; between equality as end and as means; between political citizenship and social inequalities; and between education as an adjustment to the capitalist social order or as a vehicle to transform it.[28] The American experience of the past two decades—one of the domestication of class combined with the exhaustion of anything like a social democratic reform impulse—has been one in which these questions have been put aside just at the moment when they have been needed most. Must we compose an elegy for schooling for all? Or shall we fight for this vision and, in so doing, broaden the possibilities of American politics and society?

NOTES

Chapter 1

1. Andrew Hacker, "The Schools Flunk Out," *New York Review of Books,* 12 April 1984, pp. 35–40; David Tyack, Robert Lowe, and Elisabeth Hansot, *Public Schools in Hard Times: The Great Depression and Recent Years* (Cambridge: Harvard University Press, 1984); Diane Ravitch, *The Troubled Crusade: American Education, 1945–1980* (New York: Basic Books, 1983); Sara Lawrence Lightfoot, *The Good High School: Portraits of Character and Culture* (New York: Basic Books, 1983); James S. Coleman, Thomas Hoffer, and Sally Kilgore, *High School Achievement: Public, Catholic, and Private Schools Compared* (New York: Basic Books, 1982); The National Commission on Excellence in Education, *A Nation at Risk: The Imperative for Educational Reform* (Washington, D.C.: U.S. Government Printing Office, 1983); Task Force on Education for Economic Growth, *Action for Excellence* (Washington, D.C.: Education Commission of the States, 1983).

2. Marvin Lazerson, "Revisionism and American Educational History," *Harvard Educational Review* 43 (1973): 269–83.

3. Lawrence A. Cremin, *Traditions of American Education* (New York: Basic Books, 1977), 37.

4. Harold L. Wilensky, *The Welfare State and Equality: Structural and Ideological Roots of Public Expenditures.* (Berkeley: University of California Press, 1975), 3–7.

5. R. H. Tawney, *The British Labor Movement* (New Haven: Yale University Press, 1925), 124.

6. Before opinion is registered, opinion must be formed. What is evident today, if one compares the practical workings of democracy with the anticipations of it formed by its earlier pioneers, is that it is precisely in the weakness of the means by which men are prepared to form an intelligent opinion, in the liability of the individual to be overwhelmed by mass suggestions which he has not learned to criticise, in his reluctance to undertake on his own account the painful process of analysis, and in the ease with which, as a consequence, he succumbs to the great modern art of organizing delusion through the press, that one capital weakness of our society is to

be found . . . . If what is desired is a community where the average citizen is healthy, alert, and responsible, and is immune to the grosser illusions of a self-complacent patriotism, then these qualities can only be cultivated by education. (Tawney, *British Labor Movement,* 125–26)

7. Ibid., 122.

8. Ibid., 121, 122.

9. Ibid., 122.

10. David Tyack, *The One Best System: A History of American Urban Education* (Cambridge: Harvard University Press, 1974), 9.

11. Jean Floud and A. H. Halsey, "Introduction," in *Education, Economy, and Society: A Reader in the Sociology of Education,* ed. A. H. Halsey, Jean Floud, and C. Arnold Anderson (New York: Free Press, 1961), 1.

12. An excellent review of these debates may be found in Jerome Karabel and A. H. Halsey, "Educational Research: A Review and an Interpretation," in *Power and Ideology in Education,* ed. Jerome Karabel and A. H. Halsey (New York: Oxford University Press, 1977).

13. Samuel Bowles and Herbert Gintis, *Schooling in Capitalist America* (New York: Basic Books, 1976).

14. Henry C. Link, *Education and Industry* (New York: Macmillan, 1923), 1; National Industrial Conference Board, *Public Schools and the Worker in New York* (New York: NICB, 1928), v.

15. Frank Tracy Carlton, *Economic Influences upon Educational Progress in the United States, 1820–1850* (New York: Columbia University Press, 1965); Diane Ravitch, *The Great School Wars: New York City, 1805–1973* (New York: Basic Books, 1973); Joel Spring, *Education and the Rise of the Corporate State* (Boston: Beacon, 1972); and Clarence Karier, Paul Violas, and Joel Spring, *Roots of Crisis: American Education in the Twentieth Century* (Chicago: Rand McNally, 1973).

16. For the classic statement of the "progressive" tradition, see E. P. Cubberley, *The History of Education* (Boston: Houghton Mifflin, 1920); see also Lawrence A. Cremin, *The Transformation of the American School: Progressivism in American Education* (New York: Alfred A. Knopf, 1961). One of the first, and best, of the "revisionist" accounts is Michael Katz, *The Irony of Early School Reform: Educational Innovation in Mid-Nineteenth Century Massachusetts* (Boston: Beacon, 1968). A contentious and far too dismissive review of this scholarly corpus is Diane Ravitch, *The Revisionists Revisited: A Critique of the Radical Attack on the Schools* (New York: Basic Books, 1978).

17. The book that most succeeds in overcoming the traditional conversation is Julia Wrigley, *Class Politics and Public Schools, Chicago, 1900–1950* (New Brunswick, N.J.: Rutgers University Press, 1982).

18. Lawrence A. Cremin, *Traditions of American Education* (New York: Basic Books, 1977), 127.

19. Bowles and Gintis, *Schooling in Capitalist America,* xvii.

20. Some social scientists reject functional accounts of the kind presented by Bowles and Gintis as constituting lazy social science because they fail to specify mechanisms of cause and effect. Such criticisms miss the point that a proposed functional explanation is no more, but also no less, than a plausible statement about social reality. It follows that such explanations are only a start. They suggest that we need theories to explain why and how functional relationships like the one Bowles and Gintis propose exists between schooling and capitalism actually work. In this light their claim that American capitalism produced public education and that, in turn, schooling has helped to underpin the capitalist system should be treated as an opportunity to develop explanations of how these connections might actually work.

For discussions of functionalism, see Arthur L. Stinchcombe, *Constructing Social Theories* (New York: Harcourt, Brace and World, 1968); Jon Elster, *Ulysses and the Sirens* (New York: Cambridge University Press, 1979); and G. A. Cohen, *Karl Marx's Theory of History: A Defence* (Princeton, N.J.: Princeton University Press, 1978).

21. Bowles and Gintis, *Schooling in Capitalist America,* 178 (italics added).

22. Ibid., 131 (italics added).

23. Ibid., 130.

24. Ibid., 224.

25. Ibid., 37 (italics added).

26. Ibid., 49.

27. Ibid., 238.

28. Ibid., 223–31; Carlton, *Economic Influences.*

29. Bowles and Gintis, *Schooling in Capitalist America,* 228.

30. See Philip R. V. Curoe, *Educational Attitudes and Policies of Organized Labor in the United States* (New York: Teachers College, 1926); and Rush Welter, *Popular Education and Democratic Thought in America* (New York: Columbia University Press, 1962).

31. Bowles and Gintis, *Schooling in Capitalist America,* 10.

32. This discussion is taken up more fully in chapter 2. Also see Ira Katznelson, *City Trenches: Urban Politics and the Patterning of Class in the United States* (New York: Pantheon, 1981), especially chap. 3.

33. Bowles and Gintis, *Schooling in Capitalist America,* 230.

Chapter 2

1. The early lead that the United States took in primary education was maintained in secondary and higher education. Although secondary school enrollment rates rarely exceeded 15 percent in western Europe in the 1930s, they had reached 70 percent in the United States. Today, over 50 percent of American high school graduates continue with their schooling, roughly three times the percentage of the same group in the major OECD countries. See John E. Craig and Norman Spear, "The Diffusion of Schooling in Nineteenth Century Europe: Toward a Model," paper presented at the annual meeting of the Social Science History Association, November 1978; see also John E. Craig, "The Expansion of Education," *Review of Research in Education* 9 (1981): 151–213.

The early founding of public schools in the United States contrasts starkly with the late development of other social policies. Not until the New Deal did the United States begin to create the kinds of social services that by then were common in much of western Europe. Today the United States is still at the bottom of comparative rankings of welfare state expenditures. It also has a relatively underdeveloped governmental capacity to shape and modify market forces by planning and by direct control of industry. See Ira Katznelson, "Considerations on Social Democracy in the United States," *Comparative Politics* 11 (October 1978): 77–99.

In tackling the question of the early enthusiasm for state schooling in the United States one must be cautious to avoid conflating the separate issues of the founding and the subsequent expansion of public education. The causes that brought public education into being may not be the same as those that later sustained its development.

2. The early educational histories of Chicago and San Francisco exhibit the three puzzles of early timing, local genesis, and cross-class support. In the formative years of both cities, when their populations were small (each had approximately fifty thousand residents in 1850) and when they faced considerable fiscal uncertainties owing to the risks associated with new urban growth and crises in the economy (1837 and 1857 were years of national economic crisis), the two cities founded public schools.

Chicago's schools received public funding even before the incorporation of the city. The Charter of 1837 and the Amendment of 1839 provided for the governance of public schools and stated that all white children would be able to attend. In San Francisco, legislation providing for free public education was enacted in 1851. Education, in short, was understood from the outset to be a legitimate function of government. Schooling would be public and would provide a common experience for primary-age white children of all social classes and ethnic and religious groups.

The founding of public schools in Chicago and San Francisco reflected the distinctive traits of American federalism. In both cities, school systems had to be created by *local* decision. In Chicago and San Francisco, moreover, the territorially based distribution of political authority was given expression in the organization of the school systems. Chicago's board of education tied governance to localities by selecting members by ward. San Francisco also emphasized localism, within a more centralized school administration, by dividing the city into eight and later twelve wards with a school director elected from each. Although these principles of organization were later challenged by reformers who sought to institutionalize at-large selection procedures for the boards of education, the ward principle remained the basic alternative model, which corresponded with the more general district organization of urban politics.

Working-class families in Chicago and San Francisco tried hard to get their children into the new schools that had been created with cross-class support. Long waiting lists were common. In his 1863 report to the legislature, San Francisco's Superintendent of Public Instruction estimated that at least 1,000 additional children would enter the public schools if there were room. Three years later he observed, "During the last year and the early part of the present, many parents were becoming discouraged from making further efforts to gain accommodation for their children and were transferring their patronage and support to private instead of Public schools." The public schools of Chicago were also unable to welcome all of the children who wanted to attend. Throughout the founding period of San Francisco's schools, school reports reiterated concern about overcrowding and the lack of school facilities. In 1857 the superintendent warned that the school system was not meeting its obligations:

> Our city ordinances require that free instruction be provided for *all* the children residing within the limits of the city, who are over the age of five years, and who desire to attend public schools; and yet there has been no time during the past two years when the number attending schools would not have been greatly increased if suitable provision could have been found to receive them. (Kathleen Gille, "The Founding Period of Chicago's Public Schools" [unpublished MS, November 1980], 6)

The situation in 1857 was probably no worse than it had been in the entire period before the Civil War. A sense of the extent of overcrowding can be gathered from a description of the first school building in the city. It was two stories high and measured sixty by eighty feet. Within three years of its opening it was forced to hold eight hundred children. During the Civil War the school population of Chicago nearly doubled, but school construction came to a halt. Although a new building program was embarked on after the war, overcrowding remained a serious problem. In 1867 the president of the board bemoaned the fact that some classrooms held seventy or eighty pupils. To deal with overcrowding at this time the principals were instructed to examine all new applicants for the lower divisions of the schools and place their names on waiting lists.

3. Lawrence A. Cremin, *American Education: The National Experience, 1783–1876* (New York: Harper & Row, 1980), ix. This volume is the second of a trilogy. The first volume covers the colonial period; the third, yet unpublished, will tell the story of the past century. An overview of the whole project may be found in Lawrence A. Cremin, *Traditions of American Education* (New York: Basic Books, 1977).

Cremin follows in the tradition of Emile Durkheim, the only major social theorist of the late nineteenth and early twentieth centuries to examine the place of education in society systematically. Durkheim linked education to morality and its reproduction. The aim of education was to inculcate within individuals the "system of ideas, sentiments, and practices which express in us . . . the group or different groups of which we are a part; these are religious beliefs, moral beliefs and practices, national or occupational traditions, collective opinions of every kind." (Emile Durkheim, *Education et Sociologie* [Paris: Alcan, 1922], 119–20; cited in Steven Lukes, *Emile Durkheim: His Life and Work* [New York: Harper & Row, 1972], 111).

Cremin's and Durkheim's approaches share an emphasis on motivation and volition and, perhaps more important, an understanding that education as a process is comprehensible only in a macrosocial context. The grand volumes of Cremin's *American Education,* albeit stressing the role of ideas and the influence of key individual thinkers, provide a rich example of an attempt to locate education generally, and state schooling in particular, in a vast network of organizations, cultures, and practices. Implicit is the idea, found also in Durkheim, that education reflects, sustains, and only modestly alters the structure of society as a whole. Further, the determination of education is acknowledged to be complex, reflecting both society's generalized self-conception, its economic, political, and social goals, and the diversity of milieus in society. In this way the study of schooling holds up a mirror to society, both as the society's values say it is and wish it to be and as society is actually experienced and lived.

4. Cremin, *American Education,* vol. 1, 192–93.

5. Geraldine Murphy, "Massachusetts Bay Colony: The Role of Government in Education" (Ph.D. diss., Radcliffe College, 1960).

6. Cremin, *American Education,* vol. 1, 538.

7. An exceptionally important and controversial discussion of these themes may be found in Carl E. Kaestle and Maris A. Vinovskis, *Education and Social Change in Nineteenth Century Massachusetts* (Cambridge: Cambridge University Press, 1980).

8. Cremin, *American Education,* vol. 2, 180. For an influential discussion of the shift from private to state-sponsored schooling, see also Albert Fishlow, "Levels of Nineteenth-Century American Investment in Education," *Journal of Economic History* 26 (1966): 418–36.

9. Samuel E. Bowles and Herbert Gintis, *Schooling in Capitalist America* (New York: Basic Books, 1976); Michael B. Katz, *The Irony of Early School Reform* (Cambridge: Harvard University Press, 1968).

The story of how schooling became institutionalized in Chicago at mid-century is in part a tale of the direct impact of New England and middle Atlantic educators in these new cities. After the Blackhawk Wars of 1831–32, migration patterns into northern Illinois altered. Before the Indians were pushed across the Mississippi and before the Great Lakes became navigable, white settlement was restricted mainly to southern Illinois. In the 1830s, growing numbers of settlers from New England and New York began to arrive in Chicago, and the town grew rapidly from 200 residents in 1833 to more than 4,100 in 1837. The first tuition schools in Chicago were created by Granville Sproat of Boston and Eliza Chappell of New York City (who were among the first to secure a public subsidy for children unable to pay). The key amendments to the city charter concerned with school finance in the late 1830s were written by J. Young Scammon of Maine. The first agent of the city's school fund was from Connecticut; and the city's first mayors and the leaders of the state educational convention of 1846 were all from the East.

In the mid-1850s, when school officials were seeking a method to bring order to the rapidly growing system of public schools, they turned to a solution that had been adopted in the East: establishing the post of superintendent of schools. They hired John Dore from the Boylston Street School in Boston, who served for two years. He was replaced by William Harvey Wells, former editor of *The Massachusetts Teacher,* president of the Massachusetts state teachers' association, and head of a public school in Westfield, Massachusetts.

San Francisco's school system was likewise founded by educators from the East. There the central figure was John Swett, a native of New Hampshire who had taught for six years in his home state and in Massachusetts before moving to California. James Denman, another prominent figure in the Bay Area's schools, was from New York. One of the earliest teachers in the system, John Pelton, came from Massachusetts, where he had been the principal of the Phillips Free School at Andover. Further, as in Chicago, the great majority of school board members were from New England and New York.

10. In 1859 then superintendent Denman noted in his annual report, "We have been favored in the establishment of our schools with the models of the Boston and New York schools." The 1865 superintendent's Report noted that, "Recognizing the superior excellence of schools of Boston and Chicago, the Board has labored to make schools exhibit the merits of the models." At that time the schools were explicitly following the curriculum of Chicago's public education system.

11. Perhaps the best study of the founding of the Chicago school system is still Hannah B. Clark, *The Public Schools of Chicago* (Chicago: University of Chicago Press, 1897). The first twenty-five pages offer a concise summary of the founding period with particular emphasis on comparing Chicago to school systems in the eastern states. Other useful sources include J. Currey Seymour, *Chicago: Its History and Its Builders* (Chicago: S. J. Clarke, 1912), especially 296–98; Henry E. Dewey, "The Development of Public School Administration in Chicago" (Ph.D. diss., The University of Chicago, 1937); and Mary Herrick, *The Chicago Schools: A Social and Political History* (Beverly Hills, Calif.: Sage, 1971). It is also instructive to read the annual superintendent's reports for the founding era.

12. See Herrick, *Chicago Schools,* 23–25; Clark, *Public Schools,* 12, 27; and Dewey, "Public School Administration," 92.

13. Cited in Gille, "Founding Period."

14. The council appointed a board of inspectors to supervise school administration. Each school district elected three trustees, who reported to the inspectors and who hired teachers and provided for school accommodations. School taxes were levied by the vote of citizens in each school district. These tax funds complemented the school land fund controlled by a Commissioner of Common School Lands.

15. Significant treatments of the founding of the schools of San Francisco include Victor Shradar, "Ethnic Politics, Religion, and the Public Schools of San Francisco, 1849–1933" (Ph.D. diss., Stanford University, June 1974); Miriam Mead Hawley, "Schools for Social Order: Public Education as an Aspect of San Francisco's Urbanization and Industrialization Processes" (M.A. thesis, San Francisco State College, June 1971); and Mildred Purnel Martin, "City Government in San Francisco: A Half Century of Charter Development" (M.A. thesis, University of California, Berkeley, April 1911).

16. Clark, *Public Schools,* 18.

17. Rush Welter, *Popular Education and Democratic Thought in America* (New York: Columbia University Press, 1962), 104.

18. James W. Sanders, "The Education of Chicago Catholics: An Urban History" (Ph.D. diss., The University of Chicago, 1970), 33–38.

19. Cited in Sanders, "An Urban History," 22.

20. Bessie Louise Pierce, *A History of Chicago,* vol. 2 (New York: Alfred A. Knopf, 1957), 379.

21. Cited in Sanders, "An Urban History," 24–25.

22. Herrick, *Chicago Schools,* 61.

23. Lee Steven Dolson, "The Administration of the San Francisco Public Schools, 1847–1947" (Ph.D. diss., University of California, Berkeley, 1967), 55; and John Swett, *History of the Public School System in California* (Berkeley: Bancroft Library Archives, University of California, 1872), 116.

24. An editorial on the common school appearing in the official newspaper of the archdiocese, *The Monitor,* affirmed "that the state should place primary education within

the reach of all its citizens and that the majority of schools should be public or under the supervision of the State, we believe to be desirable and we consider that if reasonable measures be taken to respect the religious and moral convictions of parents, the State cannot fairly be charged with infringing on their rights by doing so." At the same time, the editorial argued that "it is an injustice to those Catholics, Methodists, or Episcopalians, who, through religious convictions, refuse to make use of the public schools, to refuse help to those institutions which alone they can use—thus imposing on them a double tax for the education of their children" (*The Monitor,* 25 January 1868).

25. R. A. Burchell, *The San Francisco Irish, 1848–1880* (Berkeley: University of California Press, 1980), 165.

26. The discussion that follows is indebted to two first-rate studies, currently in press, by Mary Jo Maynes, who has shared them with us in manuscript draft: *Schooling and Social History: Recent Interpretations of the Expansion of Elementary Schooling in Western Europe in the Eighteenth and Nineteenth Centuries;* and *Schooling for the People: Comparative Local Studies of Schooling History in France and Germany, 1750–1850.*

27. Maynes, *Schooling and Social History* (in draft).

28. Ibid.

29. Ibid.

30. A lucid discussion of these issues may be found in Marzio Barbagli, *Education for Unemployment: Politics, Labor Markets, and the School System—Italy, 1859–1973* (New York: Columbia University Press, 1982).

31. See Michalina Vaughn and Margaret Scotford Archer, *Social Conflict and Educational Change in England and France, 1789–1848* (Cambridge, Mass.: Cambridge University Press, 1971).

32. Bowles and Gintis, *Schooling in Capitalist America,* 151, 157, 158.

33. Ibid., 160–64.

34. Ibid., 178.

35. Robert Dreeben, "American Schooling: Patterns and Processes of Stability and Change," in *Stability and Social Change,* ed. Bernard Barber and Alex Inkeles (Boston: Little, Brown, 1971), 117.

36. Alexander James Field, "Economic and Demographic Determinants of Educational Commitment: Massachusetts, 1855," *Journal of Economic History* 39 (June 1979): 453–54; and Kaestle and Vinovskis, *Education and Social Change,* 167.

37. Kaestle and Vinovskis, *Education and Social Change,* 33–42.

38. Ibid., 42.

39. Field, "Educational Commitment," 448.

40. Ibid., 454.

41. Ira Katznelson, *City Trenches: Urban Politics and the Patterning of Class in the United States* (New York: Pantheon, 1981), 44.

42. David Tyack, "Ways of Seeing: An Essay on the History of Compulsory Schooling," *Harvard Educational Review* 46 (August 1976): 367.

43. See R. Freeman Butts, "Public Education and Political Community," *History of Education Quarterly* 14 (1974): 165–84; and Amy Bridges, *A City in the Republic: Antebellum New York and the Origins of Machine Politics* (New York: Cambridge University Press, 1984).

44. J. C. Dore, *First Annual Report of the Superintendent* (Chicago: Chicago Public Schools, 1854), 14–15.

45. John Swett, *A History of the Public School System of California* (San Francisco: A. L. Bancroft, 1876), 39, 46. The first part of the citation refers to the 1863 Report of the Superintendent and the second to the 1864–65 Biennial Report of the State Superintendent of Public Instruction, both of which were roles filled by Swett.

46. Relevant discussions may be found in Anthony Davies Edwards, *Language in Culture and Class* (London: Heinemann Educational Books, 1976); Carl F. Kaestle, "Conflict and Consensus Revisited: Notes toward a Reinterpretation of American Educational His-

tory," *Harvard Educational Review* 46 (August 1976): 390–96; and Katznelson, *City Trenches,* chap. 3.

47. Frank Tracy Carlton, *History and Problems of Organized Labor* (Boston: D. C. Heath, 1911), 135. Elsewhere, Carlton's formulation was more modest: "The workingmen of the country were very much alive to the benefits of a system of public schools, and . . . their influence was an important factor in hastening the development of the system" (Carlton, *Economic Influences upon Educational Progress in the United States, 1820–1850* [New York: Teachers College Press, 1965], 92–93).

48. Bridges provides a useful summary discussion in *A City in the Republic.*

49. Philip R. V. Curoe, *Educational Attitudes and Policies of Organized Labor in the United States* (New York: Teachers College Press, 1926), 190–91. See also Sidney L. Jackson, *America's Struggle for Free Schools: Social Tension and Education in New England and New York, 1827–1842* (Washington, D.C.: American Council on Public Affairs, 1941).

50. Katznelson, *City Trenches,* 64.

51. Ibid., chap. 3.

52. Thomas W. Laquer, "Working Class Demand and the Growth of English Elementary Education," in *Schooling and Society: Studies in the History of Education,* ed. Lawrence Stone (Baltimore: Johns Hopkins University Press, 1976), 195. See also J. S. Hurt, *Elementary Schooling and the Working Classes, 1860–1918* (London: Routledge and Kegan Paul, 1979).

53. Herrick, *Chicago Schools,* 61; Chicago Public Schools, *Annual Report of the Superintendent* (Chicago: City of Chicago, 1866, 1867); and Kathleen Gille, "Chicago Public School Curriculum and the Teaching of German" (unpublished MS, December 1980).

54. City of San Francisco, *Annual Report of the Superintendent* (San Francisco: San Francisco Public Schools, 1867); Hawley, "Schools for Social Order," 52–53; and Dolson, "San Francisco Public Schools," 192.

55. City of San Francisco, *Annual Report of the Superintendent* (San Francisco: San Francisco Public Schools, 1858, 1864).

56. This discussion is drawn from Kathleen Gille, "High Schools in Chicago in the Late 1800's" (unpublished MS, October 1980).

Chapter 3

1. Although high schools had been established in both cities soon after the founding of the school systems, enrollment figures indicate that only a select few received secondary education. Of the fourteen- to seventeen-year-olds in Chicago's high school population in the 1890s only 6 percent had been of public school students. No more than 4 percent of public school students in San Francisco attended high school at any point in the nineteenth century. High schools expanded significantly after 1900, but it was not until 1940 that they became mass institutions. See Chicago Board of Education, *Annual Reports,* 1870, 1895; and Miriam Mead Hawley, "Schools for Social Order: Public Education as an Aspect of San Francisco's Urbanization Process" (M.A. thesis, San Francisco State College, 1971).

2. See Ira Katznelson, *City Trenches: Urban Politics and the Patterning of Class in the United States,* (New York: Pantheon, 1981), chap. 3.

3. Jules Tygiel, "Workingmen in San Francisco, 1880–1901" (Ph.D. diss., University of California, Los Angeles, 1977), 233, 286.

4. Thomas L. Philpott, *The Slum and the Ghetto: Neighborhood Deterioration and Middle-Class*

Reform, Chicago, 1880–1930 (New York: Oxford University Press, 1978), 6–41. Spatial distinctions between work and home in Chicago were less sharp than in San Francisco. The belt of immigrant workers that surrounded Chicago's core was also the site of factories, warehouses, railroad yards, and stores. Chicago's failure to develop more spatial functional specificity was due to the much greater immigration that the city attracted. Although the earliest immigrants gradually left for the newer outlying sections of the city, newcomers immediately replaced them, so that the mixture of land uses that had characterized the earlier period persisted to a greater extent than in San Francisco, where immigration tapered off in the 1880s. In both cities, however, the growth of new residence communities and the development of at least some functional specificity in older areas attested to the emergence of a qualitatively different American city.

5. In San Francisco, the Union Labor Party, an organization aiming to become the party of labor, was formed in 1901. Although it did not initially attract union support, within several years the ULP did become a major political vehicle for labor, particularly for the Building Trades Council and its leader P. H. McCarthy. See Michael Kazin, "Barons of Labor: The San Francisco Building Trades, 1896–1922" (Ph.D. diss., Stanford University, 1983), especially chap. 7, and Edward J. Rowell, "The Union Labor Party of San Francisco, 1901–1911" (Ph.D. diss., University of California, Berkeley, 1938).

6. The best source on trade union history in San Francisco during this period is Ira Cross, *A History of the Labor Movement in California* (Berkeley: University of California Press, 1935). Peter Varcados, "Labor and Politics in San Francisco, 1880–1892" (Ph.D. diss., University of California, Berkeley, 1968), is also helpful, as is Jules Tygiel, "Workingmen in San Francisco, 1880–1901." For the development of the San Francisco Labor Council see Robert Verner Ohlson, "The History of the San Francisco Labor Council" (M.A. thesis, University of California, Berkeley, 1938), 4–10. Kazin, "Barons of Labor," 44, 321, discusses the early years of the Building Trades Council. The politics of the late 1870s is discussed in Ralph Krauer, "The Workingmen's Party of California," *Pacific Historical Review* 13 (1944): 279–91. For an analysis of politics during the 1880s see William A. Bullough, *The Blind Boss and His City: Christopher Augustine Buckley and Nineteenth-Century San Francisco,* (Berkeley: University of California Press, 1980); and Alexander B. Callow, Jr., "San Francisco's Blind Boss," *Pacific Historical Review* 25 (1956): 261–79. Steven P. Erie, "The Development of Class and Ethnic Politics in San Francisco, 1870–1910: A Critique of the Pluralist Interpretation" (Ph.D. diss., University of California, Los Angeles, 1975), contains useful information on the characteristics of the workforce as well as trade unions and political parties.

7. Claudins O. Johnson, *Carter Henry Harrison I: Political Leader* (Chicago: University of Chicago Press, 1928), 189.

8. The trade union movement in late-nineteenth-century Chicago is analyzed in several sources. David M. Behen, "The Chicago Labor Movement, 1870–1896: Its Philosophical Bases" (Ph.D. diss., University of Chicago, 1953), stresses the ideological aspects of labor activism. Jack Bizjack, "The Trade and Labor Assembly of Chicago, Illinois" (M.A. thesis, The University of Chicago, 1969), is a useful discussion of trade unions. David J. Hogan, "Capitalism and Schooling: A History of the Political Economy of Education in Chicago, 1880–1930," (Ph.D. diss., University of Illinois, 1978), contains information on the characteristics of the work force and some background on labor organizations. The politics of the period is best treated in Bessie L. Pierce, *A History of Chicago,* vol. 3 (New York: Alfred A. Knopf, 1957), which also has chapters on the labor movement. Claudins O. Johnson, *Carter Henry Harrison I: Political Leader* (Chicago: The University of Chicago Press, 1928), is the most important source on politics in the 1880s.

9. Peter De Boer, "A History of the Early Compulsory School Attendance Legislation in Illinois" (Ph.D. diss., University of Chicago, 1968), 38.

10. Quoted in Edith Abbot, *Truancy and Non-Attendance in Chicago's Schools* (Chicago: University of Chicago Press, 1917), 85.

11. *The Plebeian,* 25 July 1871.

12. Quoted in John Swett, *History of the Public School System in California* (San Francisco: A. L. Bancroft, 1876), 64.

13. California Superintendent's Report, 1871, 92.

14. *The Monitor,* 2 December 1871.

15. *The Plebeian,* 4 August 1871; *The People's Journal,* 11 March 1871.

16. David Hogan, "Capitalism and Schooling: The Political Economy of Public Education in Chicago, 1880–1930," 207.

17. Quoted in Liz Borowitz, "Compulsory Attendance Legislation in Illinois, 1889–1893" (Paper, University of Chicago, 1979) 4.

18. Peter De Boer, "A History of the Early Compulsory School Attendance Legislation in Illinois," 300–301, 320–21, 344–46.

19. Abbott, *Truancy and Non-Attendance in Chicago's Schools,* 440–46.

20. San Francisco Superintendent of Schools, *Annual Report,* 1878.

21. Steven Philip Erie, "The Development of Class and Ethnic Politics in San Francisco, 1870–1910: A Critique of the Pluralist Interpretation;" Jules Tygiel, "Workingmen in San Francisco, 1880–1901," 45.

22. San Francisco *Call,* 2 November 1902, 30 July 1903, 7 December 1903; *The Coast Seamen's Journal,* 21 June 1905.

23. Mary I. Herrick, *The Chicago Schools: A Social and Political History* (Beverly Hills, Calif.: Sage, 1971), 61; Miriam Mead Hawley, "Schools for Social Order," 75.

24. Chicago Board of Education, *Annual Report,* 1867, 191–92.

25. San Francisco *Call,* 9 November 1880.

26. *Chicago Tribune,* 4 January 1893.

27. *Chicago Tribune,* 11 January 1893, 13 January 1893, 12 February 1893, 18 February 1893.

28. Hogan, "Capitalism and Schooling," 52–53.

29. Chicago *Inter-Ocean,* 20 March 1893.

30. Hogan, "Capitalism and Schooling," 56.

31. *Chicago Tribune,* 23 February 1893.

32. *Chicago Tribune,* 9 March 1893, 25 April 1893, 28 April 1893, 12 May 1893; Chicago Board of Education *Proceedings,* 1893, 424–25.

33. *Shop and Senate,* 6 December 1873; *Truth,* 7 March 1883.

34. *Knights of Labor,* 4 September 1886.

35. Ibid., 26 January 1889.

36. Hogan, "Capitalism and Schooling," 251.

37. *Merchants Association Review,* December 1896.

38. San Francisco Board of Education, *Report of the Committee on Manual Training,* 14 March 1894, 16.

39. *Organized Labor,* 31 March 1900, 16 May 1903.

40. See chap. 6 for a discussion of the controversy over the Cooley bill.

Chapter 4

1. *Report of the Educational Commission of the City of Chicago* (Harper Commission Report), Chicago, 1899, 41–42.

2. Ellwood Cubberly, "The School Situation in San Francisco," *Educational Review* 21 (April 1901): 364–81.

3. U.S. Bureau of Education, *Bulletin no. 46* (The Claxton Report), 1917, 98–99.

4. David Hogan, "Capitalism and Schooling: A History of the Political Economy of Education in Chicago, 1880–1930" (Ph.D. diss., University of Illinois, 1978).

5. Frances Fox Piven and Richard A. Cloward, "Social Policy and the Formation of Political Consciousness," in *Political Power and Social Theory,* vol. 1, ed. Maurice Zeitlin (Greenwich, Conn.: JAI Press, 1980), 127–31.

6. Julia Wrigley, *Class Politics and Public Schools: Chicago, 1900–1950* (New Brunswick, N.J.: Rutgers University Press, 1982), 102–6.

7. San Francisco, Board of Education, *Annual Reports;* Chicago, Board of Education, *Annual Reports.*

8. Diane Ravitch, *The Revisionists Revisited: A Critique of the Radical Attack on the Schools* (New York: Basic Books, 1979), 15–18.

9. Lawrence A. Cremin, *The Transformation of the School: Progressivism in American Education, 1876–1957* (New York: Alfred A. Knopf, 1961).

10. Cf. Suzanne Berger, "Introduction," in *Organizing Interests in Western Europe,* ed. Suzanne Berger (Cambridge, Mass.: Cambridge University Press, 1981).

11. Martin J. Schiesl, *The Politics of Efficiency* (Berkeley: University of California Press, 1977), 131.

12. Ibid., 162; also 73, 81, 83, 84, 158. See also Kenneth Fox, *Better City Government: Innovation in American Urban Politics, 1850–1937* (Philadelphia: Temple University Press, 1977).

13. David Rogers, *110 Livingston Street: Politics and Bureaucracy in the New York City School System* (New York: Random House, 1968); Marilyn Gittel, *Participants and Participation: A Study of School Policy in New York City* (New York: Praeger, 1967).

14. Not all of the scholarship on schooling and reform is silent on the subject of organizational imperatives. Selwyn Troen, for one, in his study of nineteenth- and early-twentieth-century public schooling in St. Louis, argues that because the public schools had an interest in expanding their own domain they had an interest in developing rational legal bureaucratic forms. He observes, "It was imperative to restructure school management if the system were to be able to proceed with the program of expansion it embarked on after the turn of the century" (Selwyn K. Troen, *The Public and the Schools: Shaping the St. Louis System, 1838–1920* [Columbia: University of Missouri Press, 1975], 208).

15. San Francisco, Board of Education, *Annual Reports.*

16. Chicago, Board of Education, *Annual Reports.*

17. Troen, *Public and the Schools,* 226.

18. Piven and Cloward, "Social Policy," 124.

19. A notable exception is William J. Reese's excellent article " 'Partisans of the Proletariat': The Socialist Working Class and the Milwaukee Schools, 1890–1920," *History of Education Quarterly* 21 (1981): 3–50. Reese examines the (partially successful) attempts by the Milwaukee socialists to bridge the categories of labor and ethnicity and to forge a broad agenda of working-class educational concerns during the Progressive Era. However, the atypical nature of their effort in the American context and its ultimate fragility attest to the dominance of the fractured sense of class that has characterized the American working class.

20. Piven and Cloward, "Social Policy," 124.

21. Julia Wrigley, "Comment on 'Social Policy and the Formation of Political Consciousness,' " in *Political Power,* ed. Zeitlin, 153ff.; see also Wrigley, *Class Politics and Public Schools.*

22. David Tyack, *The One Best System: A History of American Urban Education* (Cambridge, Mass.: Harvard University Press, 1974), 78.

23. Robert Reid, "The Professionalization of Public School Teachers: The Chicago Experience, 1895–1920" (Ph.D. diss., Northwestern University, 1968), 41.

24. Mary Herrick, *The Chicago Schools: A Social and Political History* (Beverly Hills, Calif.: Sage, 1971), 111.

25. Robert Nottenburg, "The Relationship of Organized Labor to Public School Legislation in Illinois, 1880–1948" (Ph.D. diss., University of Chicago, 1950), 153.

26. Forrest Crissey, *The Making of an American School Teacher* (Chicago: C. M. Barnes Co., 1906), 48.

27. Reid, "Professionalization of Public School Teachers," 48, 71–72.

28. Ibid., 127.

29. The literature on teachers in San Francisco in this period is sparse. Lee Stephen Dolson, "The Administration of the San Francisco Public Schools, 1847–1947" (Ph.D. diss., University of California, Berkeley, 1964), 369–73, discusses the first effort of teachers to unionize. Victor Shradar, "Ethnic Politics, Religion and the Public Schools of San Francisco, 1849–1933" (Ph.D. diss., Stanford University, 1974), is a good source of information on teacher-board relations. See also his article "Ethnicity, Religion, and Class: Progressive School Reform in San Francisco," *History of Education Quarterly* 20 (1980): 385–401. *The Early History of Teachers Organizations and First Year Book of the Teachers' Association of San Francisco* (December 1928) provides an introduction to the early teachers' organizations in San Francisco. For the early years of the San Francisco Federation of Teachers Local 61 see the correspondence between AFT national president Charles Stillman and local president Paul J. Mohr in the Archives of Labor History and Urban Affairs, University Archives, Wayne State University.

30. Dolson, "Administration of San Francisco Public Schools," 369–73.

31. Shradar, "Ethnic Politics," discusses the political dominance of the Irish in San Francisco politics. See also Michael Kazin, "Barons of Labor: The San Francisco Building Trades, 1896–1922" (Ph.D. diss., Stanford University, 1983), especially 417.

32. William Issel, "Class and Ethnic Conflict in San Francisco Political History: The Reform Charter of 1898," *Labor History* 18 (1977): 341–59.

33. *The Labor Clarion* 17, no. 36 (1918):13.

34. Michael P. McCarthy, "Businessmen and Professionals in Municipal Reform: The Chicago Experience, 1887–1920" (Ph.D. diss., Northwestern University, 1970), 67–81.

35. Reid, "Professionalization of Public School Teachers," 167.

36. *Illinois State Federation of Labor Weekly Newsletter,* 28 August 1915, cited in Reid, "Professionalization of Public School Teachers," 172.

37. Reid, "Professionalization of Public School Teachers," 192.

38. Cited in Wrigley, *Class Politics and Public Schools,* 136–37.

39. Ibid., 139.

40. Ibid., 144–45.

41. On McAndrew's superintendency, see Wrigley, *Class Politics and Public Schools,* chap. 5.

42. Shradar, "Ethnic Politics," 132.

43. On this dispute, see Shradar, "Ethnic Politics," 133–43.

44. On the rift between the Labor Council and the Building Trades Council see Jules Tygiel, "Workingmen in San Francisco, 1880–1901" (Ph.D. diss., University of California, Los Angeles, 1977). An excellent history of the Building Trades Council in this era including a discussion of McCarthy's administration is presented in Kazin, "Barons of Labor." See also Millard Robert Morgen, "The Administration of P. H. McCarthy, Mayor of San Francisco, 1910–1912" (M.A. thesis, University of California, 1948). For the progressive-labor alliance in California, see George E. Mowry, *The California Progressives* (Berkeley and Los Angeles: University of California Press, 1951), 147–51; Alexander Saxton, "San Francisco Labor and the Populist and Progressive Insurgencies," *Pacific Historical Review* 34 (1965): 437; Mary Ann Mason Burki, "The California Progressives: "Labor's Point of View," *Labor History* 17 (1976): 24–37; and Kazin, "Barons of Labor," 460–61.

45. See the Stillman-Mohr correspondence.

46. See the editorials favoring vocational education in *The Labor Clarion,* 2 March 1917;

16 March 1917; 8 March 1918; 14 June 1918. Correspondence between the Labor Council and school officials confirms labor's dissatisfaction with the school department on this issue. See Labor Council files, Bancroft Library. Although the Building Trades Council stood to gain as much (perhaps more) by the institution of vocational education in this era of employer offense, the Building Trades Council's political ties to the ethnic patronage regime that was being challenged were much stronger than were the Labor Council's. The BTC had demonstrated some support for progressive Republicans, but its involvement with such politics was considerably less that that of the Labor Council. See Kazin, "Barons of Labor," 460–61. See also the discussion in chapter 6.

47. Shradar, "Ethnic Politics," 145–48.

Chapter 5

1. Robert Alford and Roger Friedland, "Nations, Parties, and Participation: A Critique of Political Sociology," *Theory and Society* 1 (1974): 320.

2. Charles Noble, "The Welfare State and the Problem of Reform: The Case of OHSA," paper presented to the meetings of the American Political Science Association, September 1983.

3. Diane Ravitch, *The Great School Wars* (New York: Basic Books, 1974), chaps. 21 and 22. Two notable exceptions to this omission are the excellent discussion of Chicago school politics in the 1930s in Julia Wrigley's *Class Politics and Public Schools: Chicago 1900–1950* (New Brunswick, N.J.: Rutgers University Press, 1982) and David Tyack, Robert Lowe, and Elisabeth Hansot's survey of the impact of the Great Depression on American schools in *Public Schools in Hard Times: The Great Depression and Recent Years* (Cambridge, Mass.: Harvard University Press, 1984).

4. David Rogers, *110 Livingston Street: Politics and Bureaucracy in the New York City School System* (New York: Vintage, 1968); Marilyn Gittell, *Participants and Participation: A Study of School Policy in New York City* (New York: Praeger, 1968); Mario Fantini, Marilyn Gittell, and Richard Magat, *Community Control and the Urban School* (New York: Praeger, 1970.)

5. Wallace S. Sayre and Herbert Kaufmann, *Governing New York City: Politics in the Metropolis* (New York: Norton, 1965); J. David Greenstone and Paul Peterson, *Race and Authority in Urban Politics: Community Participation and the War on Poverty* (Chicago: The University of Chicago Press, 1976); James Q. Wilson, *The Amateur Democrat* (Chicago: The University of Chicago Press, 1962); Norman I. Fainstein and Susan F. Fainstein, *Urban Political Movements: The Search for Power by Minority Groups in American Cities* (Englewood Cliffs, N.J.: Prentice-Hall, 1974); Alexander B. Callow, Jr., ed., *American Urban History* (New York: Oxford University Press, 1973).

6. Theodore Lowi, *At the Pleasure of the Mayor: Patronage and Power in New York City, 1898–1958* (New York: Free Press, 1964), especially chaps. 4, 5, 8, and 9.

7. Alex Gottfried, *Boss Cermak of Chicago* (Seattle: University of Washington Press, 1962), 210–11.

8. George D. Strayer, *Report of the Survey of the Schools of Chicago,* vol. 5 (New York: Columbia University Press, 1932), 58.

9. Cited in Stephen D. London, "Business and the Chicago Public School System, 1890–1966" (Ph.D. diss., University of Chicago, 1968), 81–82.

10. Comptroller, City of Chicago, *Seventy-fourth Annual Report* (Chicago: Department of Finance, 1930), 14.

11. Mary J. Herrick, *The Chicago Schools: A Social and Political History* (Beverly Hills, Calif.: Sage, 1971), 180, 185–86.

12. William H. Stuart, *The Twenty Incredible Years* (Chicago: M. A. Donahue, 1935), 86; London, "Business and Chicago Public Schools," 86; Herbert D. Simpson, *Tax Racket and Tax Reform in Chicago* (Chicago: The Institute for Economic Research, Northwestern University, 1930), 169.

13. Simpson, *Tax Racket and Reform,* 169.

14. Julia Wrigley, *Class Politics and Public Schools: Chicago, 1900–1950* (New Brunswick, N.J.: Rutgers University Press, 1982), 209; Gottfried, *Boss Cermak,* 247.

15. Wrigley, *Class Politics and Public Schools,* 212.

16. Simpson, *Tax Racket and Reform,* 185–86.

17. Wrigley, *Class Politics and Public Schools,* 212.

18. Herrick, *Chicago Public Schools,* 194.

19. London, "Business and Chicago Public Schools," 90.

20. Wrigley, *Class Politics and Public Schools,* 213–14.

21. London, "Business and Chicago Public Schools," 97–98.

22. Cited in James S. Hazlett, "Crisis in School Government; An Administrative History of the Chicago Public Schools, 1933–1947" (Ph.D. diss., University of Chicago, 1968), 37.

23. Wrigley, *Class Politics and Public Schools,* 216; Francis M. Landwermeyer, "Teacher Unionism—Chicago Style" (Ph.D. diss., University of Chicago, 1978), 94.

24. Fred W. Sargent, "The Taxpayer Takes Charge," *Saturday Evening Post,* (14 January 1933), 80; Wrigley, *Class Politics and Public Schools,* 214.

25. Herrick, *Chicago Public Schools,* 199; Wrigley, *Class Politics and Public Schools,* 216.

26. Wrigley, *Class Politics and Public Schools,* 216; London, "Business and Chicago Public Schools," 216.

27. Wrigley, *Class Politics and Public Schools,* 217.

28. London, "Business and Chicago Public Schools," 106.

29. Wrigley, *Class Politics and Public Schools,* 218.

30. Wrigley, *Class Politics and Public Schools,* 218; Herrick, *Chicago Public Schools,* 209–10; Hazlett, "Crisis in School Government," 46–47.

31. Wrigley, *Class Politics and Public Schools,* 221–23.

32. U.S. Bureau of the Census, *The Sixteenth Census of the United States,* vol. 2, part 1, 659.

33. Lee Stephen Dolson, "The Administration of the San Francisco Public Schools, 1847–1947" (Ph.D. diss., University of California, Berkeley, 1965), 495.

34. *Statistical Reports of the San Francisco Public Schools,* 1930, 1940.

35. Memorandum from Monsignor Cantwell, 10 September 1930, Chancery Archives, Archdiocese of San Francisco.

36. *San Francisco Examiner,* 3 November 1930.

37. Preston Devine, "The Adoption of the 1932 Charter of San Francisco" (M.A. thesis, University of California, 1933); *San Francisco Examiner,* 6 November 1930.

38. *San Francisco Examiner,* 14 May 1931; Dolson, "San Francisco Public Schools," 520.

39. *San Francisco Examiner,* 2 November 1932; Dolson, "San Francisco Public Schools," 524.

40. *San Francisco Examiner,* 8 September 1933.

41. *San Francisco Chronicle,* 13 September 1933; quoted in Dolson, "San Francisco Public Schools," 528–29.

42. Dolson, "San Francisco Public Schools," 532–34.

43. Ibid., 546.

44. Royle D. Delmatier, Clarence F. McIntosh, and Earl G. Walters, *The Rumble of California Politics, 1848–1970* (New York: John Wiley and Sons, 1970), 171.

45. See Frederick M. Wirt, *Power in the City* (Berkeley: University of California Press, 1974), on fragmentation; See Devine, "Adoption of the 1932 Charter," on the struggle for the Charter of 1932.

46. Wrigley, *Class Politics and Public Schools*, 240; Hazlett, "Crisis in School Government," 227–28.

47. *New World*, 21 April 1933, cited in James W. Sanders, "The Education of Chicago Catholics: An Urban History" (Ph.D. diss., University of Chicago, 1970), 314; Hazlett, "Crisis in School Government," 228.

48. Gottfreid, *Boss Cermak*, 161; John Allswang, *A House for All Peoples: Ethnic Politics in Chicago, 1890–1936* (Lexington, University Press of Kentucky, 1971), 152–62.

49. Wrigley, *Class Politics and Public Schools*, 217.

50. Martin Levit, "The Chicago Citizens Schools Committee (M.A. thesis, University of Chicago, 1947), 52.

51. Emma Levitt, "The Activities of Local Teacher Organizations in Chicago since 1929" (M.A. thesis, University of Chicago, 1936), 17–18; Hazlett, "Crisis in School Government," 58.

52. Wrigley, *Class Politics and Public Schools*, 233–34.

53. Quoted in Bernard Patrick Knoth, " 'Many and Diverse Forces': A Study of the 1933 Chicago Public School Crisis with Special Regard for the Role of Organized Labor" (MS, University of Chicago, Autumn 1979), 47.

54. Wrigley, *Class Politics and Public Schools*, 240; *Federation News*, 29 July 1933, 1.

55. Herrick, *Chicago Public Schools*, 165.

56. *Federation News*, 29 July 1933, 5.

57. Ibid.

58. Wrigley, *Class Politics and Public Schools*, 233.

59. Memo from Mr. Andriano, 22 March 1935; Memorandum from Andrew F. Burke, 22 March 1935; Memorandum to Bishop Connolly from Mr. Lally, 5 September 1942, Chancery Archives, Archdiocese of San Francisco.

60. J. M. Graybiel to John A. O'Connell, 6 November 1934; Lillian B. Olney to John A. O'Connell, 2 June 1935, Files of the San Francisco Labor Council, Bancroft Library, Berkeley, California.

61. *San Francisco Examiner*, 1 May 1935, 6 June 1935; Dolson, "San Francisco Public Schools," 611–12.

62. *The American Teacher* 15, no. 8 (May 1931): 1.

63. J. M. Graybiel to John A. O'Connell, 6 November 1934, Files of the San Francisco Labor Council, Bancroft Library, Berkeley, California.

64. San Francisco Public Schools *Bulletin*, 2 September 1935, 1.

65. The San Francisco Board of Education, *Minutes*, 3 August 1937, 14 September 1937.

66. San Francisco Unified School District, Citizens Committee for the Study of Teachers' Salaries, *Report*, 1929; *The Labor Clarion*, 1 May 1931.

67. *The Labor Clarion*, 26 February 1932, 10; San Francisco Federation of Teachers President Dole to John A. O'Connell, 9 March 1932, Files of the San Francisco Labor Council, Bancroft Library, Berkeley, California.

68. Memorandum from Father Connolly, n.d., Chancery Archives, Archdiocese of San Francisco.

69. Grace E. King to Daniel C. Murphy, 10 May 1938, John A. O'Connell to the San Francisco Board of Education, 1 June 1938, Files of the San Francisco Labor Council, Bancroft Library, Berkeley, California.

70. *The Labor Clarion*, 23 February 1934.

71. Hazlett, "Crisis in School Government," 221–22.

72. National Commission for the Defense of Democracy through Education of the National Education Association, *Certain Personnel Practices in the Chicago Public Schools* (Washington, D.C.: National Education Association of the United States, 1945), 67.

73. National Commission for the Defense of Democracy . . . , *Personnel Practices*, 65–66.

74. Landwermeyer, "Teacher Unionism," 134.

75. Hazlett, "Crisis in School Government," 269.

76. Wrigley, *Class Politics and Public Schools,* 253–54.

77. Hazlett, "Crisis in School Government," 276.

78. Ibid., 278–81.

79. Ibid., 287.

80. Ibid., 287–88.

81. Wrigley, *Class Politics and Public Schools,* 254; Hazlett, "Crisis in School Government," 290–91.

82. Wrigley, *Class Politics and Public Schools,* 254.

83. Herrick, *Chicago Public Schools,* 278; Robert F. Pearse, "Studies in White Collar Unionism: The Development of a Teachers' Union" (Ph.D. diss., University of Chicago, 1950), 205–6.

84. *San Francisco Examiner,* 27 October 1943, 7 June 1947.

85. *The Labor Clarion,* 20 October 1939, 8 October 1943; *The New York Times,* 24 October 1943; *San Francisco Examiner,* 30 October 1943. In 1943 each candidate could boast some labor support; even employers' candidate Lapham had a labor committee headed by a representative from the San Francisco Building and Construction Trades Council although that council did not officially endorse him. *The New York Times,* 24 October 1943.

86. *San Francisco Examiner,* 27 June 1944.

87. Mary Ellen Leary, "Mr. San Francisco," *Saturday Evening Post,* November 11, 1944, 18–19, 89–90.

88. *San Francisco Examiner,* 9 July 1942.

89. *San Francisco Examiner,* 5 May 1943.

90. Ibid.

91. *San Francisco Examiner,* 15 February 1944.

92. Clyde M. Hill, "Administrative Organization Study, San Francisco Unified School District" San Francisco: The San Francisco School Survey, (mimeo, 1944), 2–7.

93. *San Francisco Examiner,* 7 May 1943.

94. *San Francisco Examiner,* 12 May 1943.

95. Dolson, "San Francisco Public Schools," 650.

96. *San Francisco Examiner,* 20 December 1944.

97. Dolson, "San Francisco Public Schools," 650.

98. *San Francisco Examiner,* 6 February 1947.

99. *San Francisco Examiner,* 7 June 1947.

100. *San Francisco Examiner,* 1 July 1947, 15 July 1947.

Chapter 6

1. Marvin Lazerson and W. Norton Grubb, *American Education and Vocationalism: A Documentary History, 1870–1970* (New York: Teachers College Press, 1974), 17–28.

2. On manual training see chapter 3. See also Marvin Lazerson, *Origins of the Urban School: Public Education in Massachusetts, 1870–1915* (Cambridge, Mass.: Harvard University Press, 1971), especially chaps. 3–6.

3. Layton S. Hawkins, Charles A. Prosser, and John C. Wright, *Development of Vocational Education* (Chicago: American Technical Society, 1951), 63; Lawrence A. Cremin, *The Transformation of the School: Progressivism in American Education, 1876–1957* (New York: Alfred A. Knopf, 1961), 39, 54–55.

4. Quoted in Lazerson and Grubb, *American Education and Vocationalism,* 21.

5. Lazerson and Grubb, *American Education and Vocationalism,* 20–21.

6. U.S. Congress, Senate, Document no. 936, 62nd Cong., 2nd sess., 1912, 11–19. See also the testimony of AFL representative Grant Hamilton in the *Report of the Commission on National Aid to Vocational Education, vol. 2: Hearings before Commission* (Washington, D.C.: U.S. Government Printing Office, 1914), 181–86.

7. Mary Herrick, *The Chicago Schools: A Social and Political History,* (Beverly Hills, Calif.: Sage, 1971), 403.

8. San Francisco Board of Education, *Annual Reports,* 1928, 72; 1930, 68.

9. Quoted in Hawkins, Prosser, and Wright, *Development of Vocational Education,* 97.

10. *San Francisco News,* 17 June 1930.

11. City Club of Chicago, *Report on Vocational Training in Chicago and Other Cities* (Chicago: City Club of Chicago, 1912), 38.

12. Ibid., 32.

13. Ibid., 74–75.

14. *Chicago Tribune,* 14 January 1913.

15. The Commonwealth Club of California, *Transactions* 5, no. 2 (April 1910): 37.

16. Julia Wrigley, *Class Politics and Public Schools, Chicago, 1900–1950* (New Brunswick, N.J.: Rutgers University Press, 1982), 61.

17. David Hogan, "Capitalism and Schooling: The Political Economy of Public Education in Chicago, 1880–1930" (Ph.D. diss., University of Illinois, Champaign, 1978), 443.

18. Paul H. Douglas, *American Apprenticeship and Industrial Education* (New York: Columbia University Press, 1921), chap. 3.

19. Wrigley, *Class Politics and Public Schools,* 61.

20. Commonwealth Club, *Transactions* 9, no. 12 (November 1914): 667–68.

21. Hogan, "Capitalism and Schooling," 296.

22. Wrigley, *Class Politics and Public Schools,* 64.

23. Ibid., 46–47.

24. Ibid., 62.

25. Ibid., 67.

26. Ibid., 82.

27. Ibid., 66.

28. Joseph Rathnau, "The Cooley Vocational Bill, 1912–1917" (Ph.D. diss., University of Chicago, 1973). Appendix I, 497–519, contains a copy of the bill.

29. Wrigley, *Class Politics and Public Schools,* 97.

30. Ibid., 97; Illinois State Federation of Labor, *Proceedings of the 32nd Annual Convention,* 52.

31. Illinois State Federation of Labor, *Proceedings of the 32nd Annual Convention,* 52.

32. John Dewey, "An Undemocratic Proposal," in *American Education and Vocationalism: A Documentary History, 1870–1970* (New York: Teachers College Press, 1974), 143–47.

33. Cited in Wrigley, *Class Politics and Public Schools,* 124.

34. Rathnau, "Cooley Vocational Educational Bill," 462.

35. Ibid., 139–45.

36. Wrigley, *Class Politics and Public Schools,* 85–87.

37. Ibid.

38. Herrick, *Chicago Schools,* 119.

39. Commonwealth Club, *Transactions* 5, no. 2 (April 1910): 38.

40. William Haber, *Industrial Relations in the Building Industry* (Cambridge, Mass.: Harvard University Press, 1930), 402; Robert Edward Lee Knight, *Industrial Relations in the San Francisco Bay Area 1900–18* (Berkeley: University of California Press, 1960), 103–4, 124–27, 139–66, 381; and Michael Kazin, "Barons of Labor: The San Francisco Building Trades, 1896–1922" (Ph.D. diss., Stanford University, 1983), 41–53.

41. See, for example, the remarks of James W. Kerr in Commonwealth Club, *Transactions* 5, no. 2 (April 1910): 659.

42. Hill, *San Francisco School Survey,* 4.

43. Commonwealth Club, *Transactions* 9, no. 12: 618.

44. Ibid., 645.

45. Ibid., 619.

46. Ibid., 620.

47. Ibid. 10, no. 16 (January 1916): 645–46.

48. Lee Stephen Dolson, "The Administration of the San Francisco Public Schools, 1847–1947" (Ph.D. diss., University of California, Berkeley, 1965), 370.

49. Ibid., 381–82.

50. Ibid., 381.

51. See Robert Verner Ohlson, "The History of the San Francisco Labor Council" (M.A. thesis, University of California, Berkeley, 1940), 87–109; Kazin, "Barons of Labor," 478–529; Knight, *Industrial Relations,* 299–368, for the open-shop campaign that culminated in the American Plan in the early 1920s.

52. See *The Labor Clarion,* 2 March 1917.

53. Ibid.

54. Ibid., 16 March 1917.

55. Ibid., 8 March 1918.

56. Ibid., 14 June 1918.

57. Ibid., 8 March 1918.

58. Ibid.

59. Commonwealth Club, *Transactions* 14, no. 15 (February 1920): 599.

60. San Francisco Labor Council to George E. Gallagher, President, Board of Education, 10 March 1919, Files of the San Francisco Labor Council, The Bancroft Library.

61. Alfred Roncovieri to San Francisco Labor Council, 29 October 1920, Files of the San Francisco Labor Council, Bancroft Library.

62. Ibid.

63. See the discussion in chapter 4.

64. Victor Shradar, "Ethnic Politics, Religion and the Public Schools of San Francisco, 1849–1947" (Ph.D. diss., Stanford University, 1974), 132.

65. Alfred Roncovieri to the San Francisco Labor Council, 29 October 1920, Files of the Labor Council, Bancroft Library.

66. The Building Trades Council's decision to stick with reform opponents probably reflects a desire to remain with traditional political allies in a period when the building trades, more than any other unions, were under severe employer pressure to break the closed shop.

67. Dolson, "Administration of San Francisco Public Schools," 459–60.

68. *The Labor Clarion,* 3 September 1937.

69. See Arthur G. Wirth, *Education in the Technological Society: The Vocational-Liberal Studies Controversy in the Early Twentieth Century,* (Scranton: Intext Educational Publishers, 1972), chap. 9, for a discussion of John Dewey's views on "the 'vocational' as a means for liberalizing education."

70. Kazin, "Barons of Labor," 526; Haber, *Industrial Relations,* 146.

71. Quoted in Haber, *Industrial Relations,* 146, 423.

72. Haber, *Industrial Relations,* 146.

73. Selden C. Menefee, *Vocational Training and Employment of Youth,* Works Projects Administration, Research Monograph 25 (Washington, D.C.: U.S. Government Printing Office, 1942), xix.

74. John D. Russell and Associates, *Vocational Education,* Staff Study no. 8, Advisory Committee on Vocational Education (Washington, D.C.: U.S. Government Printing Office, 1938), Appendix A, "The Experience of Labor with Trade and Industrial Education," by Howell H. Broach and Julia O'Connor Parker, 241–89: Lazerson and Grubb, *American Education and Vocationalism,* 42.

75. Menefee, *Vocational Training,* xix.

76. Ibid., xv.

77. Chicago Board of Education, *Report of the Superintendent of Schools,* 1937–38, pp. 420–22.

78. Ibid., 420–21.

79. See National Education Association, *Proceedings of the 69th Annual Meeting,* 739.

80. James S. Hazlett, "Crisis in School Government, Chicago, 1933–47" (Ph.D. diss., The University of Chicago, 1968), 122.

81. Chicago, *Report of the Superintendent,* 1936–37, p. 271.

82. Ibid.

83. Hazlett, "Crisis in School Government," 137.

84. Chicago *Daily News,* 11 November 1937, 1, 3.

85. Herrick, *Chicago Schools,* 229–30.

86. Hazlett, "Crisis in School Government," 135–37.

87. Chicago, *Report of the Superintendent,* 1940–41, p. 499.

88. San Francisco *News,* 17 June 1930.

89. *The Labor Clarion,* 3 September 1937.

90. San Francisco *News,* 17 May 1930.

91. San Francisco Board of Education, *Minutes,* 23 January 1940.

92. *San Francisco Public Schools Bulletin,* 16 November 1936.

93. *The Labor Clarion,* 3 September 1937.

94. San Francisco Board of Education, *Statistical Report of the San Francisco Public Schools, 1939–40,* 15.

95. San Francisco *News,* 28 November 1941.

96. Ibid., 9 May 1941.

97. San Francisco *Chronicle,* 9 July 1941.

98. San Francisco Board of Education, *Minutes,* 6 May 1941.

99. San Francisco *News,* 9 May 1941.

100. Ibid., 29 January 1941; *The Labor Clarion,* 19 June 1942.

101. Dolson, "Administration of San Francisco Public Schools," 587.

102. San Francisco *Examiner,* 18 March 1942, 19 March 1942.

103. Ibid.

104. *The Labor Clarion,* 13 February 1942.

105. San Francisco *News,* 10 February 1943; Dolson, "Administration of San Francisco Public Schools," 592–93.

106. Dolson, "Administration of San Francisco Public Schools," 593.

107. San Francisco *Call-Bulletin,* 27 August 1945.

108. Lazerson and Grubb make the same point about the 1917 debates over the Smith-Hughes Act in *American Education and Vocationalism,* 33.

Chapter 7

1. For a useful discussion, see Raymond Williams, *The Long Revolution* (New York: Harper & Row, 1961), 125–65.

2. See, for example, the remarks of Kenneth B. Clark, in "Education of the Minority Poor: The Key to the War on Poverty," in *The Disadvantaged Poor: Education and Employment,* Third Report of the Task Force on Economic Growth and Opportunity (Washington, D.C.: Chamber of Commerce of the United States, 1966), 175.

3. Robert Dahl, "Decision-Making in a Democracy: The Supreme Court as a National Policy-Maker," *Journal of Public Law* 6 (Fall 1957): 279–95; Richard Funston, "The Supreme Court and Critical Elections," *The American Political Science Review* 69 (September 1975): 795–811.

4. See Diane Ravitch, *The Troubled Crusade: American Education 1945–1980,* (New York: Basic Books, 1983), chap. 4, for a discussion of the issues leading up to the *Brown* decision.

5. U.S. Bureau of the Census, *The Sixteenth Census of the United States,* vol. 2, pt. 1, 114; *Eighteenth Census of the United States,* vol. 1, pt. 6, 141.

6. David Wellman, "Negro Leadership in San Francisco" (M.A. thesis, University of California, Berkeley, 1966), 22–25; Frederick M. Wirt, *Power in the City* (Berkeley: University of California Press, 1974), 254.

7. Larry Cuban, *Urban School Chiefs under Fire* (Chicago: University of Chicago Press, 1976), 71. David Kirp's "School Desegregation in San Francisco, 1962–76" in Allan P. Sindler ed., *America in the Seventies,* (Boston: Little, Brown, 1977) is a concise yet thorough analysis of the politics of race and schooling in San Francisco for this entire period with special emphasis on the role of the courts. Kirp's *Just Schools: The Idea of Racial Equality in American Education* (Berkeley: University of California Press, 1982), chap. 6, covers much the same material taking the analysis up to 1981.

8. John Kaplan, "San Francisco," in *Affirmative School Integration,* ed. Roscoe Hill and Malcolm Teeley (Beverly Hills, Calif.: Sage, 1967), 67.

9. See the account of the struggle over the new Central Junior High School in Kaplan, "San Francisco," 70–2; Robert L. Crain, *The Politics of School Desegregation* (Chicago: Aldine Publishing Co., 1968), 83–85; Robert D. Lee, "Ideology and Decision-Making in the San Francisco Public Schools" (Ph.D. diss., Syracuse University, 1967), 156–62.

10. Lee, "Ideology and Decision-Making," 169–70.

11. Wellman, "Negro Leadership in San Francisco," 3; Richard Young, "The Impact of Protest Leadership on Negro Politicians in San Francisco," *Western Political Quarterly* 22, no. 1 (March 1969): 101; Wirt, *Power in the City,* 257.

12. *San Francisco Examiner,* 19 August 1965, 13.

13. Gary Orfield, *Must We Bus? Segregated Schools and National Policy* (Washington, D.C.: The Brookings Institution, 1978), 158; U.S. Bureau of the Census, *Eighteenth Census of the United States,* vol. 1, pt. 15, 107.

14. Cuban, *Urban School Chiefs under Fire,* 9–10; Gary Orfield, *The Reconstruction of Southern Education* (New York: Wiley Interscience, 1969), 155.

15. Cuban, *Urban School Chiefs,* 10; Orfield, *Reconstruction of Southern Education,* 155–56.

16. Cuban, *Urban School Chiefs,* 17–19.

17. Orfield, *Reconstruction of Southern Education,* 162–63.

18. Kirp, *Just Schools,* 90–91; Robert E. Jenkins, *Educational Equality/Quality: Report no. 1 . . . Program Alternatives* (San Francisco Unified School District, December 1967), 25–40; Robert E. Jenkins, *Educational Equality/Quality: Report no. 2* (San Francisco Unified School District, February 1969), 7–11.

19. *San Francisco Examiner,* 28 February 1968; Stephen Saul Weiner, "Educational Decisions in an Organized Anarchy" (Ph.D. diss., Stanford University, 1973), 51.

20. *San Francisco Examiner,* 28 February 1968, 28 January 1970, 10 February 1970; Weiner, "Educational Decisions," 51.

21. See Kirp, *Just Schools,* 93–107.

22. See Orfield, *Reconstruction of Southern Education,* 164–207.

23. See also Ravitch, *Troubled Crusade,* 163–65, on the respective roles of federal agencies and the courts in enforcing the provisions of Title VI.

24. Paul Peterson, *School Politics: Chicago Style* (Chicago: University of Chicago Press, 1976), chap. 7.

25. Weiner, "Educational Decisions," 252, 310, 181–82; Norman Almeida Fernandes, "The San Francisco Board of Education and the Chinese Community: Segregation-Deseg-

regation, 1850–1975" (Ph.D. diss., University of Denver, 1976), 131–32; Kirp, *Just Schools,* 100–106.

26. Kirp, *Just Schools,* 108.

27. Ibid., 107–10.

28. Kirp, "School Desegregation," 146.

29. *San Francisco Chronicle,* 31 December 1982, 3 January 1983.

30. Orfield, *Must We Bus?,* 174.

31. Diana Pearce, Joe D. Darden, and Reynolds Farley, "Housing and School Desegregation in Metropolitan Chicago: Report to the Chicago Board of Education," 19 February 1981, 7.

32. U.S. Bureau of the Census, *Tenth Census of the United States, 1870,* vol. 1, *Population,* 102.

33. Atlanta City Council Minutes, 26 November 1869; Alexa Bensen, "Race Relations in Atlanta As Seen in a Critical Analysis of the City Council Proceedings and Other Related Works, 1865–1877" (M.A. thesis, Atlanta University, 1966), 28; Melvin W. Ecke, *From Ivy Street to Kennedy Center* (Atlanta: Board of Education, 1972), 11.

34. Atlanta Board of Education, *Annual Report,* 1883, 10.

35. Grisby H. Wooton, Jr., "New City of the South, Atlanta 1843–1873" (Ph.D. diss., University of Maryland, 1977), 365.

36. *Atlanta Constitution,* 23 September 1972; Atlanta City Council minutes, 22 September 1972, 27 November 1972, 29 September 1972, 11 October 1972.

37. Eugene J. Watts, "Characteristics of Candidates in City Politics: Atlanta, 1865–1903" (Ph.D. diss., 1969), 196–205.

38. Clarence Albert Bacote, "The Negro in Atlanta Politics," *Phylon* 16 (1955): 335; Asa Gordon, *The Georgia Negro* (Ann Arbor, Mich.: Edwards Press, 1937), 152.

39. Bacote, "Negro in Atlanta Politics," 336.

40. Philip N. Racine, "Atlanta Schools: A History of the Public School System, 1869–1955" (Ph.D. diss., Emory University, 1969), 41; Watts, "Characteristics of Candidates," 217–18.

41. Atlanta Board of Education minutes, 26 November 1913.

42. Walter White, *A Man Called White: The Autobiography of Walter White* (New York: Random House, 1948), 29–31.

43. Ibid., 33.

44. Joseph W. Newman, "A History of the Atlanta Public School Teachers Association, Local 89 of the American Federation of Teachers, 1919–1956," (Ph.D. dissertation, Georgia State University, 1978), 243–44; Racine, "Atlanta Schools," 256–57.

45. Ecke, *Ivy Street to Kennedy Center,* 69–70; Racine, "Atlanta Schools," 116.

46. U.S. Bureau of the Census, *Ninth Census of the United States,* 1870, vol. 1, 91; *Tenth Census of the United States,* 1880, vol. 1, 416, 447; *Eleventh Census of the United States, Compendium,* 541.

47. Delilah L. Beasley, *The Negro Trail Blazers of California* (Los Angeles: Times, 1919), 181.

48. Francis N. Lortie, Jr., "San Francisco's Black Community, 1870–1890: Dilemmas in the Struggle for Equality" (M.A. thesis, San Francisco State University, 1970; reprinted by R and E Research Associates, San Francisco, 1973), 14.

49. Ibid., 53.

50. Charles Wollenberg, *All Deliberate Speed: Segregation and Exclusion in California Schools, 1855–1975* (Berkeley: University of California Press, 1976), 18.

51. Ibid., 18, 20; Lortie, "San Francisco's Black Community," 14.

52. Wollenberg, *All Deliberate Speed,* 25.

53. San Francisco, Superintendent of Public Instruction, *Annual Report,* 1875, 59; 1880, vol. 1, 416, 447.

54. U.S. Bureau of the Census, *Twelfth Census of the United States,* 1900, cxix.

55. Mary Herrick, *The Chicago Schools: A Social and Political History* (Beverly Hills, Calif.: Sage, 1971), 53.

56. U.S. Bureau of the Census, *Twelfth Census of the United States,* 1900, cxix.; *Fifteenth Census of the United States,* vol. 3, pt. 1, 363.

57. Allan H. Spear, *Black Chicago: The Making of a Negro Ghetto, 1890–1920,* (Chicago: University of Chicago Press, 1967), 44.

58. St. Clair Drake and Horace B. Cayton, *Black Metropolis* (New York: Harcourt Brace, 1945), 204; John Echeverri-Gent, "School Politics in Chicago and the Rise of the Democratic Machine," in *Surviving Economic Depression and Racial Unrest: Urban Schools and Working Class Organizations, 1930–1970,* Interim Report of the National Institute of Education (Chicago: National Opinion Research Center, 1980), chap. 3. The following paragraphs that discuss blacks in Chicago schools are drawn from Echeverri-Gent.

59. Michael Wallace Homel, "Negroes in the Chicago Public Schools, 1910–1941" (Ph.D. diss., University of Chicago, 1972), 45–82.

60. Ibid., 120.

61. Ibid., 110–11.

62. Ibid., 256.

63. Alexander Saxton, *The Indispensable Enemy: Labor and the Anti-Chinese Movement in California* (Berkeley: University of California Press, 1971), 7.

64. Saxton, *Indispensable Enemy,* 106; Francis Young Chang, "A Study of the Movement to Segregate Chinese Pupils in the San Francisco Public Schools up to 1885" (Ph.D. diss., Stanford University, 1936), 229–30.

65. Saxton, *Indispensable Enemy,* 17.

66. San Francisco, Superintendent of Public Instruction, *Annual Report,* 1865, 32; 1869, 43.

67. Chang, "Movement to Segregate Chinese Pupils," 294–98.

68. Wollenberg, *All Deliberate Speed,* 37.

69. San Francisco *Call,* 8 July 1982, 5 August 1982.

70. Chang, "Movement to Segregate Chinese Pupils," 294–96.

71. Ibid., 306.

72. Wollenberg, *All Deliberate Speed,* 40–43.

73. Ruth Haines Thompson, "Events Leading to the Order to Segregate Japanese Pupils in San Francisco Public Schools" (Ph.D. diss., Stanford University, 1931), 76.

74. San Francisco, Superintendent of Public Instruction, *Annual Report,* 1890, 24–25.

75. San Francisco *Call,* 19 June 1902.

76. Wollenberg, *All Deliberate Speed,* 44.

77. Ibid., 44–45.

78. Quoted in ibid., 40.

79. Thompson, "Order to Segregate Japanese Pupils," 45.

80. Ibid., 143.

81. Wollenberg, *All Deliberate Speed,* 49–51.

82. U.S. Senate, "Japanese in the City of San Francisco, California: From the President of the United States, Transmitting the Final Report of Secretary Metcalf," Washington, D.C.: U.S. Senate, 59th Congress, Second Session, Doc. 147, 1906, 4.

83. Wollenberg, *All Deliberate Speed,* 53.

84. Thompson, "Order to Segregate Japanese Pupils," 127; Wollenberg, *All Deliberate Speed,* 54.

85. Wollenberg, *All Deliberate Speed,* 55.

86. Ibid., 61; George Kennan, *Outlook* 86, no. 5 (1 June 1907): 247–50.

87. Wollenberg, *All Deliberate Speed,* 66–68.

88. Ibid., 72–73.

89. United States, *Reports of the Immigration Commission,* vol. 23, (Washington, D.C.: U.S. Government Printing Office, 1911), 183–84.

90. Thompson, "Order to Segregate Japanese Pupils," 160.

91. William J. Wilson, *The Declining Significance of Race: Blacks and Changing American Institutions* (Chicago: University of Chicago Press, 1978).

92. Ibid., 121.

Chapter 8

1. Rick Atkinson, "New Segregation in the Old South," *The Washington Post*, national weekly edition, 16 April 1984, p. 9.

2. Atkinson, "New Segregation," see also Walter Goodman, *"Brown* v. *Board of Education:* Uneven Results 30 Years Later," *New York Times*, 17 May 1984, sec. B, p. 18.

3. Goodman cites data from studies by the Joint Center for Political Studies. A discussion of these trends in one northern Manhattan school district may be found in Ira Katznelson, *City Trenches: Urban Politics and the Patterning of Class in the United States* (New York: Pantheon, 1981), chap. 7.

4. A good discussion of these issues may be found in David Tyack, Robert Lowe, and Elisabeth Hansot, *Public Schools in Hard Times: The Great Depression and Recent Years* (Cambridge, Mass.: Harvard University Press, 1984), chap. 5.

5. Sara Rimer, "Coping with Realities at School in the Bronx," *New York Times*, 16 May 1984, sec. B, p. 1.

6. Tyack et al., *Public Schools in Hard Times*, 214.

7. An important discussion of these issues may be found in Raymond Williams, *Marxism and Literature* (Oxford: Oxford University Press, 1977).

8. David Rogers, *110 Livingston Street: Politics and Bureaucracy in the New York City School System* (New York: Vintage Books, 1969).

9. Charles E. Silberman, *Crisis in the Classroom: The Remaking of American Education* (New York: Random House, 1970), 62, 53–54.

10. Diane Ravitch, *The Troubled Crusade: American Education 1945–1980* (New York: Basic Books, 1983), 326.

11. See Paul E. Peterson, *Making the Grade* (New York: Twentieth Century Fund, Task Force on Federal Elementary and Secondary Educational Policy, 1983); Task Force on Education for Economic Growth, *Action for Excellence* (Washington, D.C.: Education Commission of the States, 1983); National Commission on Excellence in Education, *A Nation at Risk: The Imperative for Educational Reform* (Washington, D.C.: U.S. Government Printing Office, 1983).

12. A useful and provocative overview is provided by Andrew Hacker, "The Schools Flunk Out," *The New York Review of Books*, 12 April 1984, pp. 35–40.

13. Tyack et al., *Public Schools in Hard Times*, 215.

14. Education, David Tyack and his colleagues observe, "has been one means of redistributing a rudimentary form of opportunity. Scarcity today poses hard choices amid the paradox of seeking to make the school an agent of equalization in a struggling market society" (Tyack et al., *Public Schools in Hard Times*, 225).

15. We do not mean to exaggerate the extent to which American common schools actually were common and equal. More frequently than not the practice of American schooling violated the ideological norm. But the standard of common schooling has been significant, as has its link to participatory understandings of citizenship.

16. Ravitch, *The Troubled Crusade*, 330; Tyack et al., *Public Schools in Hard Times*, 215.

17. A discussion of these changes may be found in Katznelson, chap. 3; see also R. J. Johnston, *The American Urban System: A Geographic Perspective* (New York: St. Martin's Press, 1982), especially chapter 6.

18. Perhaps the single most impressive case study of these processes at work is Olivier Zunz, *The Changing Face of Inequality: Urbanization, Industrial Development, and Immigrants in Detroit, 1880–1920* (Chicago: University of Chicago Press, 1982).

19. A recent study of Suffolk County, east of New York City on Long Island, found that only one in five workers commuted to employment in the city; three of five worked within the county. The area's 1970 population of over 1,120,000 constituted the country's third-ranked consumer market together with its Nassau County neighbors to the west. Because so much new housing construction is located in Suffolk County, as in other similar rapidly growing regions, there is a huge market for mortgages and loans, often

insured by the federal government, which has attracted many banks. "Consequently, Suffolk represents a highly significant sector of the nation for the realization of banking profits and a source of capital" (Mark Gottdiener, *Planned Sprawl: Private and Public Interests in Suburbia* [Beverly Hills, Calif.: Sage, 1977], 40).

20. Susan S. Fainstein and Norman Fainstein, "Economic Change, National Policy, and the System of Cities," in Susan S. Fainstein et al., *Restructuring the City: The Political Economy of Urban Redevelopment* (New York: Longman, 1983), 4.

21. Franklin James, "Economic Distress in Central Cities," in Robert Burchell and David Listokin, eds., *Cities under Stress: The Fiscal Crises of Urban America* (New Brunswick, N.J.: Rutgers University Center for Urban Policy Research, 1981).

22. Gottdiener, *Planned Sprawl,* 104, 94.

23. Gottdiener, *Planned Sprawl,* 111.

24. Johnston, *American Urban System,* 237. Education, of course, is one of the dominant forms of spending for any local government. The wide differences in resources and tax burdens affect the ability of local districts to provide decent schooling for their residents.

25. Some of the current difficulties of American education are shared by other Western societies. Discussing trends in all the societies of western Europe and North America, Swedish analyst Torsten Husen took note of a transnational educational crisis: "By the mid-1970's a sombre mood had replaced the strong commitment to education of the mid-1960's. Euphoria gave way to disenchantment." Educators were caught in a cross-fire between conservatives who blamed schools for lacking discipline, for lax standards, and for ignoring the gifted, and critics of the left who thought of schools as innately oppressive and as the handmaidens of capitalist hierarchy (Torsten Husen, *The School in Question: A Comparative Study of the School and Its Future in Western Societies* [London: Oxford University Press, 1979], 10–19). Husen also took note of the proliferation of study commissions as an indicator of the decline in support, the loss of faith in schooling as an instrument of social equity, and budgetary cuts.

26. Ravitch, *The Troubled Crusade,* 330; Tyack, Lowe, and Hansot, *Public Schools in Hard Times,* 215.

27. R. H. Tawney, "An Experiment in Democratic Education," in *The Radical Tradition* (London: Penguin Books, 1966), 76.

28. A thoughtful discussion of these issues may be found in the volume written by the Education Group, Centre for Contemporary Cultural Studies, *Unpopular Education: Schooling and Social Democracy in England Since 1944* (London: Hutchinson, 1981). See also Andrei S. Markovits, "Educational Reform and Class Cleavages in Social Democratic Regimes: The Case of Sweden," paper prepared for delivery at the September 1976 Chicago meetings of the American Political Science Association.

INDEX

225–26n2; economic history of, 93; establishment of public school system in, 30, 35, 225–26n2; establishment of vocational education in, 167–68; ethnic apathy to school issues in, 135–36; expansion of public schools in, 58, 59t, 97t, 100–102; failure to pass business-backed reform in, 114; first compulsory education laws in, 71; first superintendent of schools in, 50; foreign-born population of, 96; great fire of 1871, 63; and Harper Commission, 88, 89; and Heald Committee, 143–44; high school attendance in, 153, 230n1; Industrial Club of, 127, 155; institutionalization of schooling in, 227–28n9; labor and vocational education in, 153; Labor Council of, 74, 114, 119; labor groups in politics in, 80; labor movement in, 67; labor participation in vocational education in, 176; lack of organized political base to reform movements in, 124–25; manual training in schools in, 81–82; and Otis Law, 118; politics of race and education in, 181; postwar educational reform in, 149; primary school systems in, 23; public school funding in, 225–26n2; racial education issues in, 182–83, 186–87; reexamination of training in public schools, 168–69; role of business groups in school reform in, 95; school enrollment in, 96, 230n1; school expenditures in, 97t, 101–2, 128–29, 137; school land fund, 34–35; school reform as a labor issue, 89, 90, 92, 104–6, 107; school reform movement in, 88; school segregation in, 184, 187, 193–94, 195–96, 196–97; school system compared to San Francisco, 55; school systems in, between postrevolution and antebellum, 33; and spatial distinctions between work and home, 230–31n4; teacher participation in school reform in, 108–9; trades organizations in, 66; tuition schools of, 227n9; under Mayor Kelly administration, 126, 135, 136–37, 142, 143, 144; union movement in late-nineteenth-century, 231n8; unions in, 79–80, 139, 155, 156; vocational education issue in, 153, 156, 162–63; voting strength of blacks in, 196–97; Woman's Club of, 71

Chicago Daily News, 170
Chicago Federation of Labor (CFL): back-

ing of teachers' demands for higher pay, 109–10; membership of, 117; opposition to establishment of general superintendent office, 144; support of reassessment drive of 1927, 136–37; vocational education and, 155, 170
Chicago Manual Training School, 81
Chicago Teachers Federation (CTF), 109, 114, 115, 117, 127, 159
Chicago Teachers' Union, 144, 145, 170
Chicago Tribune: attack on foreign language instruction by, 77, 78; litigation against, 111; support of manual training by, 80
Child labor, 72, 73–74; legislation, 74, 85
Chinese, 64, 73–74, 203; access to public education, 197; economic and social position of, 197–98; establishment of first school, 198; opposition against, 73; opposition to busing in San Francisco, 188; requests of, to attend public schools, 198–99, 200; residence pattern of, in San Francisco, 63; separate schools for, 199–200
Church: responsibility for schooling, 31–32; *see also* Catholic church; Protestant church
Citizen's Association of Chicago, 80
Citizens' Save Our Schools Committee, 136
Citizen's School Committee of Chicago (CSC), 136, 141, 142–45
Citizenship, 24, 47, 52, 54, 75, 86, 98; black American demands for, 26; and denial of rights to minorities, 203; equality of, 10; and rights for minorities, 207; schooling committed to, 4
City Club of Chicago, 159
City formation: development of public schooling and, 35–36
Civil Rights Act of 1964, 186
Civil rights movement, 180, 182, 204; boycotts and sit-ins of, 185
Civil War, *see* Antebellum period
Clark, Hannah B., 228n11
Class, 19; capitalist, 19; conflict in Chicago and effect on public education, 105–6; distinction, 10; divisions and role in organizing national politics, 122; formation, 23, 24, 63–64; in political conflicts, 11; and residential communities, 219; in school disputes, 13, 26; segregation, 8; and struggle in founding of public education, 46; *see also* Social class; Working class